MY GREATEST DAY
IN BASEBALL

MY GREATEST DAY
IN
BASEBALL

As Told to

JOHN P. CARMICHAEL

Sports Editor of the CHICAGO DAILY NEWS
and many other noted sports writers

---

47 DRAMATIC STORIES
BY 47 FAMOUS STARS

GROSSET & DUNLAP *Publishers* NEW YORK

MANUFACTURED IN THE UNITED STATES OF AMERICA

CONTENTS

v

GROVER CLEVELAND ALEXANDER

as told to Francis J. Powers

Grover Cleveland Alexander, born February 26, 1887, in St. Paul, Nebraska, thrilled two generations of fans with his effortless pitching grace. He pitched the Phillies to their first pennant in 1915, and later came on to help the Cardinals to their flags of 1926 and 1928. In 20 years "Old Pete" compiled 373 victories in 686 games. Poor in health during his last few years, Alex passed away on November 4, 1950.

MY GREATEST day in baseball has to be the seventh game of the 1926 World Series between the Cards and Yankees. If I picked any other game the fans would think I was crazy. I guess just about everyone knows the story of that game; it has been told often enough. How I came in as a relief pitcher in the seventh inning, with two out and the bases filled with Yankees, and fanned Tony Lazzeri to protect the Cards' 3–2 lead. Actually, that was my greatest game, for it gave me not one, but three, thrills. But if it wasn't I'm stuck with it like George Washington with the hatchet.

There must be a hundred versions of what happened in the Yankee Stadium that dark, chilly afternoon. It used to be that everywhere I went, I'd hear a new one and some were pretty far-fetched. So much so that two-three years ago I ran across Lazzeri in San Francisco and said: "Tony, I'm getting tired of fanning you." And Tony answered: "Maybe you think I'm not." So I'd like to tell you my story of what took place in that game and the day before.

There are stories that I celebrated that night before and had a hangover when Manager Rogers Hornsby called me from the bull pen to pitch to Lazzeri. That isn't the truth. On Saturday, I had beaten the Yankees 10–2 to make the series all even. To refresh your memory on the series, the Yankees won the opener and we took the next two. Then the Yanks won two straight and needed only one more for the world's championship and I beat 'em in the sixth.

In the clubhouse after that game, Hornsby came over to me and said: "Alex, if you want to celebrate tonight, I wouldn't blame you. But go easy for I may need you tomorrow."

I said: "Okay, Rog. I'll tell you what I'll do. I'll ride back to the hotel with you and I'll meet you tomorrow morning and ride out to the park with you." Hell—I wanted to win that series and get the big end of the money as much as anyone.

Jesse Haines started the seventh game for us, pitchin' against Waite Hoyt. We figured Jesse would give the Yanks all they could handle. He was a knuckle-baller and had shut 'em out in the third game. Early in the game Hornsby said to me: "Alex, go down into the bull pen and keep your eye on Sherdel [Willie] and Bell [Herman]. Keep 'em warmed up and if I need help I'll depend on you to tell me which one looks best."

The bull pen in the Yankee Stadium is under the bleachers and when you're down there you can't tell what's going on out on the field only for the yells of the fans overhead. When the bench wants to get in touch with the bull pen there's a telephone. It's the only real fancy, modern bull pen in baseball. Well, I was sitting around down there, not doing much throwing, when the phone rang and an excited voice said: "Send in Alexander."

I don't find out what happened until the game is over. Haines is breezing along with a 3–2 lead when he develops a blister on the knuckle of the first finger of his right hand. The blister breaks and the finger is so sore he can't hold the ball. Before Rog knows it the Yanks have the bases filled.

I take a few hurried throws and then start for the box. There's been a lot of stories about how long it took me to walk from the bull pen to the mound and how I looked, and all that. Well, as I said, I didn't know what had happened when I was called.

So when I come out from under the bleachers I see the bases filled and Lazzeri standing in the box. Tony is up there all alone, with everyone in that Sunday crowd watching him. So I just said to myself, "Take your time. Lazzeri isn't feeling any too good up there and let him stew." But I don't remember picking any four-leaf clovers, as some of the stories said.

I get to the box and Bob O'Farrell, our catcher, comes out to meet me. "Let's start right where we left off yesterday," Bob said. Yesterday [Saturday] Lazzeri was up four times against me without getting anything that looked like a hit. He got one off me in the second game of the series, but with one out of seven I wasn't much worried about him, although I knew that if he got all of a pitch, he'd hit it a long piece.

I said okay to O'Farrell. We'll curve him. My first pitch was a curve and Tony missed. Holding the ball in his hand, O'Farrell came out to the box again. "Look, Alex," he began. "This guy will be looking for that curve next time. We curved him all the time yesterday. Let's give him a fast one." I agreed and poured one in, right under his chin. There was a crack and I knew the ball was hit hard. A pitcher can tell pretty well from the sound. I spun around to watch the ball and all the Yankees on bases were on their way. But the drive had a tail-end fade and landed foul by eight-ten feet in the left-field bleachers.

So I said to myself, "No more of that for you, my lad." Bob signed for another curve and I gave him one. Lazzeri swung where that curve started but not where it finished. The ball got a hunk of the corner and then finished outside. Well we were out of that jam but there still were two innings to go.

I set the Yanks down in order in the eighth and got the first two in the ninth. And then Ruth came up. The Babe had scored the Yanks' first run of the game with a tremendous homer and he was dynamite to any pitcher. I didn't take any chances on him but worked the count to three and two, pitching for the corners all the time. Then Babe walked and I wasn't very sorry either when I saw him perched on first. Of course Bob Meusel was the next hitter and he'd hit over 40 homers that season and would mean trouble.

If Meusel got hold of one it could mean two runs and the series, so I forgot all about Ruth and got ready to work on Meusel. I'll never know why the guy did it but on my first pitch to Meusel, the Babe broke for second. He (or Miller Huggins) probably figured that it would catch us by surprise. I caught the blur of Ruth starting for second as I pitched and then came the whistle of the ball as O'Farrell rifled it to second. I wheeled around and there was one of the grandest sights of my life. Hornsby, his foot anchored on the bag and his gloved hand outstretched was waiting for Ruth to come in. There was the series and my second big thrill of the day. The third came when Judge Landis mailed out the winners' checks for $5,584.51.

I guess, I had every thrill that could come to a pitcher except one. I never pitched a no-hit game. I pitched 16 one-hitters during my time in the National League and that's coming pretty close, pretty often.

You know you think of a lot of funny things that happened in baseball, sittin' around gabbing like this. I remember

THE BOX SCORE
(October 10, 1926)

St. Louis	A.B.	R.	H.	P.	A.	New York	A.B.	R.	H.	P.	A.
Holm, cf.	5	0	0	2	0	Combs, cf.	5	0	2	2	0
Southworth, rf.	4	0	0	0	0	Koenig, ss.	4	0	0	2	3
Hornsby, 2b.	4	0	2	4	1	Ruth, rf.	1	1	1	2	0
Bottomley, 1b.	3	1	1	14	0	Meusel, lf.	4	0	1	3	0
Bell, 3b.	4	1	0	0	4	Gehrig, 1b.	2	0	0	11	0
Hafey, lf.	4	1	2	3	0	Lazzeri, 2b.	4	0	0	2	1
O'Farrell, c.	3	0	0	3	2	Dugan, 3b.	4	1	2	2	3
Thevenow, ss.	4	0	2	1	3	Severeid, c.	3	0	2	3	1
Haines, p.	2	0	1	0	4	Adams	0	0	0	0	0
Alexander, p.	1	0	0	0	0	Collins, c.	1	0	0	0	0
						Hoyt, p.	2	0	0	0	1
						Paschal	1	0	0	0	0
						Pennock, p.	1	0	0	0	1
Totals	34	3	8	27	14	Totals	32	2	8	27	10

Adams ran for Severeid in 6th.
Paschal batted for Hoyt in 6th.

St. Louis	0	0	0	3	0	0	0	0	0—3
New York	0	0	1	0	0	1	0	0	0—2

Errors—Koenig, Meusel, Dugan. Runs batted in—O'Farrell, Thevenow (2), Ruth, Severeid. Two-base hit—Severeid. Home run—Ruth. Sacrifice hits— Haines, Koenig, Bottomley. Sacrifice fly—O'Farrell. Struck out—By Haines 2, by Alexander 1, by Hoyt 2. Bases on balls—Off Haines 5, off Alexander 1. Hits—Off Hoyt, 5 in 6 innings; off Pennock, 3 in 3 innings; off Haines, 8 in 6 2-3 innings; off Alexander, 0 in 2 1-3 innings. Winning pitcher—Haines. Losing pitcher—Hoyt.

when I was with the Cubs, and I was with them longer than any other club, we were playing the Reds in a morning game on Decoration Day. The game was in the 11th when I went up to bat and I said: "If they give me a curve ball, I'll hit it in the bleachers. My wife's got fried chicken at home for me." They gave me a curve and I hit 'er in the bleachers.

LUKE APPLING

as told to John C. Hoffman

An institution passed from Chicago's South Side when Lucius Benjamin Appling, born April 2, 1909, in High Point, North Carolina, laid aside the tools he had so capably used at Comiskey Park. "Old Aches and Pains," he was called, but there was very little Luke couldn't do with a bat and a glove, in his 19 years' service with the White Sox. Luke went straight from Oglethorpe University to the big leagues, but in 1951 he was finally sent to the minors —as manager of the Memphis Chicks of the Southern Association.

MAN, I've been in 2372 major league ball games and I've played 2198 at shortstop and you ask me to tell about my greatest baseball game.

Well, let's see, I'll have to do some thinking about that. I can remember a lot of games in which I didn't do so well or I booted one at the wrong time. Those are the ones you remember most, because they are the ones you'd like to forget. I don't guess I'll ever forget some of them. They hurt and the pain is lasting. It's almost twenty years, now, since I first joined the White Sox from down in Georgia, but that isn't such a long time, believe me, when you think back and reckon about the things you'd like to do all over again.

I suppose a guy can't be around so long and not have a few real good days. The game I'll always regard as my greatest was one we played August 5, 1933, in St. Louis.

There are four things I'll remember most about that game. One was that I made five hits—three doubles and two singles —against the Browns. Another was that it was terribly hot. A third was that I will always believe I should have been credited with a sixth hit my last time at bat. And, finally, Bump Hadley had been riding me pretty hard about not being able to hit to left field.

There were other games, too, like the one in which I hit a home run against Rube Walberg to beat the Athletics. Then there was a time in 1949 in which I broke up a game in New York with a home run off Joe Page of the Yankees. Those things always make you feel good inside, especially when they win for your team. And they help to balance the scale against the things you don't do when you lose.

A day I'll always have to remember as the one which gave me the feeling that the world was right was August 6, 1949. It had seemed like a game that would never arrive, because it was my 2154th at shortstop and that set a new major league record. But the thing that stands out most in my memory is that Rabbit Maranville, who had held the old record, was there and he took it like the great little guy that he is. He had worked just as hard as I had for that record and I don't think he ever expected it would be broken.

I say the game was a long time arriving, not because it had taken almost twenty years, but because every time it would seem within easy grasp something would happen. Some statistician would find where somebody else had played a game that wasn't in one record book or another. Then, when I was all set to break the record in Philadelphia, it rained and the occasion had to be delayed until we reached Washington.

One of the happiest days I can remember is one the White Sox, fans and baseball writers, staged for me in June, 1947. I can truthfully say I have never appreciated anything more in my life, but I guess they thought Ol' Luke was about through. The baseball writers gave me a rod and reel, a really good one.

Then there was the night—January 22, 1950—when the baseball writers presented me with the J. Louis Comiskey award for what they called long and meritorious service to baseball. I guess if I don't get through playing ball pretty soon the next thing they'll give me will be a Mickey Finn.

There's been a lot of kidding about my age and some say I taught Abner Doubleday the rudiments of the game, but I was through teaching when he came along. Some people think thirty-nine years is a long time, but I like the age. That's why I have been celebrating my thirty-ninth birthday anniversary, now, for four or five years and will do so again.

Before I stray too far from my greatest game, though, I'd better get back to August 5, 1933. If you think I'm old, you must remember that that was exactly 112 years after the death of Napoleon and 198 years after the birth of Daniel Boone.

I can still hear Bump Hadley riding me about not being able to hit to left field. And for a while in that game, it looked as if he was right. He kept throwing pitches outside so I'd hit to right field. He was not perturbed in the first inning when I hit a line drive over first base for my first double.

I got my second double in the fourth inning and it went to right field. Jackie Hayes singled and we got our second run of the game. As I rounded third, Hadley gave me the works.

"You couldn't throw a ball to left field," he moaned.

I just laughed and told him I was going to pull his next pitch into left field. I was up again in the fifth and this time I singled, but again it went to right field. It was a high pitch outside and I guess I was lucky, but there were other hits by Mule Haas, Earl Webb, Jimmie Dykes and Charley Berry and we scored four runs to lead the Browns, 6 to 5.

When he saw my single going into right field, Bump yelled, "That's where you will always hit them."

I made up my mind I was going to hit one to left field if it took all summer. So the next time up in the sixth inning, I doubled through short for my third double. But by this time Bump had been taking such a beating that I didn't have the heart to kid him about my hit to left field.

Well, they took him out of the game and I wasn't up again until the ninth inning. This time I hit a slow roller down the third base line. Storti came in fast for the ball, made a grab for it, but I was on first before he could pick it up.

I thought for sure it would be scored a hit and it made me feel pretty good to think I had made six hits in one game. But that night when I looked at the box score in the paper I saw where I had been credited with five hits. But that didn't spoil it for me. Five hits is enough for anybody in one game.

The only thing I regretted was that we finally lost the game in the twelfth inning. Earl Webb kicked one in the ninth to let the Browns score the tying run after two were out and after three hours under the blistering heat, Red Faber finally was the loser in the twelfth inning when big Ed Wells won his own game with a double.

Well, I suppose that would have to be regarded as my greatest game.

There was still another game which sticks in my memory, not because of any wonderful achievements, but because it helped us beat old Red Ruffing, who was then in his prime. Many guys consider it a great day if they hit a homer or two and that does help to brighten things, but this one brought nothing much more spectacular than a lot of foul balls and a base on balls. You see, I don't hit many home runs, so I have to think about foul balls.

We were playing in the Yankee Stadium one day and Ruffing was pitching against us. He was a tough guy to hit in those days and nobody would beat him very often.

The first two batters reached base—I've forgotten how—and then it was my turn to bat. Red threw a couple of pitches across and I thought they were going to be balls, but before I knew it he had two strikes on me. Now it was up to me to either make sure the next pitches were balls or at least foul them off so he wouldn't strike me out.

I think Red figured he had me in a bad spot and he was eager to get that third strike. He threw strikes, too, but luckily I fouled off four or five of them. They just weren't the kind of pitches I liked, so I had to do something to keep from being called out on strikes.

Then I think he thought I might go for a bad pitch, so he threw a couple of balls outside and low and finally the count was three and two. I fouled off a couple more and by now I think Red was slightly disgusted with the whole business. Anyhow, he missed the plate with a fourth ball and I walked.

Little Mike Kreevich was the next hitter with the bases full. He slammed out a double to score three runs and that was enough for Big Red.

I heard later that, as he passed through the Yankee dugout, somebody asked Red what happened. It was unusual for Ruffing to be knocked out in those days.

"Why, that —— Appling wore me out," he grunted. Red didn't know it, but I was worn out too. He had me worried.

I've been kidded a lot about the number of foul balls I hit and how much it costs the club to supply new balls. I do hit a lot of foul balls, but I don't think I do it intentionally. There's just something in my swing which causes me to hit to right and by accident I get quite a few base hits that way.

I remember one day I had some friends up from Georgia and I asked Joe Berry, our traveling secretary, for a couple of tickets to the game. He became involved in something else and forgot to leave them. I wound up buying the tickets.

That same day I hit about two dozen foul balls into the

THE BOX SCORE

(August 5, 1933)

CHICAGO (A)	A.B.	R.	H.	P.O.	A.	ST. LOUIS (A)	A.B.	R.	H.	P.O.	A.
Swanson, rf.	7	1	1	3	0	Storti, 3b.	5	1	1	1	4
Haas, cf.	5	2	2	5	0	West, cf.	5	3	4	4	0
Webb, 1b.	5	1	1	14	0	Reynolds, lf.	5	1	1	5	0
Simmons, lf.	6	1	1	3	0	Campbell, rf.	5	0	1	4	0
Appling, ss.	6	3	5	3	4	Burns, 1b.	5	2	3	18	0
Dykes, 3b.	5	1	3	0	2	Melillo, 2b.	6	2	3	1	7
Hayes, 2b.	6	0	2	2	8	Shea, c.	6	0	0	2	1
Berry, c.	6	0	1	4	1	Hadley, p.	2	0	1	0	1
Durham, p.	2	0	1	0	0	McDonald, p.	0	0	0	0	0
Heving, p.	3	0	0	0	0	Stiles, p.	0	0	0	0	0
Faber, p.	1	0	0	0	1	Wells, p.	2	0	1	0	0
						Levey, ss.	6	1	1	1	3
						a Garms	1	0	0	0	0
						b Gullic	1	0	0	0	0
Totals	52	9	17	*34	16	Totals	49	10	16	36	16

a b Pinch hitters.

CHICAGO (A)	1	0	0	1	4	3	0	0	0	0	0	0— 9
ST. LOUIS (A)	1	0	2	2	0	2	0	0	2	0	0	1—10

*One out when winning run scored.

Errors—Storti 2, Appling 2, Webb. Runs batted in—Simmons, Appling 3, Hayes 2, Dykes 2, Berry, Reynolds, Burns, West 2, Levey 2, Hadley, Wells. Sacrifice—West. Two base hits—Appling 3, Swanson, Simmons, Reynolds, Hadley, West, Wells. Three base hits—West 2. Home run—West. Double play —Dykes, Hayes to Webb. Strikeouts—Hadley 1, Heving 4. Bases on balls— Hadley 3, Faber 3. Hits off—Durham 5 in 3 (none out in 4th), Heving 8 in 5 2-3, Faber 3 in 2 2-3, Hadley 13 in 5 2-3, McDonald 1 in 1-3, Stiles 2 in 2, Wells 14 in 9 2-3. Winning pitcher—Wells. Losing pitcher—Faber. Time—3:00.

stand, costing the club about $30. Joe still laughs about that and accuses me of having done it on purpose. I had told some of the players I was going to do that to get even, but in this game you just can't call your shots that good. If you could, every game you played would be your greatest.

EWELL BLACKWELL

as told to Tom Swope

*Ewell (The Whip) Blackwell,
was one of the most feared right-
handers in the game when he
was at his peak for the Cincinnati Reds in the late '40s. Ralph
Kiner, National League homer
champ of that era, rated
him the most difficult
pitcher he ever faced.
Blackwell pitched for a
chronic second-division
team and a serious kidney oper-
ation destroyed his effectiveness
after a comparatively short career. He might easily have been
one of the all-time bests. A Cali-
fornian, Blackwell finished up
with a brief appearance in the
American League with the
Yankees and Kansas City. His
most effective pitch was a three-
quarters delivery at blinding
speed which the batters saw only
at the last moment, if at all.*

EVERY day on which I pitched for the Cincinnati Reds while
running up a string of 16 consecutive victories, each a completely pitched game, in 1947, stands out as a great one in my
baseball career.

The greatest, though, was not a great day but a great night.

That was the night of June 18 when I managed to hold the Boston Braves hitless while winning No. 8 of my string of 16 in a row.

I wasn't the only Red to make that a great night. Our whole team put on a great show. Maybe we figured we had to treat the crowd of slightly more than 18,000 to baseball fireworks to make up for the absence of the usual fireworks program Cincinnati's club was in the habit of shooting off before each night game at Crosley Field, our home park.

For a long time that evening it was uncertain if we would have a game at all. Rain fell almost up to game time, eliminating the fireworks from the pre-game activities. However, the rain stopped in time for Ed Wright, Boston's starting pitcher, and myself to take our usual pre-game warm ups and play got under way almost two minutes ahead of the scheduled starting time of 8:30.

The management of the Cincinnati club, with the aid of the umpires who that night were Al Barlick behind the plate, Artie Gore on first base, and Babe Pinelli on third base, "sneaked" those two minutes in the hope of getting the game completed should more rain fall.

Once we got started, though, the rain remained in the clouds and we went through the contest without any delays for weather, completing the game in an hour and fifty-one minutes.

A north wind blew across the field, making the 66-degree weather feel cooler than it was. That wind was against the right-handed batters but was favorable to those swinging from the left side of the plate. Four of Boston's first five hitters batted left-handed as did four of Cincinnati's nine starters. Our left-handed swingers found it comparatively easy to get hits off the pitching of Wright, Walter Lanfranconi and Anton Karl but luck rode with me in the pinches and some hot shots from the bats of the Boston batters were gathered in by my mates.

'Bama Rowell, playing left field for the Braves and batting third, gave me as much trouble that night as almost all the other Braves put together. He hit my pitching for three wicked line drives but all were caught, each by a different Red.

I started the game knowing my fast ball was hopping as much as it ever has before or since and soon found out that my curve wasn't much good. My catcher, Ray Lamanno, also found this out early so he wisely called for fast balls practically the entire game.

Every pitch I delivered was in keeping with the sort Lamanno had signalled for the first time he gave me the sign. I never once shook him off. My fast one was jumping so much when the game started I walked Tommy Holmes, Boston's leadoff man, before I began properly gauging the hop on it plus the distance the wind was carrying the ball off line.

Johnny Hopp then followed with a sacrifice. That put Holmes on second. Not another Brave reached second until I walked both Phil Masi and Sibbi Sisti with one out in the eighth when my fast one was jumping slightly outside the strike zone. Second was as far as those two runners got.

Holmes, in the first, Masi and Sisti, in the eighth, and Hopp, in the seventh, all of whom walked, were the only Braves to get on base. The Reds fielded perfectly behind me.

After Hopp had sacrificed Holmes to second base in the first inning, I got my first big break of the night. Rowell followed with a wicked liner. But shortstop Eddie Miller swallowed up the ball in his big hands, tossed to Zientara and Holmes was doubled off second base.

Our side then came to bat and in no time at all had a winning lead. Frankie Baumholtz, our right fielder, opened with a single to left, the first of four hits he made in five swings that night. After Zientara had struck out, Grady Hatton waited out Wright for a walk and Young then stepped into a 1–1 pitch and drove it into the right field bleachers for three runs.

Came the eighth inning and Young again hit a three-run homer into the same bleachers, clouting this one off a 3–1 pitch by Karl.

The final score was 6 to 0, so Young drove in all of the game's runs to make it one of the great performances of his career.

With those opening three runs posted on the board, the Braves went down one, two, three through the sixth inning. Rowell hit his second hot drive of the game for the third out of the fourth inning, a liner which Bert Haas, playing center field, captured without too much trouble.

Holmes opened the seventh with a wicked shot toward third. My roomie, Grady Hatton, with whom I then shared a bachelor apartment in Cincinnati, gathered in the ball and pegged Holmes out at first base.

Hopp here drew my second walk of the game and then Rowell really blasted one. For a while it appeared the ball might be going to clear the screen and land in the right field bleachers. But the pill didn't rise enough to do that. Baumholtz ran back, leaped high and picked the ball off the screen and that crisis was over.

Following my two walks to Masi and Sisti in the eighth, Connie Ryan hit a fly to left which was easy pickings for Augie Galan and Frank McCormick, batting for Lanfranconi, slammed a wicked liner but right at Hatton.

After Holmes had started the ninth with a grounder to Hatton, Hopp bunted in front of the plate. For an instant it appeared the ball might go for a scratch hit. But Lamanno jumped out from back of the bat, pounced on the ball, threw hard and true to Young, and Hopp was nipped.

Then up stepped Rowell, the fellow who had given me the most trouble all through the game. I knew that if I got him out my first major league no-hit game would be over and done with.

It was no secret to myself or anyone else in the park that night that I was one out removed from a no-hitter when

Rowell came to bat in the ninth. As a boy I used to read about pitchers who had pitched hitless games saying they didn't know the opposition had failed to hit safely until after the game when their mates rushed up to congratulate them and the crowd gave them an ovation.

Cincinnati's park, though, was one of the first in which each team's hits and errors were posted on the scoreboard all through the game along with the runs so the scoreboard showed that big zero in Boston's hit column all the way for myself and all others to see.

Rowell wasn't going to let me get away with a no-hitter if he could help it so he was up there swinging from his heels in the ninth. He fouled off two fast balls for two strikes and I was one strike away from a no-hitter. My next pitch was another fast one, high and outside. Rowell bit. He swung and missed, the ball plunked into Lamanno's big glove and my no-hitter had become a fact.

There was plenty of shouting and cheering in our clubhouse after the Reds reached it. Flashlight bulbs popped as the photographers snapped photos of me hugging Lamanno and Young, kissing a ball and doing all the stunts the photographers could think of.

The telephone rang and I was called to the phone. It was one of my friends in the rooftop press box who had to start pounding out the news immediately to be sent over the country on the telegraph wires. He wanted to know how I felt, what my best pitches had been and what I thought about my next start.

You know, Johnny Vander Meer, one of the first to grab my hand after the game, had pitched two successive no-hitters for the Reds against Boston and Brooklyn in June, 1938, the one at Brooklyn coming in that city's first night game. It was a cinch my next start would be against Brooklyn.

"I'll be trying for another just like this one my next time out," I shouted into the telephone, not in any spirit of bragging but just because I felt so good and so happy I was confident I could at least come close to another no-hitter against the Dodgers.

I came closer than I expected.

In the first game of a double-header at Cincinnati the afternoon of Sunday, June 22, 1947, I started off by throwing a called third strike past Eddie Stanky and until there was one out in the ninth I had the Dodgers hitless and held to three walks with the Reds again giving me errorless support. Then Stanky spoiled my bid for a second successive no-hitter with a ground ball which I should have fielded and turned into an out.

And had I done so I would have made it two no-hitters in succession because the next batter, little Albert Gionfriddo who later was to make the star fielding play of the 1947 World Series for the champion Dodgers, followed with a fly to Haas. That would have been the third out of the game had I fielded Stanky's ninth-inning effort.

Stanky hit directly back at my feet. Some observers in the crowd of more than 31,000 believe I missed fielding Stanky's ball because I am so tall at six feet, five inches, that I couldn't bend down low enough to get my hands on the ball. That wasn't the case. I had my glove down low enough to have fielded the ball but misjudged its speed and its hop and lifted my gloved hand an instant too soon and the ball passed under my glove, through my legs and on out into center field.

After Gionfriddo had flied out Jackie Robinson clipped a clean single to center and Carl Furillo grounded out to Young to end the game. So it was a two-hitter instead of a second successive no-hit game. But had I fielded Stanky's single, Robinson never would have come to bat to make the second hit.

I'm proud, of course, of my no-hitter of June 18 and my close bid for two successive hitless games but I'm prouder of the fact that every one of my string of sixteen successive victories that season was a completely pitched game, that five of the sixteen were shutouts and that the Giants had to go ten innings on July 30 to stop my winning streak in a 5–4

THE BOX SCORE
(June 18, 1947)

BOSTON (N)	A.B.	R.	H.	P.O.	A.	CINCINNATI	A.B.	R.	H.	P.O.	A.
Holmes, rf.	3	0	0	3	0	Baumholtz, rf.	5	2	4	3	0
Hopp, cf.	2	0	0	3	0	Zientara, 2b.	3	0	1	2	2
Rowell, lf.	4	0	0	0	0	Hatton, 3b.	1	2	1	1	4
R. Elliott, 3b.	3	0	0	1	1	Young, 1b.	5	2	2	9	1
Torgeson, 1b.	3	0	0	8	3	Haas, cf.	4	0	0	3	0
Masi, c.	2	0	0	2	1	Galan, lf.	5	0	2	4	0
Sisti, ss.	2	0	0	3	4	Miller, ss.	5	0	0	2	1
Ryan, 2b.	3	0	0	4	1	Lamanno, c.	3	0	1	2	1
Wright, p.	0	0	0	0	0	Blackwell, p.	4	0	1	0	2
Lanfranconi, p.	2	0	0	0	1						
a McCormick	1	0	0	0	0						
Karl, p.	0	0	0	0	0						
Totals	25	0	0	24	11	Totals	35	6	12	27	11

a Batted for Lanfranconi in 8th.

BOSTON (N)	0	0	0	0	0	0	0	0	0—0	
CINCINNATI	3	0	0	0	0	0	0	3	x—6	

Errors—Sisti 2. Runs batted in—Young 6. Home runs—Young 2. Sacrifices —Hopp, Zientara 2. Double plays—Miller and Zientara; Ryan, Sisti and Torgerson. Left on base—Boston 3, Cincinnati 13. Bases on balls—Blackwell 4, Wright 3, Lanfranconi 1, Karl 3. Strikeouts—Blackwell 3, Wright 1. Hits off— Wright 3 in 1 1-3, Lanfranconi 6 in 5 2-3, Karl 3 in 1. Hit by pitcher—Wright (Haas). Losing pitcher—Wright. Umpires—Barlick, Gore and Pinelli. Time— 1:51. Attendance—18,137.

game in which Buddy Kerr drove in the winning run by hitting a 3–2 pitch into center for a single with two out in the extra round. After that hit I fanned Bobby Thomson but that strikeout came too late.

LOU BOUDREAU

as told to Ed McAuley

For one brilliant season Louis Boudreau was Frank Merriwell reincarnated. Born July 1917, in Harvey, Illinois, Boudreau was appointed Cleveland pilot in 1941, when only 25, the youngest big league manager in history. Boudreau's take-charge performance in 1948, when he batted, fielded and masterminded the Indians to a world championship, is truly one of baseball's most magnificent one-man achievements.

Boudreau managed for a number of American League clubs and finished his field career with the Chicago Cubs. He is now a popular broadcaster in the Windy City.

BASEBALL has given me a large lockerful of emotional souvenirs since the night in 1939 when Ray Mack and I—co-featured with Tony Galento—arrived from Buffalo to become full-fledged members of the Cleveland Indians.

Not all of my happiest memories are connected with personal accomplishment. I had the good fortune to play shortstop in four no-hit games delivered by Cleveland pitchers, two by Bob Feller and one each by Don Black and Bob Lemon.

Joe Gordon and Ken Keltner, my veteran teammates of the infield, have given me many a thrill, and the roots of my hair still tingle when I recall some of the relief pitching miracles of Russ Christopher and Satchel Paige.

On the personal side, when I am asked to name my greatest game, I think quickly of a belly-slamming stop I made behind second base one day in Yankee Stadium. That one started a double play and saved a big ball game, but the kick came in the sudden realization that all those Yankee rooters —there must have been more than 70,000 of them—were on their feet, giving the enemy shortstop an ovation.

Then there was the afternoon of August 8, 1948, the season when the pennant almost literally rode on every pitch. I was in the third day of a week's layoff ordered by the club physician after I injured my ankle, knee and shoulder in a collision with Gil Coan of the Washington Senators.

The Yankees were in town for a Sunday double-header and 73,484 spectators paid their way into our mammoth Stadium. Glumly, I looked on from the bench as the visitors shelled their way into a 6–1 lead.

But in our half of the seventh, Keltner walked and Johnny Berardino hit a home run. Eddie Robinson followed with a homer to leave us only two runs behind. Then Jim Hegan singled, Allie Clark walked and Dale Mitchell singled.

The bases were filled, we were back in the ball game. It was Thurman Tucker's turn to bat, but I decided a right-handed pinch hitter might have a better chance against the Yankees' great southpaw, Joe Page.

Our best right-handed hitter—the official averages said— was a fellow named Boudreau. I grabbed a bat and clumped out of the dugout as the public address announcer started to say: "Your attention, please. Now batting for . . ."

If he finished the sentence, he wasted his breath. Never before or since have I heard such a thrilling roar from a baseball crowd. There was a lump in my throat as I faced

Page, but I was calm enough to know I mustn't hit the pitch he wanted me to hit. I let the first two go by, then pulled one into left field for a single that tied the score. We went on to win that game, then took the second one also. It was— with one exception—the biggest day of our drive to the championship.

The one exception was October 4, 1948, when we moved into Boston for the only title play-off in the history of the American League. In view of the importance of the game to so many people, to say nothing of the impact of my entire career, I suppose I'd have to place that contest with the Red Sox at the top of my list of thrills.

Most fans are familiar with the extraordinary emotional background against which I led my club onto the field that historic afternoon. For Joe McCarthy, the Boston manager, the game was tremendously important—but no more so than a dozen others in which that genius of the dugout had figured during his long career.

For me, it was make or break. I had convinced myself long before that Bill Veeck, then the Indians' president and by no means the country's greatest admirer of my managerial moves, would trade me or buy up my contract if I failed to produce the pennant. I believed that every move I made was a life-or-death move so far as my future with the Indians was concerned.

Many times, in common with all other managers, I have planned just as carefully and thought just as hard as I planned and thought that day, only to have my strategy look silly. But that day, everything worked.

In the first place, I had decided that big Gene Bearden, our freshman southpaw, represented the best hope of our tired pitching staff. That was a gamble, especially in Fenway Park, but Gene didn't let me down.

In the second place, I had the good fortune to park one of Dennis Galehouse's pitches in the very first inning in that fish net beyond the close left field fence. We were a long way from home, but it's always comforting, especially in a game like that one, to get in the first punch.

The Sox quickly regained that run and we went into the fourth inning deadlocked at 1–1. I led off with a single to left. Gordon also singled, moving me to second. With Keltner at bat, I was tempted to order the orthodox sacrifice bunt —but only tempted. At that stage of the game, I decided to play for a big inning.

Seldom in baseball history has a manager's judgment been so quickly or so spectacularly justified. Keltner not only "hit away." He hit the ball far over that left field fence for his 31st home run of the season. We had a lead of 4 to 1 and, with Bearden pitching with the nonchalance of a veteran in a meaningless exhibition, the pennant race, to all practical purposes, was over.

We got another run that inning, then I hit my second homer of the day in the fifth. The Red Sox got two in the sixth, but we added single runs in both the eighth and ninth. I managed to single in my last turn at bat, so wound up with a perfect afternoon, two home runs, two singles and an intentional pass.

We won the game, 8 to 3, and with it Cleveland's first pennant in twenty years. When Keltner fielded Birdie Tebbetts' grounder and fired the ball to Eddie Robinson for the last putout of the game, I rushed to the box where Della, my wife, was sitting, but neither of us could say a word. I just threw my arms around her and kissed her as hard as I could.

MORDECAI BROWN

as told to Jack Ryan

Mordecai Peter Centennial Brown was known as "Three-Fingers" because an accident had destroyed half the index finger of his pitching hand. Nevertheless, he was the ace of the Chicago Cub staff between 1906 and 1911, pitching his last game in 1916. Born October 19, 1876, in Nyesville, Indiana, Three-Finger Brown died on February 14, 1948.

WHEN Manager Frank Chance led the Chicago Cub team into New York the morning of October 8, 1908, to meet the Giants that afternoon to settle a tie for the National League pennant, I had a half-dozen "black hand" letters in my coat pocket. "We'll kill you," these letters said, "if you pitch and beat the Giants."

Those letters and other threats had been reaching me ever since we had closed our regular season two days before in Pittsburgh. We'd beaten the Pirates in that final game for our 98th win of the year and we had waited around for two days to see what the Giants would do in their last two games with Boston. They had to win 'em to tie us for the National League championship.

Well, the Giants did win those two to match our record of 98 wins and 55 losses so a playoff was in order. I always thought that John McGraw used his great influence in National League affairs to dictate that the playoff must be held on the Giants' home field, the Polo Grounds.

I'd shown the "black hand" letters to Manager Chance and owner, Charley Murphy. "Let me pitch," I'd asked 'em, "just to show those so-and-sos they can't win with threats."

Chance picked Jack Pfeister instead. Two weeks before, Pfeister had tangled with Christy Mathewson, McGraw's great pitcher, and had beaten him on the play where young Fred Merkle, in failing to touch second on a hit, had made himself immortal for the "boner" play. Since Mathewson had been rested through the series with Boston and would go against us in the playoff, Chance decided to follow the Pfeister-Mathewson pitching pattern of the "boner" game. I had pitched just two days before as we won our final game of the schedule from Pittsburgh.

Matter of fact, I had started or relieved in 11 of our last 14 games. Beyond that I'd been in 14 of our last 19 games as we came down the stretch hot after the championship.

In our clubhouse meeting before the game, when Chance announced that Pfeister would pitch, we each picked out a New York player to work on. "Call 'em everything in the book," Chance told us. We didn't need much encouragement, either.

My pet target was McGraw. I'd been clouding up on him ever since I had come across his sly trick of taking rival pitchers aside and sort of softening them up by hinting that he had cooked up a deal to get that fellow with the Giants. He'd taken me aside for a little chat to that effect one time, hoping that in a tight spot against the Giants I'd figure I might as well go easy since I'd soon be over on McGraw's side.

Sure, it was a cunning trick he had and I didn't like it. So, the day after he'd given me that line of talk I walked up to him and said: "Skipper, I'm pitching for the Cubs this afternoon and I'm going to show you just what a helluva pitcher you're trying to make a deal for." I beat his Giants good that afternoon.

But that was early in the season and I want to tell you about this playoff game. It was played before what everybody said was the biggest crowd that had ever seen a baseball game. The whole city of New York, it seemed to us, was clear crazy with disappointment because we had taken that "Merkle boner" game from the Giants. The Polo Grounds quit selling tickets about 1 o'clock, and thousands who held tickets couldn't force their way through the street mobs to the entrances. The umpires were an hour getting into the park. By game time there were thousands on the field in front of the bleachers, the stands were jammed with people standing and sitting in aisles, and there were always little fights going on as ticket-holders tried to get their seats. The bluffs overhanging the Polo Grounds were black with people, as were the housetops. The elevated lines couldn't run for people who had climbed up and were sitting on the tracks.

The police couldn't move them, and so the fire department came and tried driving them off with the hose, but they'd come back. Then the fire department had other work to do, for the mob outside the park set fire to the left-field fence and was all set to come bursting through as soon as the flames weakened the boards enough.

Just before the game started the crowd did break down another part of the fence and the mounted police had to quit trampling the mob out in front of the park and come riding in to turn back this new drive. The crowds fought the police all the time, it seemed to us as we sat in our dugout. From the stands there was a steady roar of abuse. I never heard anybody or any set of men called as many foul names as the Giants' fans called us that day from the time we showed up till it was over.

We had just come out onto the field and were getting settled when Tom Needham, one of our utility men, came running up with the news that, back in the clubhouse he'd overheard Muggsy McGraw laying a plot to beat us. He said the plot was for McGraw to cut our batting practice to about four minutes instead of the regular 10, and then, if we protested to send his three toughest players, Turkey Mike Donlin, Iron Man McGinnity and Cy Seymour charging out to pick a fight. The wild-eyed fans would riot and the blame would be part on us for starting it and the game would be forfeited to the Giants.

Chance said to us "Cross 'em up. No matter when the bell rings to end practice, come right off the field. Don't give any excuse to quarrel."

We followed orders, but McGinnity tried to pick a fight with Chance anyway, and made a pass at him, but Husk stepped back, grinned and wouldn't fall for their little game.

I can still see Christy Mathewson making his lordly entrance. He'd always wait until about 10 minutes before game time, then he'd come from the clubhouse across the field in a long linen duster like auto drivers wore in those days, and at every step the crowd would yell louder and louder. This day they split the air. I watched him enter as I went out to the bull pen, where I was to keep ready. Chance still insisted on starting Pfeister.

Mathewson put us down quick in our first time at bat, but when the Giants came up with the sky splitting as the crowd screamed, Pfeister hit Fred Tenney, walked Buck Herzog, fanned Bresnahan, but Kling dropped the third strike and when Herzog broke for second, nailed him. Then Turkey Mike Donlin doubled, scoring Tenney and out beyond center field a fireman fell off a telegraph pole and broke his neck. Pfeister walked Cy Seymour and then Chance motioned me to come in. Two on base, two out. Our warmup pen was out in right center field so I had to push and shove my way through the crowd on the outfield grass.

"Get the hell out of the way," I bawled at 'em as I plowed through. "Here's where you 'black hand' guys get your chance. If I'm going to get killed I sure know that I'll die before a capacity crowd."

Arthur Devlin was up—a low-average hitter, great fielder but tough in the pinches. But I fanned him, and then you should have heard the names that flew around me as I walked to the bench.

I was about as good that day as I ever was in my life. That year I had won 29 and, what with relief work, had been in 43 winning ball games.

But in a way it was Husk Chance's day.

That Chance had a stout heart in him. His first time at bat, it was in the second, the fans met him with a storm of hisses —not "boos" like you hear in modern baseball—but the old, vicious hiss that comes from real hatred.

Chance choked the hisses back down New York's throat by singling with a loud crack of the bat. The ball came back to Mathewson. He looked at Bresnahan behind the bat, then wheeled and threw to first, catching Chance off guard. Chance slid. Tenney came down with the ball. Umpire Bill Klem threw up his arm. Husk was out!

Chance ripped and raved around, protesting. Most of us Cubs rushed out of the dugout. Solly Hofman called Klem so many names that Bill threw him out of the game.

The stands behind us went into panic, they were so tickled and the roar was the wildest I ever heard when Matty went on to strike out Steinfeldt and Del Howard.

Chance was grim when he came up again in the third. Tinker had led off the inning by tripling over Cy Seymour's head. We heard afterward that McGraw had warned Seymour that Tinker was apt to hit Mathewson hard, and to play away back. Seymour didn't. Kling singled Tinker home. I sacrificed Johnny to second. Sheckard flied out, Evers walked. Schulte doubled. We had Matty wabbling and then up came Chance, with the crowd howling. He answered them again with a double, and made it to second with a great slide that beat a great throw by Mike Donlin.

Four runs.

The Giants made their bid in the seventh. Art Devlin singled off me, so did Moose McCormick. I tried to pitch too carefully to Bidwell and walked him. There was sure bedlam in the air as McGraw took out Mathewson and sent up the kid, Larry Doyle, to hit. Doyle hit a high foul close to the stand and as Kling went to catch it, the fans sailed derby hats to confuse him—and bottles, papers, everything. But Kling had nerve and he caught it.

Every play, as I look back on it, was crucial. In the seventh after Tenney's fly had scored Devlin, Buck Herzog rifled one on the ground to left but Joe Tinker got one hand and one shin in front of it, blocked it, picked it up and just by a flash caught Herzog who made a wicked slide into first.

In the ninth a big fight broke out in the stands and the game was held up until the police could throw in a cordon of bluecoats and stop it. It was as near a lunatic asylum as I ever saw. As a matter of fact the newspapers next day said seven men had been carted away, raving mad, from the park during the day. This was maybe exaggerated, but it doesn't sound impossible to anyone who was there that day.

As the ninth ended with the Giants going out, one-two-three, we all ran for our lives, straight for the clubhouse with the pack at our heels. Some of our boys got caught by the mob and beaten up some. Tinker, Howard and Sheckard were struck. Chance was hurt most of all. A Giant fan hit him in the throat and Husk's voice was gone for a day or two of the World Series that followed. Pfeister got slashed on the shoulder by a knife.

We made it to the dressing room and barricaded the door. Outside wild men were yelling for our blood—really. As the mob got bigger, the police came up and formed a line across

THE BOX SCORE
(October 8, 1908)

CHICAGO	A.B.	H.	P.	A.	NEW YORK	A.B.	H.	P.	A.
Sheckard, lf.	4	0	4	0	Tenney, 1b.	2	1	9	0
Evers, 2b.	3	1	0	3	Herzog, 2b.	3	0	1	2
Schulte, rf.	4	1	4	0	Bresnahan, c.	4	1	10	2
Chance, 1b.	4	3	13	0	Donlin, rf.	4	1	0	0
Steinfeldt, 3b.	4	1	0	3	Seymour, cf.	3	0	2	0
Hofman, cf.	0	0	0	0	Devlin, 3b.	4	1	2	0
Howard, cf.	4	0	1	0	McCormick, lf.	4	1	3	1
Tinker, ss.	4	1	1	4	Bridwell, ss.	3	0	0	1
Kling, c.	3	1	4	1	Mathewson, p.	2	0	0	3
Pfeister, p.	0	0	0	0	Doyle	1	0	0	0
Brown, p.	2	0	0	1	Wiltse, p.	0	0	0	0
Totals	32	8	27	12	Totals	30	5	27	9

Doyle batted for Mathewson in 7th.

```
CHICAGO     0 0 4 0 0 0 0 0 0—4
NEW YORK    1 0 0 0 0 0 1 0 0—2
```

Error—Tenney. Runs—Tenney, Tinker, Kling, Evers, Schulte, Devlin. Runs batted in—Donlin, Kling, Schulte, Chance (2), Tenney. Two-base hits—Donlin, Schulte, Chance, Evers. Three-base hit—Tinker. Double plays—Kling to Chance; McCormick to Bresnahan. Bases on balls—Off Pfeister, 2; off Brown, 1; off Mathewson, 1. Hit by pitcher—By Pfeister, 1. Struck out—By Mathewson, 7; by Wiltse, 1; by Pfeister, 1; by Brown, 1. Hits—Off Pfeister, 1 in 2-3 inning; off Mathewson, 7 in 7 innings. Umpires—Johnstone and Klem.

the door. We read next day that the cops had to pull their revolvers to hold them back. I couldn't say as to that. We weren't sticking our heads out to see.

As we changed clothes, too excited yet to put on one of those wild clubhouse pennant celebrations, the word came in that the Giants over in their dressing room were pretty low. We heard that old Cy Seymour was lying on the floor, in there, bawling like a baby about Tinker's triple.

When it was safe we rode to our hotel in a patrol wagon, with two cops on the inside and four riding the running boards and the rear step. That night when we left for Detroit and the World Series we slipped out the back door and were escorted down the alley in back of our hotel by a swarm of policemen.

TY COBB

as told to Francis J. Powers

A proud man to the day he died, Ty Cobb's proudest achievement was his being given the most Hall of Fame votes ever. A unanimous choice on virtually every all-time all-star team ever assembled, Cobb held a fistful of records, including games played, times at bat, runs scored, stolen bases. In the latter department he led the American League six times and his record of 96 for the year 1915 stood until 1962. He was the Detroit Tigers' greatest player, and finished with a lifetime batting mark of .367. He played until he was 42, maintaining a strong interest in the game until he died July 17, 1961.

THERE was little brotherly love toward the Detroit Tigers when our club arrived in Philadelphia on the morning of September 27, 1907. That old city was baseball mad; it was mad at the Tigers and very mad at me. The wildest race the six-year-old American League then had produced was nearing an end and the Athletics were leading the Tigers by a half game. It had been a four-way race all summer with the defending White Sox, Athletics, Tigers and Cleveland jumping in and out of first place. Now the chase had boiled down to a fight between the Tigers and Athletics and would be settled in the series which was to open the next afternoon. For there were only two series remaining for each club.

The Tigers had come fast that year to be pennant contenders. Hughie Jennings, famous shortstop of the old Baltimore Orioles, had been brought up to manage the team and his "E-yah!" and grass-picking had made him a popular figure. I was on my way to winning my first batting championship and running the bases well. We had tremendous power with Claude Rossman on first and Sam Crawford in center field and I think those Tigers really were the first of the great slugging team that later made the American League synonymous with power. We had some great pitchers but particularly Wild Bill Donovan, one of the finest men ever in the game, who won 25 games and lost only four that season. Ours was a fighting team that neither asked nor gave quarter, patterned after the old Orioles of Jennings and John McGraw.

Philadelphia resented us as upstarts, for Connie Mack still had much of the same team which won the 1905 championship and then had lost to the Giants in that famous World's Series where every game was a shutout. The Mackmen had sensational pitchers in Chief Bender, Eddie Plank, Rube Waddell and Jack Coombs and were a solid defensive team. They were hot to reclaim the championship they had lost to the White Sox the previous season.

We won the first game of the series on September 28, when George Mullin outpitched Chief Bender, and went into first place by a half-game. Then it rained and a double-header was scheduled for September 30. There was the pennant. If we won, we had only Washington and St. Louis ahead while the Mackmen had a series with Cleveland before getting to the Senators and the "Naps," as Cleveland was called in those days, were certain to give Philadelphia trouble.

When we went on the field to start play there were 30,000 fans looking on. There were 25,000 packed into old Columbia Park that had a capacity of 18,000, and the rest were crowded into windows and on the roofs of houses overlooking the field. There were fans, several rows deep, around the outfield, restrained by ropes and mounted police, and they weren't the least bit friendly. Before that afternoon was finished and we left the park in the autumn dusk with street lights aglow, I had experienced about every thrill that can come in baseball . . . or so it seemed to a 19-year-old boy.

Jennings picked Donovan to pitch for the Tigers, leading with our ace, while Mr. Mack started Jimmy Dygert, a spitballer. Mack had Eddie Plank, the southpaw who always was tough to beat, ready but decided to save him for the second game. You never saw and maybe never heard of a game like this one. It went 17 innings and took three hours and 50 minutes to play. It produced great pitching and poor pitching, long crashing hits and some of the most unusual incidents to be found outside the realm of fiction.

At the end of five innings, Philadelphia led us 7 to 1. The Athletics wasted no time in pounding Donovan. Topsy Hartsel opened with a single and stole second. Socks Seybold walked and Kid Nicholls sacrificed. Harry Davis' hit bounced off Charlie O'Leary's leg and into "Germany" Schaefer's hands but Seybold was safe at second and Hartsel scored. Murphy beat out an infield hit and then Seybold scored on Jimmy Collins' fly and Rube Oldring sent Davis home with a double into the crowd.

Jennings would have had any pitcher other than Donovan out of the game before that inning finished but Philadelphia was Bill's home town and his dad and relatives always came out to see him work so Hughie never took him out there. It looked like foolish sentiment at that moment, but proved to be a good policy three hours later.

For a few minutes in the second inning it seemed as if we would get them all back. Rossman singled and was safe at second when Dygert threw wild, after fielding Bill Coughlin's smash. Charlie Schmidt sacrificed and then O'Leary hit to the box. Dygert chased Rossman almost to the plate before throwing to Ossie Schreck and then Claude hit the Athletics' catcher so hard he dropped the ball. Dygert walked Donovan but then Rube Waddell came in, and with a pitch that broke from your waist to the ground, fanned the next two batters.

The Athletics got two more in the third, Davis hit a home run in the fifth and Collins and Oldring hit into the crowd for another score and there we were, behind six runs. But this Tiger team was a fighting team and we moved back into the game with four runs in the seventh. Two walks and an error filled the bases and then Crawford drove into the left field crowd for two bases. Another scored on my infield out and Crawford raced home while Murphy was making a great play on Rossman. Then we were only two runs behind. The Athletics scored one in their half but we scored in the eighth and went into the ninth still two runs behind.

That ninth is one inning that always will remain bright in my memory. Crawford was on first when I came to bat and I hit a home run to tie the score. Right then and there Mr. Mack forgot about saving Plank for the second game and Eddie rushed to the box and retired the next three batters. We went out in front in the 11th when I hit into the crowd after Rossman's single but we couldn't hold the lead and the Athletics tied it, largely because of a wild pitch, at 9-all.

Then the game settled down to a brilliant duel between Donovan and Plank but at the same time produced some of the greatest confusion ever seen on any field. In the 14th inning, Harry Davis hit a long fly to center field that Sam Crawford muffed and it was good for two bases. Our team claimed interference, for a policeman had stepped in front of Crawford as he was following the ball along the ropes. "Silk" O'Loughlin was umpiring behind the plate (there were only two umpires in a game at that time) and it was his play. Both teams gathered around O'Loughlin, arguing and snarling. Finally O'Laughlin called to Tommy Connolly, umpiring at first base: "Was there interference?" Without hesitation,

Tommy called: "There was." So Davis was out and that was lucky for us, since Murphy followed with a single.

During the argument with the umpires, Rossman and Monte Cross, one of the Athletics' reserve infielders, threw some punches and soon there were players and policemen all over the field. Rossman was tossed out of the game and that started a new argument. Ed Killian, a left-handed pitcher, finished the inning at first base and later Sam Crawford came in from the outfield to play the bag. After the game, Connie Mack was bitter in his denunciation of O'Loughlin and it was one of the few times when he really roasted an umpire.

There was no further scoring, although I got as far as third in our half of the 17th, and at the end of that inning the game was called with the score still 9-all. There was no second game that day; it never was played and the tie meant the championship for us. We left Philadelphia a half game in front and swept through Washington. The Athletics lost one to Cleveland and another to the Senators and we cinched the pennant in St. Louis . . . Detroit's first since 1887, when it was in the old National League.

Although I had the thrill of hitting the homer that tied the score and making two runs, the star of that game was Bill Donovan. I don't recall a similar exhibition of pitching in my 25 years in the American League. Bill allowed eight runs in seven innings and only one in the next 10 and fanned 11. The modern generation doesn't remember Donovan, but there was a pitcher with great speed, a great curve and a great heart.

The Athletics made 20 hits that day to our 15 and we had 17 runners left on base to their 13. They made six errors, so during the long afternoon there was just about everything to be found in baseball.

THE BOX SCORE
(September 30, 1907)

DETROIT	A.B.	R.	H.	P.	A.	PHILADELPHIA	A.B.	R.	H.	P.	A.
Jones, lf.	7	1	1	5	0	Hartsel, lf.	9	1	4	3	0
Schaefer, 2b.	9	1	3	3	6	Nicholls, ss.	6	1	2	4	9
Crawford, cf.-1b.	8	2	2	7	0	Seybold, rf.	6	2	1	1	0
Cobb, rf.	8	2	3	1	0	Davis, 1b.	8	3	3	19	1
Rossman, 1b.	7	1	2	13	2	Murphy, 2b.	7	1	4	2	6
Killian, 1b.	0	0	0	1	0	J. Collins, 3b.	7	1	1	3	3
Mullin, 1b.	1	0	0	0	0	Oldring, cf.	7	0	3	3	0
Downs, cf.	1	0	0	2	0	Schreck, c.	4	0	0	9	1
Coughlin, 3b.	7	0	0	1	3	Powers, c.	3	0	0	4	0
Schmidt, c.	1	0	0	3	1	Dygert, p.	0	0	0	0	0
Payne, c.	6	0	1	9	1	Waddell, p.	4	0	0	1	0
O'Leary, ss.	8	1	2	3	1	Plank, p.	4	0	1	2	1
Donovan, p.	7	1	1	3	7	E. Collins	1	0	1	0	0
Totals	70	9	15	51	21	Totals	66	9	20	51	21

E. Collins batted for Oldring in 17th.

DETROIT	0 1 0 0 0 0 4 1 2 0 1 0 0 0 0 0 0—9
PHILADELPHIA	3 0 2 0 2 0 1 0 0 0 1 0 0 0 0 0 0—9

Errors—Schmidt, Nicholls, Oldring, Schreck, Powers, Dygert (2). Two-base hits—Crawford, Cobb, O'Leary, Hartsel (3), Nicholls, Davis, J. Collins, Oldring (2). Home runs—Cobb, Davis. Hits—Off Dygert, 1 in 1-3 innings; off Waddell, 7 in 7 2-3 innings; off Plank, 7 in 8 innings. Sacrifice hits—Schmidt, Crawford, Nicholls (2), J. Collins, Powers. Stolen bases—Coughlin, O'Leary, Cobb, Hartsel. Left on bases—Detroit 17, Philadelphia 13. First base on balls—Off Donovan 3, off Dygert 1, off Waddell 1, off Plank 2. First base on errors—Detroit 4. Hit by pitcher—By Plank 1. Struck out—By Donovan 11, by Waddell 7, by Plank 3. Wild pitch—Donovan. Time—3:50. Umpires—O'Loughlin and Connolly.

DIZZY DEAN

as told to John P. Carmichael

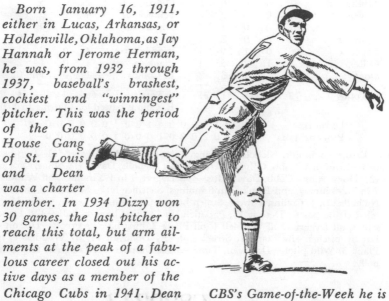

Born January 16, 1911, either in Lucas, Arkansas, or Holdenville, Oklahoma, as Jay Hannah or Jerome Herman, he was, from 1932 through 1937, baseball's brashest, cockiest and "winningest" pitcher. This was the period of the Gas House Gang of St. Louis and Dean was a charter member. In 1934 Dizzy won 30 games, the last pitcher to reach this total, but arm ailments at the peak of a fabulous career closed out his active days as a member of the Chicago Cubs in 1941. Dean moved into broadcasting. As a long-time announcer on CBS's Game-of-the-Week he is probably the country's best-known baseball telecaster.

As might have been expected, Jerome Hanna Dean did not confine himself to the traditional "Greatest Day in Baseball." He said: "I've had too derned many big days . . . lots of 'em."

I JUST wish my arm was like it was back in thirty-four. . . . I'd have me a picnic in this league. When I came up every club had three-four .300 hitters who really could powder that ball. Now? Shucks! I'd breeze home any day. I never forget

Frank Frisch the day I beat Detroit 11–0 in the last game of the World Series in 1934. We're in the clubhouse, see, celebratin' and I got a rubber tiger, all blown up, and I'm twistin' his tail and hollerin' like the rest and Frisch came by and stopped and you know what he said?

"Anybody with your stuff should have won 40 games this year instead of a measly 30," he said. "You loaf, that's the trouble. Thirty games! You ought to be 'shamed of yourself." Imagine that, and me just winning the series for him: ol' Diz out there pitchin' outta turn too, don't forget that. He wanted me to pitch although he'd said that Bill Hallahan was gonna work the last game. But he came to me the night before and he asked: "Diz, you wanna be the greatest man in baseball?" I told him I already was, but he didn't even hear me I guess, 'cause he went on: "You pitch that game tomorrow and you'll be tops." I just told him: "Gimme that ball tomorrow and your troubles are over." He wanted me to pitch I knew that. Hell, I was afraid he would let Hallahan start.

That was a big day in my life, I admit it. First World Series and all the excitement and everybody wild, and two trucks goin' up and down the streets, one playin', "Hold That Tiger" and the other tootlin' the "St. Louis Blues." I saw Babe Ruth and got his autograph, by jingo, and 'taint everybody pitches in a big series and gets Babe's name on a ball too. I liked that ol' Frisch, he was a helluva guy, but he worried all the time. He had nothin' to fret about with ol' Diz out there. You know we was leadin' 11–0 in the ninth with one out and he sent four pitchers down in the bull pen to warm up.

So help me, I thought they must be gettin' ready for the 1935 season. Eleven-nothing I got 'em and that Billy Rogell on base and Hank Greenberg came up. I already struck him out twice, no trouble 'tall, and when he came up in that ninth I hollered over to the Tiger bench, I said: "What, no pinch-hitter?" and Hank looked at me like he'd a liked to break one of them sticks over my head, but hell, he was my meat. He was easy.

You know what that Frisch did? I put two fast balls right past the letters on that Greenberg's uniform and when he missed the second one I hadda laugh. I put my glove up to my face to keep from laughin' right in his face, he looked so funny, and before I could throw any more Frisch came out. He was mad. He said: "Cut out the foolin', we got a lot at stake" and I just stood there and looked at him like he must be outta his mind . . . me leadin' 11–0 with one out in the last of the ninth. Just then Leo Durocher came in from short and he said: "Aw, what the hell, Frank, let the guy have his fun. What's the matter with you?" Well you know what Frisch told me? Yeah . . . he said: "You lose this guy and you're through." Eleven-nothing . . . I can't get over that yet. He was gonna pull me.

That Greenberg couldn't a hit that next pitch if he'd a started to swing when I wound up. Gonna pull me. He didn't even see it and the next guy was Owen and he forced Rogell and the whole thing was over. Them Tigers weren't bad; they gave us a good battle, but they were just pussy-cats with me. I don't like to brag a lot, because folks think I'm a big lunkhead or somethin', but when I had my fast ball, before I broke my toe and couldn't throw it any more, nobody hit me . . . much. You know what I did one day? I pitched a game in Boston and never took a sign or never threw nothin' but fast balls. A whole game, Bill Delancy was catchin'. I told Al Spohrer, the Braves' catcher, before the game that he could tell everybody I was gonna do that too. I beat 'em 10–0 or 13–0 . . . some score that. Just wound up and fogged that ball over.

I'll tell you another day in Boston I got a helluva kick. Remember seein' a big fat guy around with me a lot? Well, he was Johnny Perkins and he worked in a night club around St. Louis and he made this trip with us. He made me a bet I wouldn't strike out Vince DiMaggio the first time he came

up. I did and when I went back to the bench I made motions
to Perk I'd double the bet the next time. I struck him out
again and I put everything back on a third bet and I fanned
him three straight times. Then Perkins wanted to make it
all or nothin' so I took 'im and when DiMag came up again
he lifted a pop foul back of the plate. I thought Ogrodowski
was gonna catch it and I ran and hollered: "Let it go, let it
go." He couldn't get the ball anyway, as it turned out, 'cause
it hit the screen, but I'd a bumped him sure as hell if he'd
a got under it. I wanted to win that bet. I struck DiMaggio
out next pitch . . . four straight times.

I got a great kick outta the time I was traded to the Cubs,
just before the season opened in '38. All ballplayers want to
wind up their careers with the Cubs, Giants or Yankees . . .
they just can't help it. Seems like they're finally in the big
time, although of course the Cubs used to pay derned good
wages too, which they don't any more, so you couldn't help
a guy wantin' to land there. I didn't know anything about
it until I came in from the bench during a game with the
Browns right in St. Louis . . . spring series, you know . . .
and I was walkin' in the clubhouse door and somebody
grabbed my arm and it was Clarence Rowland, 'cept I didn't
know him then. He said: "Well, Diz, you belong to us now
. . . you're a Cub." Hell, I thought he was a fan and kiddin'
me and I said: "I'll see you later, bud," and went on inside.

There was a lot of newspapermen and photographers there
and I wondered what was going on, but never dreamed a
deal for me, and finally Branch Rickey came in and he whispered: "I want to see you in my office after you're dressed,"
and I said O.K., and then he called for silence and said: "We
just want to say we've made a deal with the Cubs and we have
traded this man here . . ." and he put an arm on my shoulder, but he should a put it under me 'cause I thought I'd
faint . . . "and we don't want you players to feel we're letting
you down, because we've got a man to replace him and we'll
still win the pennant."

Well, nobody seemed to know who that man to take my place was, but "Pepper" Martin, he got up on a chair, with a towel around him . . . he'd just come from the shower . . . and he made a helluva speech. He sounds like Mr. Rickey at that. I'd hate to have to listen to both of 'em in the same night. They'd have a guy really dizzy and I ain't kiddin'. He said: "Mr. Rickey, we appreciate you coming in to tell us what you've done and that we ain't going to be too bad off even if Diz here goes, that you still want us to win a pennant and we're all for you and we'll win too." Hell, I knew they couldn't win any ol' pennant without Diz, even if I was only a half a pitcher then, so when they asked me to say something for the newspapermen I said: "Well, Mr. Rickey, I predicted we'd win that flag right here in St. Louis, but now that I'm gone, we'll win it in Chicago and I'll see you get into the world series." How about that, huh, and then we back into it in Chicago? I reminded ol' Branch about that many a time, but I hadda laugh like the devil, 'cause we just made it.

That game I beat Pittsburgh in 1938 (Sept. 27) was just about as big a day as I ever remember. I never had nothin'. I wasn't even supposed to pitch. I was on the inactive list or somethin' and Gabby Hartnett came in the clubhouse that day and you know he twirls that big seegar around in that red face of his (I like ol' Gabby, even if I did call him a pickle-puss in Wichita which he was because he bawled me out right in front of all the players and people a-gazin' at me and fined me $100) and he said: "Dean, you're the pitcher" and I said: "Fine," but I thought he was kiddin' and then Larry French and Herman and them said: "He ain't foolin' Diz . . . you're pitchin'." My God, I couldn't break a pane of glass and I knew it, but I pitched.

They finally had to get me outta there in the ninth and I was leadin' 2–0 and Bill Lee went in and the first pitch he made was a wild one and a run scored, but he hung on and they didn't score again and, boy, I felt like a million. Ol' Diz saved many a game for Cardinal pitchers in his day and here was a guy who saved one for me and I told him, I said: "Lee, you're a great man," and he was a helluva guy and a swell pitcher. I always liked old Gabby, but he shouldn't have yelled at me in front of all those people in Wichita. They was a-gazin' at me like I was a freak and I don't stand for bein' shown up by nobody. The fine was all right. . . . I didn't get in until 20 minutes to 2 and we had a midnight deadline . . . but he could-a told me on the quiet.

The first game I pitched for the Cubs that year I beat Cincinnati and afterwards some of us went out and had a few beers and such, but I just went along. I didn't know what rules the Cubs had and figured these guys must know what they're doing. We had a helluva time, too, and then I beat the Cardinals and it looked like I'd have a great year, but Diz just didn't have so much left, I guess. But Mr. Wrigley told me not to worry, that he wasn't sorry he bought me and just go ahead and do the best I could and it's too bad I couldn't-a been with the Cubs when I wuz in my prime, because we'd a never got beat and I'd probably been drawin' $50,000 a year and pitchin' my arm off.

How about the time I had the run-in with Ford Frick? I'll never forget that either and I never apologized and never signed a derned letter and his secretary must-a wrote 20 different copies or somethin' for me to sign and I wouldn't. I was in a tough spot, though. See, I wuz pitchin' against Carl Hubbell here in St. Louis and he beat me 4–1. I led into the sixth or seventh and then George Barr, the umpire, called a balk on me; he said I didn't come to a stop before I threw. He was nuts, but anyway they got three runs and ol' Diz never liked to take a beatin'. No time. So I had to go to Belleville, Ill., that night to a banquet . . . promised a friend of mine there . . . and they said I said Frick and Barr were a couple of crooks. 'Course I was still pretty sore by then, too.

That was pretty strong and the Cardinals were goin' East, and when we got to Brooklyn there I was suspended without pay and supposed to apologize. Frick had me up there and waved a lot of telegrams and said this was something terrible, look what all these people had to say, and I told him: "You must live out there and wait till I get some telegrams where I live" and I got some too and they all said I never said nothin' like he was a crook and I wouldn't sign no paper, but I was in a helluva spot and don't you forget it. Frisch was crazy. I got so many laughs listenin' to him I wouldn't a signed even if I'd been wrong and once I told him I had a notion to sue the National League for slander and Frank hit the ceiling. All he wanted me to do was get back in uniform.

So Frick finally saw the error of his ways and I got back, but I had a great time not workin' for a few days. Nightclubbin' every night and a couple of times I ran into ol' Frisch and gave him a big cheery hello and I didn't pitch neither until I made sure I got paid for that time out. Well, it was June 9, 1936, when I put on the uniform and Hubbell'd beaten me May 19 in St. Louis. So here we were again and that Polo Grounds was a madhouse. I was afraid to come out of the dugout. Everybody was yellin' and throwin' things down at our bench and I waited until Frisch said: "You only got five minutes, you better warm up," so I dashed out there by home plate and warmed up and I was almost deaf from the noise when I got through.

I just went out there and pitched a cool three-hitter in the first game of a double-header and beat Hubbell 8–1 and I'd had a shutout only Durocher booted one near the end. Yes sir, ol' Jay Hanna Dean was just in ripe form that day and there was nobody gonna make a monkey outa him. I told that Durocher after the game, I said: "You oughta been more careful on that ball, I wanted to rub it in" and he said: "You rubbed it in enough, don't worry about it . . . the time to boot 'em, if you have to, is when you got runs to spare," which I guess is probably right.

Oh say, I'm forgettin' just about the best day of all, although there was nothin' like that series of 1934, but the afternoon I struck out 17 Cubs wasn't no ordinary day neither. That was July 30, 1933, and nobody's broken the record yet. Frisch had only been manager a couple of days . . . he took Street's job . . . and Guy Bush started against me and nothin' ever occurred to me 'bout this bein' a big day. Hell, Koenig doubled and Herman singled in the first inning and I was losin' 1–0 'fore we ever came to bat. Frisch had two guys warmin' up . . . he didn't know ol' Diz so well then.

We had the biggest crowd in two years in Sportsman's Park, almost 30,000, and I came in off the bench the end of the first inning and Frisch said: "I'm sendin' you to the bull pen next inning if you don't get better" and I told him: "Hell, you worry about gettin' a couple of runs. . . . I just didn't warm up good." Well, Bush was the only man I didn't strike out on the whole Cub team. I didn't know nothin' about it, understand, 'cause I was just a pitchin' away and Jimmy Wilson was catchin' and he never said a word and neither did anybody else. Hell, I might-a broke the record for consecutive strikeouts if somebody'd told me what I was doin', just like I could-a pitched a no-hit game in Brooklyn that time Paul did, 'cept nobody said nothin'. We'd a had a double no-hitter and no brothers ever did that before.

I struck out three men this day in the fifth and the eighth and ninth. Twelve of the 17 swung too at the last one. I never bothered with pitchin' high or low when I was good. . . . I just poured that ball in there, right over the plate. Koenig, Cuyler, Demaree, Hendricks and Jurges each struck out twice and I got that Babe Herman three times. He came up the fourth time and I just threw easy-like and he popped up for a change and he threw his bat away and yelled at me: "You must have a Bible in your pocket, you lucky bush so-and-so" but I didn't. It wuz only ol' Diz on one of his good days. If I'd known I was anywhere near a record I'd a struck out 20 anyway. . . . I just toyed with Bill Jurges a couple of times, figurin' he couldn't hit nothin' anyway.

Never forget the last inning. I struck out Hendricks and

Jurges and that made it 16, I found out afterwards. Charley Grimm was makin' faces over on the bench and growlin' at me about bein' a big, dumb Oklahoma busher . . . hee-hee, I never forget he yelled at me: "You look like you live in one of those Oklahoma penthouses". . . you know what that is, a pigpen with Venetian blinds, and I almost got laughin' and spoiled it all. He sent up somebody named Mosolf to pinch-hit and ol' Wilson met this guy before he got to the plate and I could hear him say: "This is a helluva place to stick you in, kid. . . . I wouldn't be surprised if the first one this dizzy moron threw was right at your ear. He don't like pinch hitters."

Mosolf never took his bat off his shoulder. Wilson'd give me the sign and then he'd straighten up and pound his glove right behind Mosolf's ear and the guy thought surer-'n-hell he was gonna get punctured and I just put three through there. Dean specials with the smoke curlin' off 'em. You'd a thought we won the World Series the way everybody pounded me on the back in the clubhouse and told me what I'd done and I was pretty proud too. But hell, there ain't no use in me tryin' to talk about a special day, 'cause every time I had a ball in my hand, and that suit on, it was my greatest day. The only time you ever feel bad is when you gotta quit.

And with every rose must grow a thorn. "I'd a given anything in the world to have beaten the Yanks that time," said Dean, referring to the World Series game in 1938, with the Cubs, when he led 3–2 into the eighth. "I didn't have nothin'. I had no license to beat anybody. But they could-a cut off my arm in that clubhouse if I'd a won that one. Diz just stubbed his toe one year too soon, in that All-Star game."

BILL DICKEY

as told to John P. Carmichael

Rated one of the game's all-time catching greats, William Malcolm (Bill) Dickey was one of the most important men ever to play for the mighty Yankees. He was a member of eight World Series teams, later managed and coached. He passed on his knowledge and savvy to such Yankee catchers of subsequent eras as Yogi Berra and Elston Howard, giving the New Yorkers an unbroken succession of all-star performers behind the plate. An iron man, Dickey caught 100 or more games thirteen straight seasons. He was elected to the Hall of Fame

six years ago. No longer a coach, Dickey is in business in Arkansas, and is scouting talent for his old club.

MY BIGGEST day? Well, I used to think it was the afternoon in 1932 when Babe Ruth didn't hit me right on the chin. I put a raw egg in one of his spikes before a game and you can imagine what happened when he set that big dog of his down inside. He really was "red" when he pulled the foot out, with egg drippin' all over and he looked around the clubhouse and yelled: "I can whip the man that did that."

Well, nobody answered and the Babe got madder 'n' madder and growled around and finally I said: "I did it, Babe," and he glared at me and took a couple of steps toward my locker and suddenly started to laugh and said: "Aw, to hell

45

with it" and changed socks and shoes. He'd a been a pretty big guy to tangle with.

A day I remember for the laugh we all got was in '30 when Bob Shawkey had the club and "Lefty" Grove was pitchin' against us. To me he was the fastest man I ever saw and he was having a field day against the Yanks. "Red" Ruffing was sittin' on the bench and just for fun he kept telling everybody: "I can't understand how you guys don't hit him. He's just nice and fast . . . boy, I like to hit those kind of pitchers. Sure wish I was in there today."

Finally we got the bags loaded in the eighth with two out and Shawkey looked down the line and motioned to Ruffing. "I know you want to take a crack at Grove," said Bob, "so pick up a bat and go up there." We all gave "Red" a big hand when he walked to the plate. Then we sat and watched. Grove threw three times. Ruffing hardly got a good look at any of 'em. He was back in a minute without ever getting the bat off his shoulder . . . three strikes and out!

That World Series of '38 with the Cubs was a honey . . . especially the day that Hack and Jurges collided going after a ground ball and Lou Gehrig scored from first base. I can still see "Diz" Dean chasin' the ball while your left fielder (Carl Reynolds) stood and watched. But I guess when you come down to it, this last World Series . . . the last game when I hit a home run . . . is the biggest day of all.

One of the newspapermen afterwards hollered at Joe McCarthy: "Hey, Joe, how about ol' Bill Dickey there," and Joe reached over and slapped me on the back and said: "Bill and I have come a long way . . . we practically started together on the Yanks." That's about right, too . . . it was the eighth series for both of us and we won out seven times. Joe and I were the old-timers of them all.

The '43 series was a tough one and some of those games could have changed scores very easily. Take that second one in which Cooper beat us 4–3. We had one run home in the ninth, a man on third and nobody out when I came to bat. I hit the hardest ball, for me, of the whole series. Caught it good . . . but it was a line drive right into the hands of Klein. Five feet either side and I'd a been on first with another run home and still no outs.

Then there was the ninth inning of the fourth game, with Russo leading 2–1. There was one gone when Marion doubled and the tying run was on second. They sent up that third-string catcher . . . oh, wait a minute, Sam Narron . . . to hit and we got two strikes on him in a hurry. Then I decided to waste one and called for a high, outside fast ball. I didn't expect him to hit at it . . . didn't want him to, in fact, because I was only setting him up for another curve. But for some reason I caught Crosetti's eye just after giving Russo the sign and motioned Frank over toward second a few steps.

It was a good thing I did, because Narron hit that outside pitch . . . pretty smart down toward second base and if Frank hadn't been over there, it'd been a hit and we'd a never got Marion at home. Even as it was Crosetti had to make a quick stop and throw. That was a hard hit ball and it was good strategy to send a fellow like Narron up because we didn't know anything about him or what he couldn't hit.

I think even if we'd lost next day, the fifth game, we still would have won the series but maybe it's just as well it didn't go any longer. You remember Cooper striking out five of us in a row at the start, including me, and he was fast. You could see he'd made up his mind to throw everything he had into that last effort and we got some good breaks. That play Crosetti made on Klein to start the fourth or fifth inning. . . . I don't see how he ever got to the ball, but he did and it got their leadoff man and gave us a margin to operate on.

Then the next frame Kurowski led off and bunted safely toward third on the first pitch. I was a little afraid of "Spud" Chandler losing his control, because I didn't think he was as sharp in either series game as in most of his season starts and sure enough he got wild and walked Ray Sanders on four pitches. There were two men on, nobody out, and no score in the game. Up came Johnny Hopp, a left-handed hitter to boot, and Chandler threw three straight balls to him.

McCarthy wig-wagged me to go out to the mound and see what happened. "Spud" said he wasn't tired or anything; he just didn't want to give Hopp a clean shot. But I told him to "come on and get the ball over" and called for a sinker. It was good for strike one, just around the knees, and, naturally, Hopp didn't swing. After all, Chandler had thrown seven straight balls. I took a chance he wouldn't even cut at the 3–1 pitch and asked for a curve. It was called strike two, so it was 3–2 and the next pitch was "for the money."

THE BOX SCORE
(October 11, 1943)

St. Louis	A.B.	R.	H.	P.	A.	New York	A.B.	R.	H.	P.	A.
Klein, 2b.	5	0	1	3	1	Crosetti, ss.	4	0	1	0	5
Garms, lf.	4	0	0	1	0	Metheny, rf.	5	0	1	1	0
Musial, rf.	3	0	0	1	0	Lindell, rf.	0	0	0	0	0
W. Cooper, c.	2	0	1	6	0	Johnson, 3b.	4	0	1	1	2
O'Dea, c.	2	0	2	2	0	Keller, lf.	3	1	1	1	1
Kurowski, 3b.	4	0	2	3	3	Dickey, c.	4	1	1	7	0
Sanders, 1b.	3	0	1	7	2	Etten, 1b.	3	0	1	11	1
Hopp, cf.	4	0	0	1	0	Gordon, 2b.	2	0	0	6	6
Marion, ss.	3	0	1	2	3	Stainback, cf.	3	0	1	0	0
M. Cooper, p.	2	0	0	0	1	Chandler, p.	3	0	0	0	2
Walker	1	0	1	0	0						
Lanier, p.	0	0	0	0	1						
Dickson, p.	0	0	0	1	0						
Litwhiler	1	0	1	0	0						
Totals	34	0	10	27	11	Totals	31	2	7	27	17

Walker batted for M. Cooper in 7th.
Litwhiler batted for Dickson in 9th.

St. Louis	0 0 0 0 0 0 0 0 0—0
New York	0 0 0 0 0 2 0 0 0—2

Errors—Crosetti, W. Cooper. Runs batted in—Dickey (2). Earned runs—New York 2. Left on bases—New York 9, St. Louis 11. Double plays—Crosetti to Gordon to Etten, Klein to Marion to Sanders. Struck out—Chandler 7, M. Cooper 6, Lanier 1. Bases on balls—Chandler 2, M. Cooper 2, Lanier 2, Dickson 1. Hits—Off M. Cooper, 5 in 7 innings; Lanier, 2 in 1 1-3; Dickson, 0 in 2-3. Wild pitch—M. Cooper. Losing pitcher—M. Cooper. Umpires—Rommel (A. L.), Reardon (N. L.), Rue (A. L.), Steward (N. L.). Time—2:24.

It was . . . but for our money. I signaled for a fast ball and Chandler threw one at least a foot off the plate, outside. The bases should have been loaded with nobody gone. I don't know why Hopp swung at the ball, but he did . . . and fanned. There was one of the two big breaks of the whole series in our favor; that one and the day in New York when Lindell knocked the ball out of Kurowski's hands. Anyway, with Hopp gone, we got the next two easily.

There were two out in the sixth when Keller bounced the ball between first and second for a hit and I came up. I wasn't trying to outguess Cooper. I wasn't trying to hit the ball out of the park either. I wanted a fast ball and I only wanted to meet it, just so it would go safe. Well, I got it . . . and hit it good, but not hard. At least I didn't think so, but when I was running to first I saw the ball heading for the roof and Earl Combs (Yank coach) yelled at me: "You got one, Bill." But the only thing I thought was: "We'll get a run, anyway, for 'Spud' and maybe it'll be enough." Then I saw Art Fletcher (at third) wavin' his cap and I knew it was a home run.

It didn't mean so much at the time; it wasn't until that night, when I was in bed that I began to realize I'd won the game and the series with one blow and we were champions again and I'd had a pretty darn good season for an old man who'd been playing up there 16 years.

JOE DiMAGGIO

as told to Fred Down

Joseph Paul DiMaggio, the famed "Yankee Clipper" was born November 25, 1914, and was a product of the San Francisco sandlots, like so many other diamond greats.

Hampered by injuries during a brilliant career, he nevertheless made the Hall of Fame shortly after he became eligible in the balloting.

In 1941 he established one of baseball's great marks, hitting safely in 56 consecutive games. He was selected Most Valuable Player three times before he hung up his pinstripe flannels for good following the 1951 season. Still vitally interested in the game, DiMaggio is a spring-time batting coach for his old club.

I'D BE a heel if I didn't list October 1, 1949, as one of the greatest days a baseball player ever knew. It was a day on which the fans chose to honor me. And before it was over I had a lump in my throat the size of Ted Williams' batting average.

It was assumed that the American League pennant race would be over when the day was picked originally. It wasn't, of course. We were one game behind the Red Sox with two to play. We had to beat them twice and they had their two best pitchers ready to throw at us.

It would be folly to attempt to list all the things the fans gave me. And it would not be fair to list some and leave others out. The record speaks for itself. There must have been one hundred presents. I wouldn't attempt to estimate their value in money. Whatever that might be they had a greater value.

My mother and family occupied a box seat behind the Yankee dugout and I couldn't help thinking of them while Mel Allen, who was the master of ceremonies, reeled off presents and tributes to me. I couldn't help thinking, too, of my teammates. They had stood up all season despite 70-odd injuries. I knew every man was certain the Red Sox were not going to "steal" the prize from us at the very end and I knew every man was waiting impatiently for the game to begin.

I like to think that the long delay caused by "my day" did not affect their play. I cannot be sure of that, of course. There must have been times when they thought, "Come on, give the guy his presents and get on with the game. There is a pennant to be won."

Maybe they would have won that game more easily if there had been no "Joe DiMaggio Day." But it was enough to me—and I think to them—that they did win. Joe Page came on to stop the Red Sox cold for the last six and one third innings. The race was tied and we went on to break the tie once and for all the next day.

That, then, was one of my "greatest thrills." Ted Williams says he would rather win the batting title than gain the most valuable player award because the title is something you earn yourself and the most valuable award something which someone gives to you. I realize what he is driving at. But I would not trade any batting title I ever won for that day which the fans gave me.

I'd have to consult the record book to tell you when I won the batting title. But I'll never have to check the book to tell you about those 70,000 fans who came to Yankee Stadium that day for the express purpose of honoring me.

There was another crowd on another day which I'll never forget either. Which brings me to my "other greatest thrill."

This one is not as easy to tell you about. It is always simple to tell about the homers you hit and the games you won. It is more difficult to talk about the strikeouts and the defeats. Especially when you try to explain the thrill in it.

For the record the day was Sunday, October 3, 1948. The setting was Fenway Park in Boston. The crowd was about 31,000 and it had come to see Yankee blood.

We could no longer win the pennant. Jack Kramer had beaten us, 5 to 1, the day before. It was between Cleveland and Boston with Cleveland leading the Sox by one game. The Red Sox could gain a tie and force a play-off by beating us providing Cleveland lost to Detroit. So those 31,000 fans were watching two games that day—one on the field and one on the scoreboard.

We had nothing except satisfaction to play for. You might say there must have been a let-down in our play. But there wasn't. It is never fun to lose. Besides, the league standings did not convince us that there were two better teams in the league. Maybe we were wrong but that's the way we felt. And we thought we could go a long way toward proving our point by beating the Red Sox that day.

Well, the game is history. We got a run in the first inning when I doubled but the Sox rocked Bob Porterfield for five in the third. Joe Dobson was their pitcher but he wasn't too sharp and I knew we'd get him sooner or later.

My family was in the stands and I know they were rooting for the Red Sox. They knew I couldn't play in the World Series no matter what happened but Dom had a chance if the Sox won and Detroit beat Cleveland. And there was the score after three innings on the board—Detroit, 5, Cleveland, 0.

But Dobson was faltering and we got him in the fifth inning. Phil Rizzuto singled and Bobby Brown doubled. Then I hit one off the left field wall. That cut the margin to 5 to 4. The crowd was really going crazy.

My mother told me later that my sister Marie almost went crazy too.

"What is he trying to do?" she screamed. "Doesn't he want Dom to play in the series?"

The fact is that I probably didn't at that moment although I rooted for him the next day in the play-off.

I had charley horses in both legs and the one in my right leg hurt like fury. I know I couldn't have gone much further. I was happy that it was the last game of the season. But I wanted to stay in there. To win on the last day, if possible.

We didn't, of course. They beat us, 10 to 5. And I didn't last all the way. Bucky Harris sent Steve Souchock in to run for me after I got my fourth hit—a single—in the ninth.

I saw Souchock come out of the dugout and trot toward first.

"Bucky says you've had enough," he said.

I turned and started for the dugout. I guess I was limping pretty badly. Anyway that's what they told me later.

I'll never forget that crowd. It was standing and roaring—like one man. I tipped my cap but it didn't stop. I looked up at the stands and I never saw a more wonderful sight. There were 30,000 people giving an ovation to a guy who had tried to beat them. They were still yelling when I disappeared into the dugout; they didn't stop for another three or four minutes.

Dom and I had a reunion after it was all over.

"Well," I said. "You did it. I hope you win tomorrow."

He was looking at me kind of funny.

"That was the greatest tribute a crowd here ever gave a ball player," he said. "Everybody is talking about it."

"I guess you felt like cutting my throat when I hit that one off the wall in the fifth inning," I said. "I know Marie did."

"No," he said, and he was dead serious. "Don't ever tell Joe McCarthy this—but I felt like applauding too."

* * * * *

It wasn't difficult for me to single out that game in Fenway Park on the last day of the 1948 season as the greatest game I had ever played. After all that was the finish to one of my greatest seasons, one in which I had taken clear title to leadership in both the home run and runs batted in departments for the second time in my career, but just let me tell you about one game, rather one homer which furnished me with my most satisfying afternoon.

The 1950 season was about the longest I had known. I was in a slump from the opening bell and just did manage to untrack myself long enough in the last two weeks to push my batting average above the .300 mark, the second lowest in my career. For some a .301 average might indicate a pretty good year, but I was really below par throughout the campaign and when I did get my blows they came in bunches. It was far from a steady performance and if ever there was a hot-and-cold hitter that year, it was DiMaggio.

That we eventually won the pennant was no fault of mine. I hadn't been of much help, and a little siege of virus (how that guy follows me around!) in mid-August sapped my strength and caused me to lose weight.

The Series began in Philadelphia, and we beat Jim Konstanty, 1–0, but I might just as well have stayed in the hotel. I did draw a couple of passes, but on my other two times up I hit a couple of infield flies which my son, Joe, could have snatched. And I was much worse the next afternoon—at least for a while!

Robin Roberts and our Allie Reynolds hooked up in a ding-donger and at the end of nine innings we were all knotted at 1–1, and my streak of popups continued unbroken. There were a couple of "wicked" floaters to Mike Goliat at second base, one to Willie Jones at third base, and a "screamer" to Eddie Waitkus at first base. Up and down they went, not even going beyond the grass which borders the infield. Four times at bat in this one, twice in the first game and I hadn't even driven a ball past the Phillie inner defense. I was really burning with rage at my pitiful demonstration and I don't think I hated a guy as much as poor Roberts when I came to the plate in the 10th inning.

The Phillie right-hander slipped behind in the count at 2-and-1, and I sort of anticipated his high, hard one at this point, the pitch which had kept me popping up. And Roberts didn't disappoint me! I rifled his next pitch, and I knew it was gone. Ever see one of those taut wires at the circus which extend from the ground to the highest perch? Well, that's how that ball traveled—right into the upper left-center seats for the game-winning homer.

There was no mistaking the happiest Yankee in the clubhouse a few moments later. You'd think I had just broken Babe Ruth's record, that's how big my smile was. I had finally smacked one, and I was tingling all over. No home run ever gave me such satisfaction!

LEO DUROCHER

as told to John P. Carmichael

With time out for a short stint as a radio broadcaster, the slightly incredible Leo Ernest Durocher has been part and parcel of the major-league scene since 1928. He came up with the Yankees, moved to the National League, achieved his greatest fame with the Dodgers of the '40s. He won two pennants with the New York Giants and his greatest managerial achievement was driving the Giants to four straight victories over the Cleveland Indians in the 1954 Series. Durocher also coached the Los Angeles Dodgers, which means he has appeared in World Series as a player, manager and coach.

You mean the day I'll never forget? That's easy, brother! We've only got to go back to 1941 when Brooklyn won the pennant. It was my first flag as manager, too, and I was fired before the day was over. That's right. Won a pennant and I was fired as manager the same day. Put that down in the books.

In the first place, I didn't think I'd live to get to Boston, where we clinched the flag. I couldn't sleep nights. If you recall we played a double-header in Philly the Sunday before and we won the first game easy and I was all set to let Curt Davis go in the second one, when Larry MacPhail came in the clubhouse and asked: "Who yuh workin' this game . . . Luke Hamlin?" I said: "No, Davis," and he didn't say nothin' and walked out.

Well I got thinkin' about Davis and Hamlin and whip-sawin' myself and finally wound up with Hamlin and Lit-whiler hit a homer off him with the bags loaded in the first inning and we blew it. I was afraid to shave that night because I couldn't stop shakin' and finally I went to a barber and I thought of Casey Stengel as I got in the chair; the time he dropped two in one afternoon, walked into a shop, sat down and told the guy:

"Once over and never mind cutting my throat. I may do that myself later in the evening."

That just shows you how things were going when we got to Boston for those two games. We won the first, thanks to "Dixie" Walker's three-run triple in the eighth, and that only made things worse. I didn't close an eye all night. "Peewee" Reese had booted one to give Boston the lead and I lay awake wondering if maybe I hadn't better take him out the next day and play myself. I got up outta bed four times . . . the last time at a quarter after 5 . . . and made out different lineups. Finally I just stayed up.

Oh, how that morning dragged. Every time I picked up a paper I read where if we won and the Cards lost we were "in" and then I'd have more coffee. It was a helluva relief to get into the uniforms; just putting it on seemed to quiet me a little and I'd keep telling myself, "What you worryin' for: Wyatt's pitching and he's beaten these mugs five straight times. He'll handcuff 'em." I remember as we were walkin' out on the field, ol' Whitlow came by and maybe he figured the skipper could stand some cheering up and he put a hand on my shoulder and said: "Get me one run today. They won't score!" That's all.

We got him one right off the bat. Walker singled, went to third on two infield outs and then Medwick topped a ball toward third. I saw it might be a hard play for Tom Early, the Boston pitcher, and hollered to Joe: "Run for your life." I thought afterwards that must have sounded funny as hell, because what else would he do, but anyway he beat the play by a step and Walker came home. In the next inning Owen was on second with two out and took third as "Dixie" singled again . . . too short for Mickey to score. But Walker got himself trapped off first and maneuvered around long enough to let Owen count before he was caught.

I was feeling a little better by then and so help me if that Rowell, at second, didn't make three straight errors in the third and give us another run. You'd a thought those guys were winning a pennant. They were so damn anxious to beat us, like everybody else in the league, and they blew up. He kicked Camilli's grounder, just an easy roller, and then threw it away and he fell all over Medwick's ball and Dolph scored from second. About the time Reiser hit that homer in the seventh to make the score 5 to 0, the guys in the press box were hollerin' down that the Cards were losing 3 to 1 and somebody on our bench let out a yip and I shut him up. It was too soon to shake hands with ourselves.

That Wyatt was beautiful to watch. They got three hits off him in seven innings and not a man reached third. I never said a word to him at any time, nor to any man on the club, except to yell and holler, "Keep the 'pepper' up." Whitlow was my best pitcher. If we couldn't win with him, the chances were we couldn't win at all. The same went for the whole team. There it was on the field, the best we had. The fourth hit off Whit came by Rowell in the eighth and they sent up Frank Demaree to pinch hit. He was ready and he hit one. I can close my eyes now and see Billy Herman going for that ball.

He made the (deleted by censor) stop I've seen in many a day. He just dove, almost full length, after it and still kept his feet. That was the end. We were home. I started to laugh, like a kid who knows Santa Claus is coming that night. Wyatt went through the motions in the ninth and we carried him into the clubhouse. It's funny to see big, swearing men cry, but they did. Everybody was tired and worn and happy.

That ride to New York was something! We had a special train. We drank up $1,400 worth of beer, Scotch and champagne on the trip. Well, you were on it . . . remember when Tony Martin, the movie guy, got up to make a speech and somebody hit him smack in the face with a hot steak? The gang yelled: "Sit down, you bum, this isn't your party," and from then on it was a riot.

At New Haven the conductor got a wire from MacPhail telling him he'd board the train at 125th Street in New York. I didn't know anything about a wire, but the conductor came to me and asked if we wanted to stop there. I told him no. We knew there'd be a mob in Grand Central Station and some of the fellows wanted to get off at 125th and slip home, but I vetoed that. I told them: "I don't care if they tear your clothes off. We belong to those fans. They've been waiting 21 years for this chance to celebrate and we've gotta go through with it. There'll be no stop."

We went right on through. MacPhail was standing on the platform with Sam Breadon and Branch Rickey. They were on their way to see Rochester in the playoffs. We passed 'em up, just like that; went roaring right on and I got a glimpse of MacPhail and I said to myself: "Oh, oh, there'll be hell to pay about this." There was. I met him in a Hotel New Yorker elevator. He never said a word. Didn't congratulate me or the team or a thing; just looked at me. We got off at the same floor, walked into the same suite together, never talked.

People began to come in and he called me into another room. Still didn't say anything about the pennant. "Why

didn't you have the train stopped at 125th?" he shot at me.
I told him I didn't know he'd sent a wire; I told him why
we decided to go on through, so the players wouldn't get off.
He was plenty mad. Told me I might have called him up
and asked and a lot of junk and finally I said I was runnin'
the team, not the (deleted by censor) train and he barked
back:

"Well, you're not even runnin' the team any longer. You're
fired!"

So I said "all right" and walked out and went up to my
own room. Somebody sent up word the newsreel men were

THE BOX SCORE
(September 25, 1941)

BROOKLYN DODGERS					BOSTON BRAVES				
	A.B.	R.	H.	P.	A.		A.B.	R.	H.	P.	A.
Walker, rf.	5	1	3	3	0	Sisti, 3b.	3	0	0	1	4
Herman, 2b.	4	0	0	2	2	Dudra, 3b.	1	0	0	0	0
Coscarart, 2b.	1	0	0	0	0	Cooney, c.	1	0	0	0	0
Reiser, cf.	3	1	2	2	0	Moore, cf.	3	0	0	0	0
Camilli, 1b.	4	1	0	10	0	Hassett, 1b.	4	0	0	9	2
Medwick, lf.	4	0	1	1	0	Waner, rf.	3	0	1	1	0
Lavagetto, 3b.	2	1	0	1	4	West, lf.	4	0	2	3	0
Reese, ss.	3	0	1	2	0	Miller, ss.	3	0	0	3	0
Owens, c.	4	1	1	5	0	Roberge, 2b.	0	0	0	1	0
Wyatt, p.	4	1	1	1	0	Rowell, 2b.	3	0	2	2	0
						Berres, c.	2	0	0	5	2
						Johnson, p.	0	0	0	0	0
						Earley, p.	2	0	0	1	3
						Masi, c.	1	0	0	1	0
Totals	34	6	9	27	17	Totals	31	0	5	27	19

Demaree batted for Berres in the 8th.

BROOKLYN	1 1 1 0 0 0 2 1 0—6
BOSTON	0 0 0 0 0 0 0 0 0—0

Errors—Miller, Rowell (3). Runs batted in—Medwick, Reiser (2). Two-base
hit—West. Home run—Reiser. Stolen base—Owen. Double plays—Herman to
Reese to Camilli, Hassett to Miller to Hassett, Miller to Rowell to Hassett,
Johnson to Miller to Hassett. Left on bases—Brooklyn 7, Boston 5. Bases on
balls—Off Wyatt 1, Earley 5, Johnson 1. Struck out—By Wyatt 5, Earley 5.
Johnson 1. Hits—Off Earley, 8 in 8 innings; Johnson, 1 in 1 inning. Losing
pitcher—Earley. Umpires—Reardon, Goetz and Stewart. Time—2:08. Attendance—10,096.

waiting below and I refused to come down. I never did, either. They had to use Joe Medwick and I never saw the pictures afterward. Maybe they didn't use 'em. I stayed where I was and finally went to bed. I was so tired I coulda slept standin' up. About 3 o'clock in the morning the phone rang and it was MacPhail.

"You comin' by the office in the morning?" he asked.

Twice as mad now, because I'd been asleep, I yelled into the phone: "What for, to get my money?" and hung up. In about two minutes it rang again.

"No," he said, "I want to talk over some things about the series with you." I said: "Okay," and went back to sleep.

That's it!

JIMMIE DYKES

as told to Hal Totten

A famed A's and White Sox infielder of another era, Jimmie Dykes and his trademark, a super-length cigar, has been a part of the major-league scene for almost a half-century. He played in three World Series with the great Philadelphia Athletics teams of the early '30s, managed in Chicago, Philadelphia, Cincinnati, Baltimore, Detroit and Cleveland. A native of Philadelphia, Dykes is a long-time friend and confidant of Casey Stengel. He achieved unique distinction when he was involved in the "manager's trade," swapping jobs with Joe Gordon of the Cleveland Indians in 1960.

I'LL never forget the day I made five hits in five times at bat against the Yankees—and each on the first ball pitched. The first four were off Garland Braxton. Herb Pennock was on the mound the last time. Apparently Benny Bengough, who was catching Herb, wanted him to "hook" me, but he kept shaking off the sign.

Finally Ben let out a wild yell, "For Pete's sake, Herb, he's made four hits already." And all Herb did was grin and say: "All right; let him get another."

Then there was the time right here in Chicago when—

officially—I made three errors. The official scorer was pretty lenient, because it could have been five or six easily. And I kicked in six runs. But I got four for five that day and I remember, I drove in just one more run for the Athletics than I booted across—seven. And some woman sitting behind our bench hollered: "It's easy to see why the Old Man keeps you in there. You can't catch anything. But you sure can hit everything." Funny thing was—usually I could catch everything and couldn't hit a thing.

Then there was the fourth game of the 1929 World Series, when we went into the seventh inning losing 8 to 0, and came out in front 10 to 8. A lot of things happened in that inning. But the thing I remember most is the double I clouted off Pat Malone with the bases full.

We were licked—well licked—when we came to bat in that seventh inning. They had us 8–0, and Charlie Root was pitching like a machine. We hadn't been able to do a thing with him, and it didn't look as if we were going to.

As a matter of fact it looked so hopeless that I found out later that Connie Mack had made up his mind to let the regulars take their turns at bat in the seventh and then put in all the youngsters who hadn't ever been in a World Series, and probably never would be. But they never got to play.

We were so completely resigned to losing that game that when Al Simmons opened the big inning with a home run, the only comment anybody made on the bench was: "Well, we won't be shut out, anyway." And it wasn't as though the game didn't mean a lot, either, because, if the Cubs had won, it would have tied up the series at two games apiece. Guy Bush had beaten us the day before 3 to 1.

Nobody got very excited even when Jimmy Foxx and Bing Miller singled and I shut my eyes and got one, too. That scored Foxx. But we were still six runs behind. Then Joe Boley scored Miller with another one-base shot. But five runs are a lot of runs to overcome—especially in a World Series game. And when George Burns, batting for Eddie

Rommel, popped to English, it looked as though our fun was over.

But Max Bishop belted one and I scored. That cut the big lead in half and I think we all began to feel that we might do something now. I guess Joe McCarthy thought so, too, because he took Charlie Root out and put in crafty old Art Nehf to pitch to Mule Haas, who batted left-handed.

Then came the blow that really turned the tide in our favor. The "Donk" (Mule Haas) hit a line drive over second base. Hack Wilson started for it and then seemed blinded by the sun. Anyway, he hesitated, and the ball shot past him into deep center. Every one of us jumped to our feet and started to shout at the top of our lungs. Boley crossed the plate! Bishop scored!

The ball was coming in now. I was standing in front of the dugout yelling: "He's gonna make it! He's gonna make it! There he goes!" And as Mule slid across the plate with a home run inside the park, I clouted the player next to me across the back and yelled: "We're back in the game, boys."

Only it wasn't a player I hit. It was Connie Mack. I'd never seen him leave his seat during a game before. But here he was, standing up there leaning out of the dugout, watching Haas race to the plate. And when I smacked him, I knocked him clear out over the bats.

I was horrified and grabbed Mr. Mack and helped him to his feet. "I'm sorry," I told him—and I must have had a funny look on my face, because he smiled, reached out, patted me on the arm, and said in that quiet way of his: "That's all right Jimmie. Everything's all right. Anything you do right now is all right. Wasn't it wonderful?" So that's one time I socked the manager and got away with it.

But it wasn't over yet. Nehf gave Mickey Cochrane a pass. That brought Fred Blake into the game. And Al Simmons, up for the second time, slammed one to left for his second hit —a single. Foxx then got his second hit of the inning—a one-baser—and Cochrane scored the tying run. Only, believe it or not, I didn't know the score was tied. No, sir!

McCarthy called in big Pat Malone. And he hit Miller with a pitched ball. And when I stepped up to the plate, I had the impression that we were still one run behind, with only one out. And with the bases full, I had only one thought in mind—to hit one far enough to let that tying run score. All I wanted was a long fly.

THE BOX SCORE
(*October 12, 1929*)

ATHLETICS	A.B.	R.	H.	P.	A.	CUBS	A.B.	R.	H.	P.	A.
Bishop, 2b.	5	1	2	2	3	McMillan, 3b.	4	0	0	1	3
Haas, cf.	4	1	1	2	0	English, ss.	4	0	0	2	1
Cochrane, c.	4	1	?	9	0	Hornsby, 2b.	5	2	2	1	1
Simmons, lf.	5	2	2	0	0	Wilson, cf.	3	1	2	3	0
Foxx, 1b.	4	2	2	10	0	Cuyler, rf.	4	2	3	0	0
Miller, rf.	3	1	2	3	0	Stephenson, lf.	4	1	1	2	1
Dykes, 3b.	4	1	3	0	2	Grimm, 1b.	4	2	2	7	0
Boley, ss.	3	1	1	1	5	Taylor, c.	3	0	0	8	1
Quinn, p.	2	0	0	0	0	Root, p.	3	0	0	0	0
Walberg, p.	0	0	0	0	0	Nehf, p.	0	0	0	0	0
Rommel, p.	0	0	0	0	0	Blake, p.	0	0	0	0	0
Burns	2	0	0	0	0	Malone, p.	0	0	0	0	0
Grove, p.	0	0	0	0	0	Hartnett	1	0	0	0	0
						Carlson, p.	0	0	0	0	1
Totals	36	10	15	27	10	Totals	35	8	10	24	8

Burns batted for Rommel in 7th.   Hartnett batted for Malone in 8th.

Cubs	0	0	0	2	0	5	1	0	0— 8
Athletics	0	0	0	0	0	0	0	10	*—10

Errors—Miller, Walberg, Wilson, Cuyler. Two-base hits—Cochrane, Dykes. Three-base hit—Hornsby. Home runs—Grimm, Simmons, Haas. Sacrifice hits —Taylor, Haas, Boley. Runs batted in—Cuyler (2), Stephenson, Grimm (2), Taylor, Haas (3), Simmons, Foxx, Dykes (3), Boley. Left on bases—Chicago, 4; Philadelphia, 6. Double play—Dykes to Bishop to Foxx. Bases on balls—Off Quinn, 2; Rommel, 1; Nehf, 1. Struck out—By Quinn, 2; Walberg, 2; Grove, 4; Root, 3; Malone, 2; Carlson, 1. Hits—Off Quinn, 7 in 5 innings; Walberg, 1 in 1; Rommel, 2 in 1; Grove, 0 in 2; Root, 9 in 6 1-3; Nehf, 1 in 0; Blake, 2 in 0; Malone, 1 in 2-3; Carlson, 2 in 1. Hit by pitcher—Malone (Miller). Winning pitcher—Rommel. Losing pitcher—Blake. Umpires—Van Grafian, Klem, Dineen and Moran. Time—2:12.

Malone threw one past me and it was a strike. I knew right then that the next one would be a fast ball, too. So I got set for it and swung. I pulled it to left and was sure it was far enough to score Simmons—and, as I thought, tie it up. So I lit out for first. I didn't see what happened, but they tell me that Stephenson jumped up against the wall; that the ball hit his glove and dropped to the ground. All I know is that when I rounded first, I saw him stooping over to pick it up, so I headed for second.

Well, as it turned out, it drove in both Simmons and Foxx and those were the two runs we won by, 10 to 8. Malone struck out the last two men. But we weren't worried any more. Why? Because Mr. Mack put in Lefty Grove, and when Lefty went into a ball game, it was all over. We knew he'd set 'em down, and he did—six in a row—and struck out four of 'em. And that ended not only my biggest and most important day, but just about the biggest one in World Series history.

JOHNNY EVERS

as told to John P. Carmichael

One of the game's finest in-fielders, Johnny Evers played with his mind as well as his limited physical capabilities. Born March 21, 1883, in Troy, New York, "The Crab," as he was known, be-gan an honorable career as second baseman with the Chi-cago Cubs in 1904. He shifted to the Braves in 1914, and fin-ished out his active days with the Phillies in 1917. Evers managed both Chicago clubs before retiring from baseball. He died March 28, 1947, at the age of 61.

IT'S A long time now since the day Fred Merkle didn't touch second, but it could be a century and I'd never forget what happened. I can't get around much any more with this bum leg, so sitting in this chair day after day there's nothing much to do but live in the past. You know most of the stories after-ward said Umpire Hank O'Day walked off the field without saying a word as the fans came down on the diamond under the impression New York had won 2–1. But he didn't. He stayed right there and waited for me to make the play and told me the Giant run didn't count.

The Merkle affair occurred Sept. 23, 1908, but it was 19

days earlier, at Pittsburgh, that we really won the game at New York. The same play came up against the Pirates and O'Day was the umpire then too. Mordecai Brown was pitching for the Cubs and he'd shut out the Bucs three straight times earlier in the season. This day they hadn't scored off him again in nine innings, making it 36 frames he'd held them runless, but we couldn't get anything off Vic Willis either. In the 10th we got beat.

Fred Clarke was on third, Wagner on second and Gill on first with Wilson at the plate. Wilson singled to center and Jimmy Slagle threw the ball back to the infield as Clarke, of course, went on home. But Gill didn't go to second. He ran off the field. I got the ball and hollered to O'Day to look. He wouldn't. I stood on second and yelled that the run didn't count . . . that Gill was the third out, but Hank refused to listen. "Clarke scored before the out could have been made," he told Manager Frank Chance and pushed his way to the dressing room.

Ol' Hank was mad at me anyway for an argument we'd had in St. Louis a few weeks before and you could tell that his whole attitude was he'd be damned if that little squirt Evers was going to get him in another jam. But just the same he was a good umpire . . . if you didn't tell him so too often . . . and he realized later what had happened and in the long run we got the break when we needed it most in New York. As everybody knows, we couldn't have won the pennant if we hadn't.

There were only about 10 points between the Giants and us by Sept. 23. This was the last game of the series and McGraw sent Christy Mathewson to the mound. Jack Pfeister was pitching for us. O'Day and Bob Emslie were the umpires and there were 25,000 fans there easily. In the fifth inning we got in front when Joe Tinker hit a home run. It really was just a line drive to the outfield but Donlin tried to make a shoestring catch and the ball rolled past him and Joe got all the way around. In the next inning the Giants tied it as Her zog beat out a slow roller to Steinfeldt at third and got to second when Harry made a bad throw to first. Up came Donlin and squared himself for missing Tinker's ball with a single that scored Herzog.

So that's the way we stood going into the ninth and to show you what a pitcher's battle it was, Tinker handled 14 chances that game and I had 11 which was as many as I had in any game all season. Matty set us down one-two-three in our half and New York put on a rally. With one out, Devlin singled and McCormick slashed one right at me. It was just slow enough so the best Tinker and I could do was to get Devlin at second. Still there were two gone. Up came Merkle. He was just a rookie at that time and probably wouldn't have been playing if we hadn't had a southpaw working, but McGraw wanted to get as much right-handed hitting into his lineup as possible and anyway Fred Tenny had a bum ankle and could use extra rest, so Merkle was at first.

Well, he singled and McCormick went to third. Al Bridwell was the next hitter and he singled to center. That's where the fun began.

Artie Hofman threw the ball in as McCormick went home and Merkle jogged halfway to second. I had my eye on him, saw him stop, glance around at the fans pouring out of their seats, and start for the clubhouse beyond right field. Hofman's throw had gone over Tinker's head and rolled over to where Joe McGinnity, the Giant pitcher, was standing. Joe'd been coaching on third and he knew what was in our minds as Tinker and I raced for the ball. He got it first, but before he could get rid of the thing, Joe and I had him and we wrestled around there for what seemed to be five minutes.

We grabbed for his hands to make sure he wouldn't heave the ball away but he broke loose and tossed it into the crowd. I can see the fellow who caught it yet . . . a tall, stringy middle-aged gent with a brown bowler hat on. Steinfeldt and Floyd Kroh, a young pitcher we'd added to our staff during the summer, raced after him. "Gimme the ball for just a

minute," Steinfeldt begged him. "I'll bring it right back."
The guy wouldn't let go and suddenly Kroh solved the prob-
lem. He hit the customer right on top of that stiff hat, drove
it down over his eyes and as the gent folded up, the ball fell
free and Kroh got it. I was yelling and waving my hands out
by second base and Tinker relayed it over to me and I stepped
on the bag and made sure O'Day saw me. As I said before, he
was waiting for that very play . . . he remembered the Pittsburgh game . . . and he said: "The run does not count."
Then he walked away. But he made no attempt to continue
the game in the confusion.

There was hell a-poppin' after that. Emslie refused to take
a stand for or against O'Day. "I didn't see the play," he insisted and that's all he'd say. Mathewson and a couple of the
Giants dashed for the clubhouse and tried to get Merkle back
to second, but I was standing there with the ball before they
got him out the door. They saw it was too late, although Mc-
Graw kept hollering that the Giants had won and the fans,
who only knew the Cubs were trying to pull off some trick,
gave us a good going over. A couple of park "fly cops" which
McGraw had scattered around to "protect" the visiting players took a few pokes at Chance under the guise of keeping the
crowd back and there must have been five fist fights going on
as we finally got out of there.

Inside the clubhouse we made a horrible discovery. It was
the custom of the club in those days for some player, usually
a pitcher, who was sure of not seeing service during the game,
to take charge of a bag in which we placed our money and
valuables for safekeeping while in uniform. Kroh had been
the man in charge this day and he'd left the bag near the
bench while he went in pursuit of the ball. Then he'd forgotten all about it, and of course it was gone when he tried
to find it. We lost about $200 in cash and $5,000 in jewelry.

But at least we won the game, eventually . . . that is we
played it off Oct. 8 and Brown won, 4–2. President Harry
Pulliam of the league backed O'Day in his decision, but the

THE BOX SCORE
(*September 23, 1908*)

CHICAGO	R.	H.	P.	A.	NEW YORK	R.	H.	P.	A.
Hayden, rf.	0	0	1	0	Herzog, 2b.	1	1	1	1
Evers, 2b.	0	1	4	7	Bresnahan, c.	0	0	10	0
Schulte, lf.	0	0	1	0	Donlin, rf.	0	1	2	0
Chance, 1b.	0	1	11	1	Seymour, cf.	0	1	1	0
Steinfeldt, 3b.	0	0	1	0	Devlin, 3b.	0	2	0	2
Hofman, cf.	0	1	0	0	McCormick, lf.	0	0	1	0
Tinker, ss.	1	1	8	6	Merkle, 1b.	0	1	10	1
Kling, c.	0	1	0	1	Bridwell, ss.	0	0	2	8
Pfeister, p.	0	0	1	0	Mathewson, p.	0	0	0	2
Totals	1	5	27	15	Totals	1	6	27	14

```
NEW YORK    0  0  0  0  1  0  0  0  0—1
CHICAGO     0  0  0  1  0  0  0  0  0—1
```

Errors—Steinfeldt, Tinker (2). Home run—Tinker. Sacrifice hits—Steinfeldt, Bresnahan. Double plays—Tinker to Chance (2), Evers to Chance, Mathewson to Bridwell to Merkle. Bases on balls—Off Pfeister 2. Hit by pitcher—By Pfeister 1. Struck out—By Mathewson 9. Time—1:30. Umpires—O'Day and Emslie.

Giants protested so vigorously and long that the board of directors finally had to settle matters. I'm not so sure they would have decided in our favor at that, but Jack Ryder, the old Cincinnati writer, who is dead now, broke into the meeting and delivered a helluva speech in our favor, claiming there was no choice but to play the game over and vowing that the league would make itself a laughingstock if it let the Giants get away with a pennant on a bonehead play.

So it turned out all right for us, but one day during the off-season I ran into Roger Bresnahan, who caught Matty that afternoon, and the Giant catcher showed me a medal. It was one of 28 which John T. Brush, Giant owner, had struck off for each member of the team and showed a ballplayer with a bat in his hand and another throwing a ball and the inscription read:

"The Real Champions, 1908."

BOB FELLER

as told to Ed McAuley

One of the game's undisputed mound greats, Bob Feller had an appreciable dent put into his career by four years of active Navy service in World War II. He wound up with a total of 266 victories, might have pushed the 400 mark had his career remained uninterrupted. Possessor of a half-dozen series marks, Feller pitched three no-hitters, and a dozen one-hitters. Feller's hallmark was his blazing fastball. At its peak of efficiency it was good enough to strike out a record total of 348 batters in 1946. He is now a successful insurance executive in Cleveland and a member of the Hall of Fame.

I CAN truthfully say that I've never thrown a baseball in anger. For one thing, my tendency toward wildness has kept me concentrating as calmly as possible on the business at hand. For another, I've long been haunted by the fear of hitting the batter.

I still turn sick when I recall the picture of Hank Lieber, the New York Giants' outfielder, sprawled beside home plate after one of my curves hit him in the head in the spring of 1937. Some pitchers will tell you that the intentional "duster" is a legitimate weapon.

It is one I never used.

But there's a difference between anger and resentment, and I must confess that I was resentful when I started against the New York Yankees in their own Stadium the afternoon of April 30, 1946. Whether or not my attitude affected my pitching is a question which no one can answer. In any case, the game turned out to be the one I call the greatest of my career. When it was over, I had my second no-hitter.

The resentment which I mention was not directed against the Yankees. On the contrary, I had at least as many good friends on that fine New York team as on any of the Indians' other rivals. The Yankees just happened to furnish the opposition on a day when I wanted desperately to prove something.

I suppose the story really opens in the training season. It was to be my first full year after the war. I felt that I was far from the twilight of my career, but it was a fact that from my kid days at home in Iowa, and through six prewar years with the Indians, I had thrown a great number of baseballs at a high rate of speed. At the age of twenty-seven, I couldn't see much point in calling on the full resources of my arm on every pitch. I no longer was anxious to strike out every exhibition game opponent who stepped to the plate.

As a result, my barnstorming performances were not exactly magnificent. I was confident that I'd be ready when the bell rang, but this opinion was not shared unanimously by the reporters who watched me work. From time to time, a critic made tentative motions in the direction of a guess that I no longer could win consistently.

Such comment didn't worry me, and when I shut out the Chicago White Sox, on opening day, 1 to 0—with the help

of a miracle catch by Bob Lemon, then playing center field—
I felt that my conditioning methods had been justified.

But Virgil Trucks and his fellow-Tigers beat me in my
next start, 3 to 2, and Joe Haynes of the White Sox shut us
out, 4 to 0, the next time my turn rolled around. That did
it, at least for one wire service writer. The readers of hun-
dreds of newspapers from Coast to Coast were told by impli-
cation if not by direct statement that they could drop the
name of Feller from the list of front-rank pitchers.

I thought that the story was not only premature. I consid-
ered it unfair. I was thoroughly angry when I read the piece,
but by the time we reached New York on our first eastern
trip, my feeling had congealed into an icy determination to
let my arm deliver my rebuttal.

I wanted to pitch a great game that afternoon of April 30.
Of course, I wasn't even dreaming of a no-hitter. No pitcher
does—especially when the opposing line-up is composed of
such hitters as Joe DiMaggio, Bill Dickey, Joe Gordon, Charley Keller, Tommy Henrich, George Stirnweiss, Nick Etten
and Phil Rizzuto.

Floyd Bevens was chosen to pitch for the Yankees and the
game got under way on schedule. Rizzuto bounced out to
Ken Keltner to open the home half of the first. Stirnweiss
grounded sharply to my left and the ball skidded off the side
of the mound and squirmed toward the right of second base.
Lou Boudreau, who had started from deep short, somehow
got to that ball, cutting across behind the mound and scooping up the grounder between hops. He was traveling so fast
that he turned a somersault as he threw to Les Fleming at
first base for the put-out. I've seen Boudreau make many an
"impossible" play, but that one stands out in my memory as
his best. I thought so even at the time. I didn't know then,
of course, that it was the play which would enable me to
write a bit of baseball history.

For that was the closest the Yankees came to a base hit in
those nine rugged innings. They collected five bases on balls

and one player reached base on an error. Eleven of them were strikeout victims.

In each of the first four innings, I had a man on base by the free ticket route. In the fifth, I finally set the Yankees down in order, with Gordon flying out and Dickey and Bevens fanning. Rizzuto walked to open the sixth and Stirnweiss bunted him to second, but Henrich fouled out and DiMaggio flied out.

In the seventh, Keller, Etten and Gordon were retired in order. As I walked to the dugout, I could hear the expectant hum in the stands. There were 37,144 fans out that day. Not only did they know that I had at least an outside chance to finish with a no-hit game, but they realized they were watching an exceptional pitchers' battle. We had made a few hits off Bevens, but not a single run.

We remained scoreless in our half of the eighth. Once more I nailed the Yanks in order in their half, with Boudreau again contributing handsomely when he threw out the fleet Rizzuto from deep short.

In the top of the ninth, Frank Hayes, our catcher that day, pulled one of Bevens' pitches into the left field stands for the only run of the afternoon. We were leading now, and only the last of the ninth stood between me and my second trip to the Hall of Fame.

Only the last of the ninth. Only Stirnweiss, Henrich and DiMaggio, with Keller following if one of them reached base. I looked around at our infielders before I took my wind-up. They were grim and pale with tension. I suddenly was glad that all I had to do was pitch.

Stirnweiss hit a bounder down the first base line, but Fleming tried to start for first before he had a good grip on the ball. He fumbled for an error. Playing to get back that one big run, Henrich sacrificed. Stirnweiss was on second, with DiMaggio swinging calmly as he waited for me to return to the rubber. I don't know how long I pitched to DiMaggio. It seemed to be hours. He fouled off pitch after pitch. The

THE BOX SCORE

CLEVELAND   NEW YORK (A)

(April 30, 1946)

	A.B.	R.	H.	P.O.	A.		A.B.	R.	H.	P.O.	A.
Case, lf.	4	0	2	1	0	Rizzuto, ss.	3	0	0	5	5
Lemon, cf.	4	0	1	1	0	Stirnweiss, 3b.	3	0	0	1	2
Edwards, rf.	2	0	0	0	0	Henrich, rf.	1	0	0	0	0
Fleming, 1b.	3	0	1	9	0	DiMaggio, cf.	4	0	0	1	0
Keltner, 3b.	1	0	0	0	3	Keller, lf.	3	0	0	3	0
Boudreau, ss.	3	0	0	0	4	Etten, 1b.	3	0	0	8	0
Hayes, c.	4	1	2	12	1	Gordon, 2b.	3	0	0	3	3
Mack, 2b.	3	0	1	4	3	Dickey, c.	2	0	0	6	3
Feller, p.	4	0	0	0	1	Bevens, p.	3	0	0	0	2
Totals	28	1	7	27	12	Totals	25	0	0	27	1\

CLEVELAND   0 0 0 0 0 0 0 0 1—1
NEW YORK (A) 0 0 0 0 0 0 0 0 0—0

Errors—Fleming, Keltner, Rizzuto, Bevens. Run batted in—Hayes. Home run—Hayes. Stolen bases—Case, Henrich. Sacrifices—Boudreau, Keltner, Stirnweiss, Edwards, Henrich. Double plays—Gordon, Rizzuto and Etten; Stirnweiss, Rizzuto and Etten; Dickey and Rizzuto. Left on base—Cleveland 8, New York 5. Bases on balls—Bevens 5, Feller 5. Strikeouts—Bevens 5, Feller 11. Umpires—Rommel, Boyer and Jones. Time—2:14. Attendance—38,112.

count went to three and two. Then he grounded hard to Boudreau, who retired him as Stirnweiss moved to third.

I forgot about Stirnweiss. He wasn't likely to attempt to steal home, with Keller at the plate. Charley didn't put me through the wringer as DiMaggio had done. To this day, I can't tell you which pitch he hit, but it was an early one— and the ball bounced toward big Ray Mack, our second base- man, the same fine infielder who had made the last assist of my first no-hitter six years earlier.

Ray charged the ball and fell to his knees. That could have meant disaster, for the official scorer hardly could have charged him with an error if he had failed to complete the play. But he was up in time to make the stop. Never on any baseball field have I heard a sound so sweet as the thump of his throw in Fleming's glove.

JIMMY FOXX

as told to Lyall Smith

Only Ruth before him has hit more home runs than James Emory Foxx. His total of 534 was accumulated over a period of 20 years, and his long distance clouting helped the Philadelphia Athletics to their pennants of 1929, 1930 and 1931. After 11 years with the A's, Jimmy spent seven with the Red Sox before closing out his career in the National League. Born October 22, 1907, in Sudlersville, Maryland, Mr. Double X managed in the minors before retiring from the game.

I GUESS I've hit just about as many home runs as anyone still wearing a baseball uniform but for just one good solid punch I'd have to take the afternoon in the fifth game of the 1930 World Series when I smacked one into the stands as a personal tribute to Mr. Mack (Manager Connie Mack of the A's).

But there were other afternoons, too, that I'll never forget. Some were before that day in '30, some after but most were wound up in one way or another with Mr. Mack.

I met him the first year I ever played. That was in 1925 when the A's bought me as a kid of 17 with nothing but a bunch of muscles and a big desperate lunge at the ball.

That previous fall I'd received one of those penny post cards from Frank "Home Run" Baker who was managing a team in the Eastern League and that was a thrill, too. I was just 16 when I got this card. Baker had scribbled on the back: "Would you be interested in being a professional ballplayer? If you are contact me." Naturally I wrote him and he signed me up. That next summer he sold me to the Athletics who shipped me out for seasoning.

I was hitting pretty good then and kept right on till the A's brought me up again to help out Cy Perkins, one of the best catchers I ever saw. I didn't have much to do until 1927 when Mr. Mack stuck me over at third base. I played there a while and then Ossie Orwoll, our first baseman, got into a slump and one day after I had been warming up a pitcher in the bullpen Mr. Mack walked over to me.

"Ever play first base, Jimmy?" he asked. I told him no. "You are today," he said, and tossed me a first baseman's mitt.

That '29 season was a big one for me. I was still pretty young but I didn't have to do very much on a team that was as murderous as any I ever saw.

We had Bishop and Haas, Cochrane and Simmons, Miller and Dykes, and pitchers like Earnshaw, Ehmke, Walberg, Grove and Quinn. That was the year we breezed to an American League pennant and faced the Cubs in the Series.

In the first game I smacked a homer off Charlie Root to break a scoreless tie in the 7th inning and help us win 3–1. I hit another one in the second game when we slapped them around 9–3 and had a lot of fun in the fourth game when we made those 10 runs in the 7th inning after trailing 8–0. I didn't hit any long ones in that game but poked out a couple of singles to take part in the big spree.

But that was nothing like the buzz I got the next year when we went into the series again. The Cards had won the National title and were giving us a stiff battle. In that first

game we were up against Burleigh Grimes and his spitter. He
was tough to hit when he gave that ball a working-over and
was really putting the stuff on it that day.

In the second inning I came up after Al Simmons had
bounced out to Grimes and I stepped in to one of Burleigh's
spitters and slapped it off the right field wall over Ray
Blades' head for a triple. Bing Miller was up next. He hit a
long fly that time out to Blades again and I came in with the
first run after the catch.

I felt pretty good about that but old Burleigh wasn't
through with me yet. In the fourth I was up again right after
Simmons had poked out a home run to tie the score, but
Burleigh fooled me on a low spitter and I struck out. In the
sixth we went ahead when Maxie Bishop worked Grimes for
a walk and scored when Jimmy Dykes doubled. With two out
Burleigh walked Simmons on purpose to get at me.

I fell right into his plans and was easy for him. I was ex-
pecting him to throw me a spitter if the count was close. And
it was for I worked him up to a 3–2 with two runners on base
and two out.

Burleigh stood out there and went through his motions.
He put the glove up to his mouth, looked out at Dykes on
second, glanced over at Simmons on first. Then stepped off
the mound and turned around for another look at the scoreboard. Then he took his stance again and pitched. I was sure
it'd be a spitter, a low one around the knees like the one he
had fanned me on in the second inning. But it was a curve,
a fast hopper that came in waist high and caught me way off
balance.

Everybody was surprised for Burleigh didn't throw a curve
very often. But they weren't nearly as surprised as I was. I
stood there at the plate for a minute still trying to figure out
what had happened, but I was out.

We won that game anyway and took the second one before
moving down to St. Louis feeling pretty good. Then Wild
Bill Hallahan shut us out 5–0 before Jess Haines set us down

on four hits to beat Lefty Grove 3–1 and even up the series at two games apiece.

Well, we're in St. Louis for the fifth game and all of us are keyed up pretty high. We wanted to win that one, for any baseball man will tell you that the fifth game is the big one. If you win it you're over the hump and coasting. If you lose it—well, that's not good at all.

It's Grimes' turn again and Mr. Mack picks out big George Earnshaw to go for us. Mr. Mack took me to one side of the dugout just before the game started. "Jimmy," he said, "you watch out for that pitcher out there. He figures he has your number and I think he'll try to get to you if he gets in a pinch. And watch for that curve ball. Don't let him fool you with that spitter motion. Just because he goes through like he's going to throw it is no sign he will."

The game starts and right away you can tell it's going to be a honey. Both Grimes and Earnshaw are really tough, although Mike Cochrane gets a single for us in the first inning and Adams pokes one off Ehmke.

I come up in the second and hit the first pitch, a fast ball, out to Chick Hafey in deep left for just another out and then come up again in the fifth. I swing on the first pitch again and poke a single into center field for our second single and the third hit of the game, but it doesn't do any good and nobody scores.

I bat again in the seventh and Burleigh gets me in a 2–1 hole. I'm still thinking about a curve ball when he throws a fast one past me and all I hit was a big hunk of air.

They scared us in their half when Jimmy Wilson doubled down the line, but there were two outs and Mr. Mack waved his score card for George to walk Gelbert to get at Grimes. Burleigh hit one hard, but Mule Haas ran it down and we were out of the jam.

In the eighth we had a good chance to score when two singles and an error by Frankie Frisch loaded the bases with

THE BOX SCORE
(*October 6, 1930*)

ATHLETICS	A.B.	R.	H.	P.	A.		CARDINALS	A.B.	R.	H.	P.	A.
Bishop, 2b.	4	0	0	1	0		Douthit, cf.	4	0	0	2	0
Dykes, 3b.	3	0	0	0	1		Adams, 3b.	4	0	1	0	1
Cochrane, c.	3	1	1	7	1		Frisch, 2b.	4	0	1	3	3
Simmons, lf.	4	0	0	3	0		Bottomley, 1b.	4	0	0	9	1
Foxx, 1b.	4	1	2	12	0		Hafey, lf.	3	0	0	1	0
Miller, rf.	4	0	0	0	0		Watkins, rf.	3	0	0	1	0
Haas, cf.	4	0	1	2	0		Wilson, c.	4	0	1	9	0
Boley, ss.	3	0	1	2	1		Gelbert, ss.	2	0	0	2	8
Earnshaw, p.	2	0	0	0	4		Grimes, p.	2	0	0	0	0
Moore	0	0	0	0	0		Blades	0	0	0	0	0
Grove, p.	0	0	0	0	1							
Totals	31	2	5	27	8		Totals	30	0	3	27	13

Moore batted for Earnshaw in 8th.   Blades batted for Watkins in 9th.

ATHLETICS	0	0	0	0	0	0	0	0	2—2
CARDINALS	0	0	0	0	0	0	0	0	0—0

Error—Frisch. Home run—Foxx. Sacrifice hit—Grimes. Double play—Adams to Frisch to Bottomley. Left on bases—St. Louis 8, Philadelphia 5. Bases on balls—Off Grimes 3 (Dykes, Moore, Cochrane); off Earnshaw 3 (Gelbert 2, Hafey); off Grove 1 (Blades). Struck out—By Grimes 7 (Bishop 2, Boley, Cochrane, Earnshaw, Foxx, Miller); by Earnshaw 5 (Watkins, Bottomley 2, Adams, Hafey); by Grove 2 (Bottomley, Gelbert). Hits—Off Earnshaw 2 in 7 innings, off Grove 1 in 2 innings. Winning pitcher—Grove. Umpires—Moriarty, plate; Rigler, first; Geisel, second; Reardon, third. Time—1:53.

only one out. But Burleigh reached down into his bag of tricks to make Bishop ground to Bottomley, who forced Haas at the plate, and make Dykes hit one to Gelbert at short, who flipped to Frisch in time to force Bishop to end the inning.

Earnshaw had been lifted for a pinch hitter in that frame and Mr. Mack put in Lefty Grove, who got by the Card half, although he was nicked for a single, the third Redbird hit, by Frisch.

Then came the ninth. There still was no score. Each team had made only three hits and Grimes was bearing down. But he pitched too carefully to Cochrane and Mickey jogged down to first base on a pass. Al Simmons came up, but he undercut a spitter and lifted a high pop fly to Gelbert for the first out. That brought me up again.

I was nervous. But Grimes was cool as ice. He was deliberately slow in getting ready to pitch, so I stepped out of the box. I got some dirt on my hands and stepped in again. He raised his hand to his mouth in his spitter motion. Then he threw the first pitch. I knew in that flash second it wasn't a spitter, for it was coming in close. It was a curve and I swung!

Well, that was it. The big thrill. I heard the Athletic bench yell all at once and there it went. Some fan reached up and pulled it down when it hit in the left-field bleachers for a home run.

FRANKIE F. FRISCH

as told to Ken Smith

Frankie F. Frisch, Jr., born September 9, 1898, in New York City, came off Fordham University's campus some twenty-one years later to spark John McGraw's New York Giant infield of the early 20's. Frisch was traded to the St. Louis Cardinals, and started to lose his hair when he became manager of the rambunctious Gas House Gang in 1933. Frisch took over the managership at Pittsburgh, later broadcasting ball games before he managed the Cubs. He is a member of the Hall of Fame.

I FINALLY got to sleep on the night of October 8, 1934, in my hotel in Detroit. The next day was the most important day of my whole baseball career so far, and I knew it.

When I had been a fresh kid, with John J. McGraw's Giants in the 1921, '22, '23 and '24 World Series, I never fretted about anything. Slept like a baby and played with an abandon I wish I had had in the three Series during the '30s. McGraw and the older men like Dave Bancroft, Heinie Groh and Casey Stengel did the worrying in the old days. A young squirt isn't afraid of anything.

But in the 1930, '31 and '34 Series, the responsibility was terrific. This stuff you hear about old codgers mellowing and losing the competitive urge is the bunk. It grows stronger with age, especially when you are playing second base and managing the Gas House Gang.

Well, we were even-Stephen at three games apiece, in the 1934 Series—the Cardinals against the Tigers. You can imagine how I would feel if we blew this, of all Series, after such a Donnybrook as we had been through. I lay there in the sheets, figuring pitches for Mickey Cochrane, Charley Gehringer, Goose Goslin and Hank Greenberg, knowing that here was the one big game of my life whether I played a personal part in the playing end, or not, I don't have to thumb back and say: "Let's see, now, which WAS my biggest day?"

You can imagine what was on my mind lying there before the seventh and deciding game. Dizzy Dean had won the first for us in Detroit, 8–3. Schoolboy Rowe, who had a tremendous year with the Tigers, had beaten us the second game, 3–2, the Schoolboy retiring 22 batters in a row starting with the fourth inning. Paul Dean had won the third battle, but the Tigers had taken the fourth and fifth, and the city of Detroit was beginning to lay the red carpet.

Then Paul came back and won the sixth game with a single, 4–3, I'll never forget old Dizzy hugging Paul in the dressing room after the game, wresting him and yelping, "You're the greatest pitcher the Dean family ever had," and then Diz would pound everybody else on the back and brag about his kid brother. Diz had announced at the start of the year "me and Paul will win 50 games," and they'd darn near done it, Dean winning 30 and Paul 19. Diz had said they'd murder the Tigers in the Series, too, and now they had between them won three games—the only ones we had taken.

I remember John Carmichael coming up to me in the confusion of that dressing room after the sixth game and asking, "Dean tomorrow—the other Dean?" and me sitting there, all in from the strain, and answering "If I last till tomorrow."

Carmichael took one look at Diz charging around the room with a white pith helmet and hollering how he'd take the seventh game tomorrow. Carmichael said, "Wild horses can't keep Dean off that mound tomorrow, Frank."

I looked. Dizzy had a rubber tiger, a Detroit souvenir, by the tail and was whacking Bill DeLancey over the head with it and then throwing it into the showers at Pepper Martin. I knew inside me Diz would pitch it. He had a terrible head cold and only two days before had been knocked out running the bases, but there'd be no use fighting against it—he was the boy and the chips were sure down.

Incidentally the wolves had been on me for putting in Dizzy to run for big, slow Virgil Davis in that fourth game— the time Diz went into second so high and hard that Charley Gehringer, trying for a forceout, hit Diz in the head. But I didn't mind the criticism. We were out to win. We were the Gas House Gang and I knew Diz would give 'em something to worry about running bases as well as pitching.

Well, morning came for the big game and then at the park Diz took the ball and warmed up with what looked like 50,000 Tiger fans hooting at him, and him grinning and yelling at each of us, "I'll shut 'em out. Get me a couple of runs: that's all. I'll blank the blank-blank blankety-blanks."

Dizzy said he'd shut 'em out and he did. And with the score 0–0 to start the third he singled and stretched it to get to second.

Pepper Martin, the Wild Horse, was up next and he hit a slow hopper to Greenberg and went down so fast he beat the throw. Three years before Pepper had driven Mickey Cochrane crazy running bases in the Series between the Athletics and the Cards and now he did it again.

Then Auker walked Rothrock and the bases were full. And I was up. I couldn't let the rest of them make an old man out of the playing-manager, so I doubled and all three of 'em came in.

That was all for Auker and in came Schoolboy Rowe. Our bench stood up and gave him the "How'm-I-doin'-Edna?" chant. He had asked that during a radio interview, throwing in a little message to his girl, and the papers had been riding him about it. Rip Collins welcomed Rowe with a double and I scored. Then DeLancey doubled and Rip scored—and away went Schoolboy.

THE BOX SCORE
(October 9, 1934)

St. Louis	A.B.	R.	H.	P.	A.	Detroit	A.B.	R.	H.	P.	A.
Martin, 3b.	5	3	2	0	1	White, cf.	4	0	0	3	0
Rothrock, rf.	5	1	2	4	0	Cochrane, c.	4	0	0	2	2
Frisch, 2b.	5	1	1	3	5	Hayworth, c.	0	0	0	1	0
Medwick, lf.	4	1	1	1	0	Gehringer, 2b.	4	0	2	3	5
Fullis, lf.	1	0	1	1	0	Goslin, lf.	4	0	0	4	0
Collins, 1b.	5	1	4	7	2	Rogell, ss.	4	0	1	3	2
DeLancey, c.	5	1	1	5	0	Greenberg, 1b.	4	0	1	7	0
Orsatti, cf.	3	1	1	2	0	Owen, 3b.	4	0	0	1	2
Durocher, ss.	5	1	2	3	4	Fox, rf.	3	0	2	3	0
J. Dean, p.	5	1	2	1	0	Auker, p.	0	0	0	0	0
						Rowe, p.	0	0	0	0	0
						Hogsett, p.	0	0	0	0	0
						Bridges, p.	2	0	0	0	1
						Marberry, p.	0	0	0	0	0
						G. Walker	1	0	0	0	0
						Crowder, p.	0	0	0	0	0
Totals	43	11	17	27	12	Totals	34	0	6	27	12

G. Walker batted for Marberry in 8th.

St. Louis	0	0	7	0	0	2	2	0	0—11
Detroit	0	0	0	0	0	0	0	0	0— 0

Errors.—Collins, White, Gehringer, Goslin. Two-base hits—Rothrock (2), Fox (2), Frisch, DeLancey. Three-base hits—Medwick, Durocher. Runs batted in—Frisch (3), Collins (2), Martin, Rothrock, Medwick, J. Dean, DeLancey. Stolen base—Martin. Double play—Owen, Gehringer, Greenberg. Base on balls—Off Auker 1 (Rothrock), off Hogsett 2 (Orsatti, Martin), off Marberry 1 (Orsatti). Struck out—By Auker 1 (Martin), by Bridges 2 (J. Dean, DeLancey), by Crowder 1 (Rothrock), by J. Dean 5 (Greenberg (3), Bridges, White). Pitching records—Auker 6 hits, 4 runs in 2 1-3 innings; Rowe 2 hits in 1-3 inning; Hogsett 2 hits, 1 run in 0 inning (pitched to 4 batters); Bridges 6 hits, 4 runs in 4 1-3 innings; Marberry 1 hit, 0 run in 1 inning; Crowder 0 hits, 0 runs in 1 inning. Left on bases—St. Louis 9, Detroit 7. Earned runs—St. Louis 10, Detroit 0. Caught stealing—Orsatti. Losing pitcher—Auker. Umpires—Geisel (A. L.) home plate; Reardon (N. L.) first base; Klem (N. L.) third base. Time of game—2:19.

We kept on hitting, and Cochrane, who was fit to be asylumed by this time, kept bringing in more pitchers. Dizzy got his second hit of the inning by racing like Pepper to first on a slow grounder, bringing DeLancey in. By the time the inning was over we had seven runs and I figured maybe Dizzy would be winded by all that hitting and base running he'd done in the inning, but, heck, no. He beat the rest of the team out to position and could hardly take time to make his warmup throws.

It was like playing ball at the foot of Vesuvius. And in the sixth came the eruption. Pepper started by singling and, seeing Goslin in left juggle the throw momentarily, he went on to second. Rothrock and I went out, but Medwick lammed the ball against the screen for a double and kept on to third, sliding in hard. Marv Owen on third got the ball and stepped on Medwick's leg. Joe kicked up from his position on his back and hit Owen in the chest. They started to fight, and both teams boiled out. The panic was on, but nothing to what happened after the umpires had quieted everybody down and got the inning played out. As Medwick went out to left field the Tiger fans met him with cushions, bottles, lemons, and some of them took off their shoes and tried to bean him. They tried to climb the 18-foot wire fence to murder him. For 15 minutes the game was stopped and finally Commissioner Landis told Cochrane and me to bring Owen and Medwick up to his box. He asked Medwick, "Did you kick him?" and Joe said "You're darn right, I did!" They wouldn't shake hands and the noise got worse. Cochrane would run out and beg the bleachers to be good, but they would have none of his advice. So Landis put both Medwick and Owen out of the game and we went on to finish it.

So it ended 11–0. Dizzy had done what he said he'd do and we'd done more than he asked us.

LEFTY GOMEZ

as told to John Drohan

Vernon Louis "Goofy" Go-
mez was born November 26,
1910, in Rodeo, California.
He came to the New York
Yankees in 1930 with an un-
dernourished body, sponta-
neity of youth and reckless
abandon. He clowned his way
through the next 12 seasons,
but never neglected his trade
—pitching winning baseball
with a blazing fast ball. After
hanging up six world's series
triumphs without a loss, three
all-star game victories and a
tentful of laughs, all with the
Yankees, Lefty closed out his
career as a member of the
Boston Braves in 1943.

TO TELL the truth, in relating my biggest baseball day, I'm
torn between two loves. I'm something like the Old Soak
who never knew whether his wife told him to take one drink
and come home at 12, or take 12 and come home at 1. Of
course, there have been complaints. I've been a pitcher. On
the other hand, there was a hot day one August in Washington—and can it get hot there—when I got four for five, as
they say down at the clubhouse.

I'd like to dwell a bit on that, because those days have been
rare in my career. But inasmuch as I've drawn my best salary

88

checks for pitching, rather than hitting, I'll pass it up, much as I dislike to. However, the fact I got four for five might have had something to do with Bucky Harris resigning his job a few weeks later.

Searching the old cerebellum, I think my biggest thrill in baseball was my first World Series game. It was against the Chicago Cubs in the second game of the 1932 series.

Red Ruffing had won the first game, 12–6 from Guy Bush at the Yankee Stadium and I was to work the second against Lon Warneke, the Arkansas Humming Bird.

Joe McCarthy had us hopped up to pour it on the Cubs and lick 'em quick. He'd got the old heave-ho from the Cubs only two years before, and was anxious to get back at them. He figured he hadn't got such a good shake in Chicago and often said he'd like to get even. This was his chance.

Revenge couldn't be as sweet to him as if Rogers Hornsby had stayed as manager of the Cubs. Hornsby had succeeded McCarthy as manager of the Cubs in 1931 and then had been given the old heave-ho in his turn in August, '32. That had brought in Charley Grimm as Cub manager, and the club has turned it on hot to come down the stretch whooping and hollering and kicking everybody out of their way to grab the flag in one of baseball's best stretch drives.

The Yanks under Huggins had swept the World Series four straight from the Pirates in '27 and again from the Cards in '28, and McCarthy naturally wanted to do what Miller had done. We figured we could do it, for while Grimm had Jurges, Herman, Koenig and English with him on the infield, Cuyler, Stephenson and Demaree in the outfield, Hartnett catching and Warneke, Root, Malone, Bush, Grimes and Jakie May pitching, we had what we thought was a much stronger club, with Dickey catching, Gehrig on first, Crosetti at short, Lazzeri at second, Sewell at third, Babe Ruth, Sam Chapman and Earle Combs in the outfield and Red Ruffing, Wilcy Moore, Johnny Allen, George Pipgras and myself.

There was a lot of talk, as the second game came up, about

the kid-competition between Lon Warneke and me—two bean poles. Both of us were sophomores; he was 23, I was 21; he had won 22 that summer for the Cubs, I had managed to get by with 24 for the Yanks.

Babe Ruth was 37 and beginning to slow down in the field, but he could still flatten the ball and had hit 41 homers that year.

I remember how Ed Barrow, our general manager, kept after me all my first and second years to put on weight. It scared him when he looked at me, for I weighed only 152, which was thin enough for my height, over 6 feet. Barrow figured I couldn't last.

At the end of the first season he told me, "About 25 years ago we had a pitcher around here named Jack Chesbro, the first pitcher ever to win 16 straight games in the American League. If you'd only put on more weight you could make the fans forget Chesbro."

I wasn't any fatter my second year, '32, but I could fire the ball through a two-inch plank. Barrow, however, kept after me, and I knew during the series that I'd have to spend the winter at a health resort in California Barrow had picked out —a sort of old ladies' home where I was to fatten up.

Incidentally, I did come back to start the '33 season 20 pounds fatter and they put me to rooming with Pat Malone, whom McCarthy had bought from the Cubs, who was a fat man.

That '33 season I won only 16 and lost 10 and instead of making the fans forget Chesbro I was making 'em forget Gomez, so that winter of '33–35 I took off so much weight I showed up in '34 spring training thinner than Bill Powell— and won 26 games and lost five for an .839 percentage, the best I ever hung up.

Anyway, on September 29, 1932, when I went against Lon Warneke and the Cubs, I was thin and felt good.

I had a break, for Warneke showed up wild and kept putting men on for us to bat around, while I found I could get the ball where I wanted and where the Cubs didn't. That afternoon I fanned eight and walked only one. Guy Bush had been wild in the first game of the series and in these first two games we got 10 walks which turned into nine runs.

As I remember it, the Cubs didn't even threaten mildly after tying the score in the third, for we went ahead with a couple more in our half and wound up winning 5–2.

It wasn't any closeness of score or suspense that made it my biggest baseball day; it was simply that it was my first World Series game and I won it.

I remember Gabby Hartnett hitting one down the left field line and Ben Chapman, the fastest man in the American League, scooping up the ball and firing it to second in time for Crosetti to be waiting with it when the old "Milford Freight" came steaming into the bag.

When the rest of the Yanks got through slapping ol' Lon around about all he had left was his chaw of terbacker. And even that was pretty well used up. But if I didn't hit Lon he didn't hit me. So I guess we're even in that respect.

That one game was my only chance in the '32 series. The Babe fixed the third one up for us in Chicago by waving toward the bleachers in center field and then whacking one of Charley Root's pitches in there. Pipgras pitched us to a 7–5 win, and the next day Wilcy Moore beat Bush, Warneke, Jakie May, Bud Tinning and a great many other gentlemen whose names escape me, 13–6.

The whole series was pretty enjoyable for me. I was going with June O'Dea, prima donna of the Broadway show, "Of Thee I Sing," at the time and, hanging around the theater saw the show so often I felt I could act myself. So when bookers came to me after the series I signed up without a quiver for vaudeville monologues on a 12-week booking. I lasted three weeks, but the audiences didn't.

I knew so little about show business that one afternoon at Loew's State in New York, when the manager said, "There won't be anybody here for the supper show," I started to skip that show as a matter of course. He caught me as I was leaving for the Rodeo over at Madison Square Garden and drove me back into my dressing room, where I put on my Yankee uniform and went out and gave my monologue to three stews, two of whom were asleep when I started and the third soon was.

The year 1932 I am safe in saying saw an end to my career in the theater.

GABBY HARTNETT

as told to Hal Totten

Who can ever forget the bouncy, red-faced, foghorn-voiced backstop that was Charles Leo "Gabby" Hartnett? Born in Woonsocket, Rhode Island, December 20, 1900, Gabby was the toast of Chicago's North Side for 19 years. Blessed with a whip-like arm and tremendous batting power, Hartnett managed the Cubs for three years before playing his 20th and final season with the New York Giants in 1941, closing out his colorful career with a batting average of .299.

Do you know how you feel when you're real scared, or something BIG is going to happen? Well, that's the way I felt for one terrific minute of my biggest day in baseball—and I don't believe you'll have to guess very much as to just which day that was.

It was in 1938, September 28, the day of "the home run in the dark." But as a matter of fact, that day—that one big moment—was the climax of a series of things that had gone on for a week or more. And every one of those incidents helped to make it the biggest day in all my years in the major leagues.

The week before—on Sunday—you'll remember we had played a double-header in Brooklyn. We lost the first game 4 to 3, and we were leading the second game by two runs along about the fifth inning. It was muddy and raining and was getting dark fast. Then big Fred Sington came up with a man on base and hit a home run to tie the score.

It was too dark to play any more, so they called the game and it ended in a tie. Now—every game meant a lot to us just then. We were three and a half games behind. Winning was the only way we could hope to catch the Pirates and we were scheduled in Philadelphia the next day. So we couldn't play the game off then.

But Larry MacPhail wanted to play it. We had an open date for travel at the end of the series in Philly, and he wanted us to go back to Brooklyn and play off the tie. The boys wanted to play it, too. They figured we could win it and gain on the Pirates.

Well, I couldn't make up my mind right away, so I asked MacPhail to give me 24 hours to decide. He said he would. But I'd been figuring—you see, we had to win all three games in the series with Pittsburgh if we were to win the pennant. And I had to think of my pitchers. I had to argue with the whole ball club—they wanted to play.

But I stuck my neck out and turned it down. I'll admit that I didn't feel any too easy about it. But I had to make the decision. And I felt that we might lose that game just as easy as we could win it. So I took that chance.

Well, we sat for three days in Philly and watched it rain. Of course, Pittsburgh wasn't able to play in Brooklyn, either, and they were three and a half games in front of us. On Thursday we played the Phils twice and beat 'em both times, 4 to 0 and 2 to 1. Lee won his 20th game of the season in that first one—and his fourth straight shutout. Clay Bryant was the pitcher in the second. But Pittsburgh beat Brooklyn twice, so were still three and a half back.

The next day we won two again—and we had to come

from behind to do it. Rip Collins put the second one on ice by doubling in the ninth with the bases full to drive in three runs just as they posted the score showing that Cincinnati had beaten the Pirates. That put us within two games of the leaders. We were really rollin'.

Then we came home and on Saturday we played the Cardinals—and beat 'em 9 to 3. But the Pirates won, too. On Sunday it was the same thing—we both won. Monday Pittsburgh wasn't scheduled, so the Pirates were in the stands at Wrigley Field as we played the final of the series with St. Louis. Bill Lee was scored on for the first time in five games, but we won 6 to 3. Then came the big series—with the lead cut to a game and a half.

I stuck my neck out in the very first game of the series. Several times, in fact. I started Dizzy Dean on the mound. He hadn't pitched since September 13 and hadn't started a game since August 13. But how he pitched! Just a slow ball, control, and a world of heart.

We got him out in front in the third when Collins tripled and Jurges drove him in with a single. For five innings Dean was great. Then he seemed to tire. Lloyd Waner grounded out in that inning, and Paul Waner fouled out. Rizzo singled, but Vaughan popped to Herman. Still, I noticed that he didn't have as much on the ball.

Probably I was the only one to notice it—except maybe Diz himself. I began to worry a bit and I made up my mind right then and there that no matter how anything else was going, the minute Dean got in trouble, I was going to get him out of there. We got another run the last half of that inning. And Diz got through the seventh and eighth, although it took a great play by Dean himself to cut down a run at the plate in the eighth.

When the ninth came around I decided to play safe and started Lee warming up in the bull pen. Bill wasn't usually a good relief pitcher, but he was the best pitcher in the league, and that was a spot for the best we had.

Dean hit Vaughan to start the ninth and I was plenty uneasy. But Suhr popped out, and Jensen batted for Young and forced Arky at second. Then came little "Jeep" Handley and he hit one clear to the wall in left center for a double. That put the tying runs on second and third, and that was my cue.

Todd was up. He always hit Dean pretty good, even when Diz had his stuff—and Diz didn't have a thing then. Not only that, but Todd never hit Lee very well. So even though Lee hadn't been a steady relief pitcher, I called him in. My neck was out again. What if Todd hit one? What if Lee had trouble getting started—after all, he'd been working day after day. But—well, when it gets to the place where it means a ball game, you've got to make a change, even if the hitter socks one into the bleachers.

I'll say this for Dean—he never complained about that. He walked right in and said I'd done the right thing—that he'd lost his stuff and his arm didn't feel so good. So Lee came in. The first pitch was a strike. Todd fouled the next one off. Then Lee cut loose with as wild a pitch as I ever saw and Jensen scored. Handley went to third with the tying run. My hunch didn't look so good. But Lee wound up again; he pitched; and Todd swung and struck out. We'd won the game and were only a half game out of first place.

That brings us up to the big day. We scored in the second inning on a couple of errors. But Pittsburgh went ahead with three in the sixth. We tied it up in our half. But the Pirates got two in the eighth and led, 5 to 3. In our half Collins opened with a single and Jurges walked.

Lazzeri batted for Lee, who had gone in again that day, and doubled, scoring Rip. They walked Hack. Then Herman drove in Jurges to tie it up again, but Joe Marty—who had run for Tony—was thrown out at the plate by Paul Waner. A double play ended that round.

It was very dark by then. But the umpires decided to let us go one more. Charlie Root got through the first half of the ninth all right. In our half Cavaretta hit one a country mile to center, but Lloyd Waner pulled it down. Reynolds grounded out. And it was my turn.

Well—I swung once—and missed; I swung again, and got a piece of it, but that was all. A foul and strike two. I had one more chance. Mace Brown wound up and let fly; I swung with everything I had and then I got that feeling I was talking about—the kind of feeling you get when the blood rushes out of your head and you get dizzy.

A lot of people have told me they didn't know the ball was in the bleachers. Well, I did—maybe I was the only one in the park who did. I knew it the minute I hit it. When I got to second base I couldn't see third for the players and fans there. I don't think I walked a step to the plate—I was carried in. But when I got there I saw George Barr taking a good look—he was going to make sure I touched that platter.

That was the shot that did it. We went into first place. And while we still had the pennant to win, we couldn't be headed. We won again the next day for Bill Lee, easy—10 to 1. The heart was gone out of Pittsburgh. And we clinched the pennant down in St. Louis the next Saturday when we won and Pittsburgh lost to Cincinnati.

TOMMY HENRICH

as told to Fred Down

Thomas David Henrich, born February 10, 1916, in Massillon, Ohio, twenty-one years later became an integral part of baseball's modern wrecking crew, the New York Yankees. For eleven seasons Henrich sparkled as a heady and skillful outfielder, brilliant part-time first baseman and a batter who was feared throughout the circuit as a dangerous clutch hitter who reserved most of his hits for the moment when a game could be broken wide open. A knee ailment forced Hen-

rich's retirement. He helped coach Mickey Mantle in his first year, and was a telecaster in New York.

I GOT my greatest thrill in baseball on August 30, 1942. It probably is the last day any one would expect me to remember as thrilling.

It started out pretty much like a thousand other Sunday afternoons in the Bronx. It was hot and humid and there was a double-header at the Yankee Stadium.

The American League race had reached a familiar point. The Yankees had all but clinched the flag and the other clubs were jockeying for first-division money. We were seven games in front and were to be eight by nightfall. This was to be our sixth pennant in seven years, a string which began in 1936, the year before I joined the club, and had been broken only in 1940 by the Detroit Tigers.

Then, as now, it was great to be a Yankee and that is why I was wearing a face a mile long when I left for the Stadium. This, you see, was to be my last day as a Yankee. By midnight I would be en route to Cleveland and the U. S. Coast Guard.

The crowd already was forming outside the Stadium when I arrived a little before noon. The Tigers were our guests and while they seemed out of the race they were an interesting team which always gave us a hard time.

In the clubhouse it was the same as usual. Red Ruffing, who was to work the first game, was sitting in front of his locker reading a magazine. There were the usual chatter and jokes. I tried to look casual.

"Hey Schulte," I said to Coach John Schulte who minded the ball bag. "Give me a mess of balls, will you?"

"All you want," he said. "Today you get all you want."

But he already was leaving the clubhouse for the field and I knew he wouldn't be an easy touch. He never was.

I don't remember too much about the first game. Ruffing was no longer a 20-game winner but he knew how to pitch and he was always very effective against the Tigers. He worked fast and the Tigers never did get him into serious trouble. We won, going away, 8 to 1. I got three hits.

They threw Dizzy Trout against us in the second game and I guess you know what kind of a pitcher he was. He hadn't become a consistent winner yet but he was a big, strong guy with a lot of stuff. He could be tough when he was "on" and he always seemed to be "on" when he worked against us.

We got a run early but the Tigers hung in there and it was 3 to 2 our favor at the end of six innings. I didn't like it. One bad pitch and the Tigers could tie it up. We needed another run and I figured Trout wasn't going to get himself into serious trouble. I figured we needed to get that run with one swing and the "homer" was uppermost in my mind when my turn came to hit in the seventh.

"This could be my last swing as a Yankee," I said to myself as I left the dugout for the batter's circle. "It would be good to go out with a homer."

Then it was my turn and I threw aside the extra bats I'd been swinging and started for the plate.

"*Attention, please. . . . Attention, please. . . .*"

It was the public address system and I'll never forget the announcer's voice—hard and metallic.

"This one's not even over and there's the announcement for tomorrow's game," I said under my breath. "You'd think he could wait until we had this one won."

"*. . . Ladies and gentlemen,*" the voice went on, "*this is the last appearance of Tommy Henrich in a Yankee uniform until the war is over.*"

"O.K.," I thought, "so what if I don't hit?"

The rumble in the stands—the exact count I learned later was 50,398—seemed to start in the bleachers. But within seconds it had become the loudest roar I'd ever heard.

I tipped my cap and looked up into the stands. Everybody was standing. I kicked at the dirt and waited. The roar went on. I tipped my cap again. Still it went on. I looked out at the mound. Trout was standing there laughing. He must have known how I felt. And I knew he was thinking I'd be easy meat when I finally got into the batter's box.

"Come on, you big lug," I yelled. "Pitch! Let's get this thing over with."

He turned his back and picked up the resin bag. He was still laughing when he looked around again. The roar from the stands was as loud as ever. I wished it would stop. I never felt so helpless in my life.

"Come on, Trout," I yelled again. "Throw!"

Now Trout was about halfway from the mound to the plate and he had stopped laughing.

"What are you in such a rush about?" he yelled. "This is

THE BOX SCORE

DETROIT   NEW YORK (A)

(August 30, 1942)

	A.B.	R.	H.	P.O.	A.		A.B.	R.	H.	P.O.	A.
Bloodworth, 2b.	4	2	2	3	4	Hassett, 1b.	5	0	0	10	1
Cramer, cf.	4	1	2	3	0	Rolfe, 3b.	4	0	0	0	2
McCosky, lf.	4	0	1	2	0	Henrich, rf.	3	1	3	0	0
York, 1b.	2	0	0	9	1	DiMaggio, cf.	5	1	1	2	0
Radcliff, rf.	5	0	1	0	0	Keller, lf.	3	2	1	0	0
Ross, 3b.	5	0	0	0	2	Gordon, 2b.	4	0	1	6	4
Lipon, ss.	4	0	0	4	3	Dickey, c.	4	0	1	7	1
Riebe, c.	4	0	1	6	2	Rizzuto, ss.	4	0	0	4	6
Trout, p.	4	0	0	1	1	Breuer, p.	3	0	0	1	1
						a Selkirk	1	0	1	0	0
Totals	36	3	7	28 *	13	Totals	36	4	8	30	15

* One out when winning run scored.
a Batted for Breuer in 10th.

DETROIT   0 0 0 1 0 1 0 1 0 0—3
NEW YORK (A)   0 0 0 1 0 2 0 0 0 1—4

Errors—Rolfe, Breuer 2. Runs batted in—McCosky, Keller 2, Radcliffe, DiMaggio, Selkirk. Two base hit—Henrich. Three base hit—DiMaggio. Home run—Keller. Stolen base—Gordon. Sacrifices—York, Cramer, McCosky. Double plays—Rizzuto and Hassett; Bloodworth and York. Left on base—Detroit 9, New York 13. Bases on balls—Breuer 3, Trout 9. Strikeouts—Trout 7, Breuer 7. Passed ball—Riebe. Umpires—Rue, Grieve and Hubbard. Time—2:10. Attendance—50,398.

for you and you'll never hear anything like it again. You couldn't buy what you're getting now, so stand there and take it."

He was right, of course. I know that now. You hit a homer —win a game—maybe win a World Series game and you remember them as great thrills. But they're nothing compared to having 50,000 people you don't even know standing and giving you a send-off like I received.

No, I didn't hit that homer although the Yankees did win. The best I could do was a single—a grounder through the box. But I didn't care. I already had had my greatest thrill in baseball.

ROGERS HORNSBY

as told to Bill Van Fleet

The greatest National League batter of 'em all! Rogers Hornsby, born April 27, 1896, in Winters, Texas, conducted a reign of terror against pitchers which lasted 23 years. He hit .424 in 1924, the highest seasonal batting mark ever recorded in modern baseball history. He also led the National League in batting seven times. The Rajah played with the Cardinals, Braves, Giants, Cubs in the National League, and the Browns in the American. He also managed the Browns for five years. In the last decade of his life Hornsby served as

a coach for a number of clubs, including the Mets in their first year. He died in 1963.

THE peak of my whole baseball career came in that seventh game of the 1926 World Series. That game, and that series, is an old, old story by now because it has been told so often, but that day always will be my greatest. As playing manager of the Cardinals, I won St. Louis' first pennant in history and beat one of the finest of all Yankee teams in the same year. You couldn't ask for anything more to remember.

Mechanically, I may say right here, I played a very ordinary game. I got two singles, but neither figured in the scoring. I handled five chances without an error, but not one was a hard play. So it wasn't what I did, but what WE did, as a championship team, that will never be forgotten. Personally, I came as close to being one of the all-time goats as eventually winding up with the temporary rank of first-class hero.

Just to start from the beginning, our club was rated well from opening day that season, but for a long time we couldn't get going. We really didn't move into contention for the flag until early in September. With about two weeks to go we won two out of three from the Reds and went into the lead, but then lost three out of four in Boston and fell into second place. In Philly we rallied for five out of six and it was September 27, or thereabouts, that we beat the Giants a double-header to clinch the title. This was the team destined to out-finish the mighty Ruth and Gehrig and Bob Meusel and Lazzeri.

No question but what fandom was pulling for us. We were the newcomers to championship circles. We were brash Davids throwing rocks at the Yankee Goliaths and nobody can say we didn't give 'em a battle. The only real "cleaning" we got was the day in St. Louis when Ruth hit those three homers to score four runs and drive in four more. The other Yank wins were by Herb Pennock, 2–1 and 3–2, while Jess Haines and old Pete Alexander packed away three for us. It was Alex who had simply breezed to a 10–2 triumph in No. 6. Old Pete didn't have to bear down at all and suddenly we were at the climax. It was now or never for both. There'd be no tomorrow for either. Jess Haines, who had hurled the only shutout of the series in whipping "Dutch" Reuther, was my choice; Waite Hoyt drew the Yankee assignment. You can imagine the scene in Yankee Stadium. The very air tingled. You couldn't step on that field without experiencing a feeling that this whole setup was a grand, grand thing.

The Yanks got a run in the first. We got three in the fourth on singles by Tommy Thevenow, "Chick" Hafey and Jim

Bottomley, thanks to a couple of timely Yank misplays. Even when Joe Dugan's single and a two-bagger by Hank Severeid gave the American Leaguers another run in the sixth, I didn't particularly worry. Haines was the kind of a pitcher who could hang onto a one-run lead if it came down to it. Then he unaccountably grew wild. Standing back there as he walked the first man in the seventh I wondered if, finally, the strain was beginning to tell.

With two out, he walked three men to fill the bases. I was thinking he ought to get one out of four out, even with Lazzeri up, then I figured something had happened to Jess. I walked over to him and asked. It had. A blister had broken on the first finger from the pressure of throwing his knuckler. Because he couldn't roll the ball over that raw spot without flinching a bit, he'd lost control. We were in a tight spot. Bases full of Yanks and a fellow waiting to hit who might have extended Haines even when Jess was in perfect shape. I made the only choice I could; the only selection any manager could make. I called Alexander.

It was no spot for youth and sheer speed even if I'd had some in the bull pen. You couldn't throw the ball past the Yanks then any more than in recent years. You couldn't afford to make a mistake in this clutch and the only man available was Alex. You should have heard the rumbling through the stands.

One minute the fans had seen Alex sitting in the sun out yonder, apparently oblivious to what was going on; the next he was shambling toward the mound, the biggest man in America . . . the man of the day and the hour and the moment. What the fans didn't know was that Alex never warmed up much. He never had to. He took his time getting to the hill and, of course, what I said to him and what he answered has been written before. "We're in a tough spot," I told him, "and there's no place to put this guy." He twisted his lips into that slow, tilted smile and nodded in complete understanding of the situation as he replied: "I'll take care of that," just like he was accepting a chore to do for an old friend.

There are a few things I'd like to say about Alexander. Almost every fan has heard stories of that game, about how he still was reeling from a celebration the night before and a lot of other things. Some fans have even told me, to my face, that I had to send a cab to get him out of a barroom after the game had started. That, of course, was a downright lie. After the sixth game some friends picked Alex up and they had a few drinks at a hotel. That was only natural, and I knew where they were. But Alex was as sober as I was for the final game and everybody who knows me knows I never took a drink in my life. He never gave me a bit of trouble.

Well, there was Alex in the sunlight and there was Lazzeri. There were the base-runners straining at leashes. There was that great crowd just about smothered by the tenseness of the spot. I moved back to position and waited. The first pitch came in low and inside, a curve. As Alex threw I couldn't help noticing the honest-to-God elegance . . . that's the only word to describe it . . . with which he pitched. He was more than graceful . . . he was a gesture of perfection itself. Just the same, Lazzeri swung and got his meat-end of the bat around in time. The ball sailed for the left-field bleachers and my heart came as close to stopping as it ever will before it never beats again.

It curved foul. Not by much. No more than two feet at the most. We had been given a new lease on life; the title hadn't yet slipped out of reach. As if the pitch was something Alex had to get out of his system before he could go about his work, he mowed down Tony on two more tosses and the danger was over. The greatest pitcher of them all didn't allow a ball hit out of the infield the next two innings, but there still was a little excitement in the guise of anticlimax to come. Ruth came up in the ninth with two out and nobody on.

The count reached three and two and the Babe chose to let

the sixth pitch go by. Umpire Bill Klem called it a ball and for a minute there was an argument at the plate. Bob O'Farrell, our catcher, thought it caught a corner, but, of course, the decision stood, and Meusel was next. Nobody ever doubted but what he could blast with the best on occasion. We were scared all over again, but the Yanks came to our rescue. They decided to let Ruth run.

He went down on the first pitch just to make the surprise move as effective as possible, but O'Farrell's throw had him by 10 feet. I'll always remember putting the ball on him. He didn't say a word. He didn't even look around or up at me. He just picked himself off the ground and walked away to the dugout and I had lived through the greatest day any man could ask.

WAITE HOYT

as told to Francis J. Powers

Born September 9, 1899, in Brooklyn, New York, Waite Hoyt was the first of the "boy wonders." He signed his first big league contract when he was 16, but didn't become a standout pitcher until the Yankees bought him from the Boston Red Sox. Hoyt was a tremendous factor in the Yankee pennant eras of 1921 through 1923, and 1926 through 1928. He achieved his best seasons in 1926 and 1927. Waite has long retired from baseball and is the present broadcaster of games played in Cincinnati.

I'M ANOTHER whose greatest day was against the New York Giants and John McGraw. It was the second game of the 1921 World Series between the Giants and Yankees; New York's first nickel series and the first of the late Miller Huggins' six championship teams. The Yanks finally had "arrived" to challenge McGraw and his Giants for the supremacy of baseball right on Broadway where they had ruled so long. And it still was George M. Cohan's Broadway. As a native New Yorker and only 22, you can imagine my jubilation. I had come to the Yanks that spring from the Red Sox and had won 19 games, so I was sure Huggins would start me in the series.

I was keen to get a crack at the Giants. Besides the natural ambition to pitch in a series I had other reasons. I had been quite a pitcher in the New York Public School League and when I was only 16, my father signed a contract for me with McGraw. But McGraw didn't keep me around long. In the next three seasons I was with six minor league clubs and came back to the big leagues when the Red Sox bought me from New Orleans in '19. That was one extra reason I wanted to pitch.

Another reason developed the day before the series opened. That year the Yanks were tenants in the Polo Grounds, renting, while Col. Jack Ruppert and Capt. Til Houston planned their magnificent stadium just across the river. The Giants took their workout from 10 to 12 in the morning and then we had the field. I was warming up in the bull pen, getting ready to pitch in batting practice when I heard a hard, rasping voice at my elbow.

"So that's the young punk who expects to beat us." It was Ross Youngs talking to Frankie Frisch and if there ever was a player who typified the old Giants it was Youngs, the Texas outfielder who died all too early. It was strictly a rib, plain and unsparing, but at the time I took it as a personal insult and promised myself I'd beat those fellows.

"Hug" opened the series with Carl Mays on the mound, going against "Shufflin'" Phil Douglas. Mays' underhand delivery was sharp that afternoon and he beat the Giants 3–0. After the game "Hug" said: "You go tomorrow." My opponent was Art Nehf, a great left-hander, and we tangled three times before the series was finished. I admit I was nervous as I warmed up. There were photographers milling around, sports writers asking questions and fights in the grandstands, for New York was taking its subway series seriously. It seems to me there was a lot more belligerency in those days than now.

I got by the first inning although those first three Giant hitters, George Burns, Dave Bancroft and Frisch looked pretty terrifying. In the second, I made Youngs look bad on slow balls. I still can see Ross, crouched at the plate, his jaws set and eyes like slits. I made Earl Smith, the big and rough catcher, look worse. I began to get confidence. I had spells of wildness but I kept turning the Giants back, inning after inning. Johnny Rawlings, the fast little second baseman, clipped one that bounced over Mike McNally's head at third, and in the ninth, Frisch rifled a clean single to right. That was all the hitting the Giants did that day.

The Giants did everything they knew to get me out of the box, to get me up in the air. They even read the advertisements in the newspapers. Shortly before the series opening, I had signed a testimonial for some brand of soap. The Giants had seen the ads. McGraw never missed a trick. Once, after grounding out, when I was on my way back to the bench a cake of soap came flying out of the Giant bench and landed at my feet. That was too much. I picked up the soap and with plenty of speed fired it back and it just shaved McGraw's ear. Man, those Giants really singed my hair with their retorts—uncourteous. But it was no go; the Giants couldn't bother me that day.

Really, it was the Giants who were jittery, and they helped us to our three runs with some poor play, for we made only three hits. We got on in the fourth, when Ward opened with a Texas Leaguer, McNally hit to Nehf and both runners were safe when Art made a wild throw to Bancroft. A pass to Wally Schang filled the bases and when I grounded to Rawlings, he threw to first and Ward scored.

We got the other two in the eighth. Frisch muffed Peck's fly after some confusion with Banny, and Ruth forced Rog. When Meusel singled to center, Babe went right into third and beat Burns' throw by a hair while Bob traveled on to second. Wally Pipp hit to Rawlings and once again Johnny threw to first while Babe scored. On Nehf's next pitch,

Meusel broke for home and scored when Oil Smith muffed the ball.

I went back at the Giants and Nehf in the fifth game and won 3–1, to make the series all even. But they got me in the eighth and deciding game on a 1–0 count. I pitched a full 27 innings in the series without allowing an earned run and technically that tied the record set by Christy Mathewson in the 1905 series against the Athletics, when every game was a shutout, although ours was an eight-game series. While we lost the series, I was pretty happy with my pitching, particularly since it was against the Giants.

Now I'm going back a bit and tell you how I came back to the majors, after getting out of organized baseball and pitching for the Baltimore Drydocks. I was the property of New Orleans when Ed Barrow, then managing Boston, bought my contract. I signed on the 27th of July, 1919, with the understanding I would get a chance to pitch and not wind up as a bench jockey, which was a custom in those days.

After I had been with the Red Sox for three days, Barrow told me I'd work the next day. A nice opponent he threw me. The Tigers with Ty Cobb, Harry Heilmann and Bob Veach. I developed a headache that evening and it lasted through the next day, until game time. The game was important to me not only because it was my first start, but because I had argued with Barrow that I could win in the American League if I had the chance. Here was the chance.

I got the first two Tigers; then one reached first. Cobb up. In those days there was no whitewashed ring for the batter on deck and two-three batters could stand around swinging bats, riding the pitcher and doing almost anything to unhinge him. Cobb started on me while Veach was batting. When he came up instead of standing in the batter's box, he stood on top of the plate with his back to me and held a long conversation with Schang.

When Ty finally faced me, standing in his half crouch, I backed off the rubber. Then I threw him a slow ball that he

THE BOX SCORE
(October 6, 1921)

GIANTS	A.B.	R.	H.	P.	A.	YANKEES	A.B.	R.	H.	P.	A.
Burns, cf.	3	0	0	1	0	Miller, cf.	3	0	0	1	0
Bancroft, ss.	4	0	0	3	3	Peckinpaugh, ss.	3	0	0	3	1
Frisch, 3b.	4	0	1	3	2	Ruth, lf.	1	1	0	0	0
Youngs, rf.	2	0	0	2	0	R. Meusel, rf.	4	1	1	1	0
Kelly, 1b.	4	0	0	12	2	Pipp, 1b.	3	0	0	14	0
E. Meusel, lf.	2	0	0	0	0	Ward, 2b.	4	1	1	4	7
Rawlings, 2b.	3	0	1	2	2	McNally, 3b.	3	0	0	0	3
Smith, c.	3	0	0	1	1	Schang, c.	2	0	0	4	2
Nehf, p.	2	0	0	0	3	Hoyt, p.	3	0	1	0	2
Totals	27	0	2	24	13	Totals	26	3	3	27	15

GIANTS	0 0 0	0 0 0	0 0 0—0
YANKEES	0 0 0	1 0 0	2 *—3

Errors—Frisch, Smith, Nehf. Stolen bases—Ruth (2), R. Meusel. Double plays—Frisch to Rawlings, Rawlings to Kelly to Smith, McNally to Ward to Pipp. Struck out—By Hoyt 5. Bases on balls—Off Nehf 7, Hoyt 5. Passed ball —Smith. Umpires—Moriarity (A. L.), Quigley (N. L.), Chill (A. L.), Rigler (N. L.). Time—1:58. Attendance—34,939.

missed a foot. The crowd (all 3,000 of it) booed and Ty didn't like that a bit. He snarled something about a "fresh busher" but didn't do anything that turn. Boston was leading 1–0 in the eighth when Cobb tripled, scoring the tying run. I was learning about him rapidly.

I wasn't nervous by that time but I pitched as if I were in a coma and my prayers were as strong as my arm. So the game went into the 13th. In our half, Erve Scott reached first, with one out, and McNally ran for him. Schang hit to short and the shortstop (not Donie Bush, for Moriarity had chased him early in the game) threw to first. But McNally didn't stop at third. He lit right out for home and seemed trapped by Catcher Eddie Ainsmith and Third Baseman Bobby Jones. Suddenly Mike shot for the plate, running headlong over Ainsmith, who didn't have the ball. The game was over and I had won my first American League start, 2–1. Cobb, Heilmann and Moriarity had a fight on the way to the clubhouse but that didn't interest me—I was walking on air.

KING CARL HUBBELL

as told to John P. Carmichael

Carl Owen Hubbell, born June 22, 1903, in Carthage, Missouri, was a gangling, raw-boned southpaw who threw a deceptive screwball with matchless control, and was the mound perfectionist of the middle 30's. He led the New York Giants to three pennants and occupies a hallowed spot among Polo Ground immortals. King Carl faced his last batter in 1943, and is now chief of the San Francisco farm system.

I CAN remember Frankie Frisch coming off the field behind me at the end of the third inning, grunting to Bill Terry: "I could play second base 15 more years behind that guy. He doesn't need any help. He does it all by himself." Then we hit the bench, and Terry slapped me on the arm and said: "That's pitching, boy!" and Gabby Hartnett let his mask fall down and yelled at the American League dugout: "We gotta look at that all season," and I was pretty happy.

As far as control and "stuff" is concerned, I never had any more in my life than for that All-Star game in 1934. But I never was a strikeout pitcher like Bob Feller or "Dizzy" Dean or "Dazzy" Vance. My style of pitching was to make the other team hit the ball, but on the ground. It was as big a surprise to me to strike out all those fellows as it probably was to them. Before the game, Hartnett and I went down the lineup . . . Gehringer, Manush, Ruth, Gehrig, Foxx, Simmons, Cronin, Dickey and Gomez. There wasn't a pitcher they'd ever faced that they hadn't belted one off him somewhere, sometime.

We couldn't discuss weaknesses . . . they didn't have any, except Gomez. Finally Gabby said: "We'll waste everything except the screwball. Get that over, but keep your fast ball and hook outside. We can't let 'em hit in the air." So that's the way we started. I knew I had only three innings to work and could bear down on every pitch.

They talk about those All-Star games being exhibition affairs and maybe they are, but I've seen very few players in my life who didn't want to win, no matter whom they were playing or what for. If I'm playing cards for pennies, I want to win. How can you feel any other way? Besides, there were 50,000 fans or more there, and they wanted to see the best you've got. There was an obligation to the people, as well as to ourselves, to go all out. I can recall walking out to the hill in the Polo Grounds that day and looking around the stands and thinking to myself: "Hub, they want to see what you've got."

Gehringer was first up and Hartnett called for a waste ball just so I'd get the feel of the first pitch. It was a little too close, and Charley singled. Down from one of the stands came a yell: "Take him out!"

I had to laugh.

Terry took a couple of steps off first and hollered: "That's all right," and there was Manush at the plate. If I recollect rightly, I got two strikes on him, but then he refused to swing any more, and I lost him. He walked. This time Terry and Frisch and "Pie" Traynor and Travis Jackson all came over to the mound and began worrying. "Are you all right?" Bill asked me. I assured him I was. I could hear more than one voice now from the stands: "Take him out before it's too late."

Well, I could imagine how they felt with two on, nobody out and Ruth at bat. To strike him out was the last thought in my mind. The thing was to make him hit on the ground. He wasn't too fast, as you know, and he'd be a cinch to double. He never took the bat off his shoulder. You could have pushed me over with your little finger. I fed him three straight screwballs, all over the plate, after wasting a fast ball, and he stood there. I can see him looking at the umpire on "You're out," and he wasn't mad. He just didn't believe it, and Hartnett was laughing when he threw the ball back.

So up came Gehrig. He was a sharp hitter. You could double him, too, now and then, if the ball was hit hard and straight at an infielder. That's what we hoped he'd do, at best. Striking out Ruth and Gehrig in succession was too big an order. By golly, he fanned . . . and on four pitches. He swung at the last screwball, and you should have heard that crowd. I felt a lot easier then, and even when Gehringer and Manush pulled a double steal and got to third and second, with Foxx up, I looked down at Hartnett and caught the screwball sign, and Jimmy missed. We were really trying to strike Foxx out, with two already gone, and Gabby didn't bother to waste any pitches. I threw three more screwballs, and he went down swinging. He had set down the side on 12 pitches, and then Frisch hit a homer in our half of the first, and we were ahead.

It was funny, when I thought of it afterwards, how Ruth and Gehrig looked as they stood there. The Babe must have been waiting for me to get the ball up a little so he could get his bat under it. He always was trying for that one big shot at the stands, and anything around his knees, especially a twisting ball, didn't let him get any leverage. Gehrig apparently decided to take one swing at least and he beat down at the pitch, figuring to take a chance on being doubled if he could get a piece of the ball. He whispered something to Foxx

THE BOX SCORE
(July 10, 1934)

NATIONAL LEAGUE	A.B.	R.	H.	P.	A.	AMERICAN LEAGUE	A.B.	R.	H.	P.	A.
Frisch, 2b.	3	3	2	0	1	Gehringer, 2b.	3	0	2	2	1
W. Herman, 2b.	2	0	1	0	1	Manush, lf.	2	0	0	0	0
Traynor, 3b.	5	2	2	1	0	Ruffing, p.	1	0	1	0	0
Medwick, lf.	2	1	1	0	0	Harder, p.	2	0	0	1	0
Klein, lf.	3	0	1	1	0	Ruth, rf.	2	1	0	0	0
Cuyler, rf.	2	0	0	2	0	Chapman, rf.	2	0	1	0	1
Ott, rf.	2	0	0	0	1	Gehrig, 1b.	4	1	0	11	1
Berger, cf.	2	0	0	0	0	Foxx, 3b.	5	1	2	1	2
P. Waner, cf.	2	0	0	1	0	Simmons, cf.-lf.	5	3	3	3	0
Terry, 1b.	3	0	1	4	0	Cronin, ss.	5	1	2	2	8
Jackson, ss.	2	0	0	0	1	Dickey, c.	2	1	1	4	0
Vaughan, ss.	2	0	0	4	0	Cochrane, c.	1	0	0	1	1
Hartnett, c.	2	0	0	9	0	Gomez, p.	1	0	0	0	0
Lopez, c.	2	0	0	5	1	Averill, cf.	4	1	2	1	0
Hubbell, p.	0	0	0	0	0	West, cf.	0	0	0	1	0
Warneke, p.	0	0	0	0	0						
Mungo, p.	0	0	0	0	0						
Martin	0	1	0	0	0						
J. Dean, p.	1	0	0	0	0						
Frankhouse, p.	1	0	0	0	0						
Totals	36	7	8	27	5	Totals	39	9	14	27	14

W. Herman batted for Hubbell in 3rd and took Frisch's place in 7th.

Klein batted for Medwick in 5th.

Ott batted for Cuyler in 5th.

P. Waner batted for Berger in 5th.

Vaughan batted for Jackson in 5th.

Martin batted for Mungo in 5th.

Cochrane ran for Dickey in 6th.

Averill batted for Gomez in 4th.

AMERICAN LEAGUE	0	0	0	2	6	1	0	0	0—9	
NATIONAL LEAGUE	1	0	3	0	3	0	0	0	0—7	

Errors—Berger, Gehrig. Runs batted in—Frisch, Medwick (3), Cronin (2), Averill (3), Foxx, Simmons, Ruffing (2), Traynor, Klein. Two-base hits—Simmons (2), Averill, Cronin, Foxx, W. Herman. Three-base hits—Averill, Chapman. Home runs—Frisch, Medwick. Stolen bases—Gehringer, Manush, Traynor, Ott. Double play—Lopez and Vaughan. Bases on balls—Off Hubbell 2, Gomez 1, Warneke 3, Mungo 2, Ruffing 1, J. Dean 1, Harder 1, Frankhouse 1. Struck out—By Hubbell 6, Gomez 3, Warneke 1, Mungo 1, Harder 2, J. Dean 4. Pitching records—Hubbell, 2 hits, 0 runs in three innings; Warneke, 3 hits, 2 runs in 1 (none out in fifth); Mungo, 4 hits, 6 runs in 1; J. Dean, 5 hits, 1 run in 3; Gomez, 3 hits, 4 runs in 3; Ruffing, 4 hits, 2 runs in 1 (none out in fifth). Left on bases—American League—12. National League—5. Winning pitcher —Harder. Losing pitcher—Mungo. Umpires—Pittman (N. L.); Moriarity (A. L.); Owens (A. L.); Stark (N. L.). Time of game—2:44.

as Jim got up from the batter's circle and while I didn't hear it, I found out later he said: "You might as well cut . . . it won't get any higher." At least Foxx wasted no time.

Of course the second inning was easier because Simmons and Cronin both struck out with nobody on base and then I got too close to Dickey and he singled. Simmons and Foxx, incidentally, both went down swinging and I know every pitch to them was good enough to hit at and those they missed had a big hunk of the plate. Once Hartnett kinda shook his head at me as if to say I was getting too good. After Dickey came Gomez and as he walked into the box he looked down at Gabby and said: "You are now looking at a man whose batting average is .104. What the hell am I doing up here?" He was easy after all those other guys and we were back on the bench again.

We were all feeling pretty good by this time and Traynor began counting on his fingers: "Ruth, Gehrig, Foxx, Simmons, Cronin! Hey, Hub, do you put anything on the ball?" Terry came over to see how my arm was, but it never was stronger. I walked one man in the third . . . don't remember who it was . . . but this time Ruth hit one on the ground and we were still all right. You could hear him puff when he swung. That was all for me. Afterwards, they got six runs in the fifth and licked us, but for three innings I had the greatest day in my life. One of the writers who kept track told me that I'd pitched 27 strikes and 21 balls to 13 men and only five pitches were hit in fair territory.

WALTER JOHNSON

as told to John P. Carmichael

What a pitcher was Walter Perry Johnson! Born on November 6, 1887, in Humboldt, Kansas, the "Big Train" whipped his smoke ball past American League batters for 21 years, all with the Washington Senators. He struck out more men than any other pitcher, 3497, and his total of 414 games won is second only to Cy Young. A huge and gentle man who was always frightened that one of his serves might accidentally strike a batter and result in severe injury, Johnson was extra careful with his control and walked very few batters. After his glorious pitching ca- *reer was finished, Walter managed at Washington and Cleveland. Then he retired to his Maryland farm where he became a leader in local politics before he died on December 10, 1946.*

("As the hitter sees Johnson's arm descending, just swing," said Outfielder "Birdie" Cree years ago. "The bat will then cross the plate at about the same time the ball reaches it and, if you're lucky, you hit the ball. A fellow does not have to judge the height of the pitch . . . or if it was a curve.")

THIS won't be very original, I'm afraid (said Johnson) because there couldn't be a bigger day for me than the one everybody knows about . . . October 10, 1924, in the last

game of my first World Series. It was Weiser, Idaho, and Detroit and Washington put together; I guess you'd call it a
piece of every day for 18 years and it didn't look like I'd ever
see it come around. After all, I was 36 years old and that's
pretty far gone to be walking into the last game of a series
. . . especially when you couldn't blame people for remembering I'd lost two starts already.

You see I didn't have much besides a fast ball in my life
and there comes a time when speed alone won't stop a batter.
If a boy hasn't got real, natural speed it isn't worth his while
to try and force a fast ball, because a slow pitch and a curve
can fool a hitter better than unnatural speed. Besides, the
arm may suffer. A free, loose motion and control are the
main assets for a pitcher. That's all I ever had to amount to
anything.

Why, when I started out at 18 years of age I couldn't even
land a job on the Pacific Coast. I went to Weiser, Idaho,
because it had a semipro team and the players worked in the
mines. I won my first game 4–0 on two hits. I won the next
2–1 in 15 innings and then fanned 15 to make my string three
straight.

Weiser people began calling me "pardner" instead of
"sonny." I still was at Weiser in 1907 and had won 13 and
lost 2 when Cliff Blankenship, a Washington scout, arrived.
He'd really come out to look at Clyde Milan; I was just a
by-product of his trip.

Well, he never saw me pitch at all, but he knew my record
and offered me a job. I wouldn't take it until he'd promised
me a return ticket to California in case I failed. I joined
Washington at Detroit August 2, 1907, despite the pleas of
Weiser folk who offered to buy me a cigar stand and set me
up in business if I'd stay there. But you know how you are
at 18 . . . you want to see things.

I saw something my first start. I got beat 3–2 and Ty Cobb
and Sam Crawford bunted me all over the infield. I fell all
over myself . . . and the 1,000 people in the stands laughed

themselves sick. I was so confused I even missed the bus back to the hotel . . . and was walking there in my uniform when some fans gave me a lift.

Seventeen years later I was in a series, but I wasn't happy about it. I'd been beaten in New York for the second time by the Giants and I'll admit when I got on the train to Washington, where we were to play the seventh game, there were tears in my eyes. I was carrying my youngest boy on my shoulder and trying not to speak to people when Clark Griffith put a hand on my arm. "Don't think about it anymore, Walter," he told me. "You're a great pitcher. We all know it.

"Now tonight when we get home don't stand around the box offices buying seats for friends or shaking hands with people who feel sorry for you. I've seen many a fast ball shaken right out of a pitcher's hand. Go home and get to bed early . . . we may need you tomorrow." I told him I would.

You can imagine how "red hot" Washington was next day . . . the last game of its first World Series coming up. Thirty-five thousand people were crammed into our park. President Coolidge was there. I made myself as inconspicuous as possible on the bench, because I didn't want any sympathy . . . and I didn't even want Harris to think of me in a jam. Well, "Bucky" started Curley Ogden but pretty soon George Mogridge was in there and then "Firpo" Marberry, our big relief ace.

We were all tied up in the ninth when I came in. I'll always believe that Harris gambled on me because of sentiment, but he said no. He just told me: "You're the best we got, Walter . . . we've got to win or lose with you." So I walked out there and it seemed to me the smoke from the stands was so thick on the field that nobody could see me. I remembered thinking: "I'll need the breaks" and if I didn't actually pray, I sort of was thinking along those lines.

I was in trouble every inning. After getting Fred Lindstrom in the ninth, Frank Frisch hit a fast ball to right center

THE BOX SCORE
(October 10, 1924)

NEW YORK	A.B.	R.	H.	P.	A.	WASHINGTON	A.B.	R.	H.	P.	A.
Lindstrom, 3b.	5	0	1	0	3	McNeely, cf.	6	0	1	0	0
Frisch, 2b.	5	0	2	3	4	Harris, 2b.	5	1	3	4	1
Young, rf.-lf.	2	1	0	2	0	Rice, cf.	5	0	0	2	0
Kelly, cf.-1b.	6	1	1	8	1	Goslin, lf.	5	0	2	3	0
Terry, 1b.	2	0	0	6	1	Judge, 1b.	4	0	1	11	1
Meusel, lf.-rf.	3	0	1	1	0	Bluege, ss.	5	0	0	1	7
Wilson, lf.-cf.	5	1	1	4	0	Taylor, 3b.	2	0	0	0	3
Jackson, ss.	6	0	0	1	4	Miller, 3b.	2	0	0	1	1
Gowdy, c.	6	0	1	8	0	Ruel, c.	5	2	2	13	0
Barnes, p.	4	0	0	1	2	Ogden, p.	0	0	0	0	0
McQuillan, p.	0	0	0	0	0	Mogridge, p.	1	0	0	0	0
Nehf, p.	0	0	0	0	0	Marberry, p.	1	0	0	1	0
Bentley, p.	0	0	0	0	0	Johnson, p.	2	0	0	0	1
Groh	1	0	1	0	0	Tate	0	0	0	0	0
Southworth	0	0	0	0	0	Shirley	0	0	0	0	0
						Leibold	1	1	1	0	0
Totals	45	3	8	*34	15	Totals	44	4	10	36	14

Meusel batted for Terry in 6th.
Groh batted for McQuillan in 11th.
Southworth ran for Groh in 11th.
* One out when winning run was scored.

Tate batted for Marberry in 8th.
Shirley ran for Tate in 8th.
Leibold batted for Taylor in 8th.

NEW YORK	0 0 0 0 0 3 0 0 0 0 0 0—3
WASHINGTON	0 0 0 1 0 0 0 2 0 0 0 1—4

Errors—Jackson (2), Gowdy, Judge, Bluege (2), Taylor. Earned runs—Washington 4, New York 1. Runs batted in—Harris 3, McNeely 1, Meusel 1. Two-base hits—McNeely, Goslin, Ruel, Leibold, Lindstrom. Three-base hit—Frisch. Home run—Harris. Double plays—Kelly to Jackson, Jackson to Frisch to Kelly, Johnson to Bluege to Judge. Bases on balls—Off Ogden 1, Mogridge 1, Marberry 1, Bentley 1, Barnes 1, Johnson 3. Struck out—By Ogden 1, Mogridge 3, Marberry 3, McMillan 1, Barnes 6, Johnson 5. Hits—Off Ogden 0 in 1-3 inning, Mogridge 4 in 4 2-3, Marberry 1 in 3 innings, Johnson 3 in 4 innings, Barnes 6 in 7 2-3 innings, Nehf 1 in 2-3 inning, McQuillan 0 in 1 2-3 innings, Bentley 3 in 1 1-3 innings (one out in 12th). Winning pitcher—Johnson. Losing pitcher—Bentley. Umpires—Dinneen (A), Quigley (N.), Connolly (A), Klem (N.). Time—3:00.

for three bases. We decided to pass Ross Young and then I struck out George Kelly and "Irish" Meusel grounded to third. In the 10th I walked "Hack" Wilson and then, after striking out Travis Jackson, I was lucky enough to grab a drive by ol' Hank Gowdy and turn it into a double play.

Heinie Groh batted for Hugh McQuillan, the Giant pitcher, in the 11th and singled. Lindstrom bunted him along. I fanned Frisch, this time, on an outside pitch and once more passed Young. Kelly struck out again.

They kept after me, though. Meusel singled in the 12th, but I'd settled down to believe, by then, that maybe this was my day and I got the next three hitters. I'd tried to win my own game in the 10th with a long ball to the wall, but Wilson pulled it down. So I was up again in the 12th when it was getting pretty dark. "Muddy" Ruel had lifted a pop foul to Gowdy, who lost it, and on the next pitch Ruel hit past third for two bases. Then I sent an easy grounder to short . . . and Jackson fumbled. We all sat there staring at Earl McNeely as he hit an easy grounder to Lindstrom.

The ball never touched Fred. It hit a pebble and arched over his head into safe territory. I could feel tears smarting in my eyes as Ruel came home with the winning run. I'd won. We'd won. I felt so happy that it didn't seem real. They told me in the clubhouse that President Coolidge kept watching me all the way into the clubhouse and I remember somebody yelling: "I bet Cal'd like to change places with you right now, Walter."

A long time later Mrs. Johnson and I slipped away to a quiet little restaurant where I used to eat on Vermont Avenue, in Washington, and do you know that before we were through with our dinner 200 telegrams had been delivered there. I never thought so many people were pulling for me to win, because the Giants were pretty popular. When we packed up and went home to Kansas we had three trunks full of letters from fans all over the world.

RALPH KINER

as told to Les Biederman

Holder of a host of home-run records, Ralph Kiner looms as the greatest slugger in Pittsburgh history. He totaled 369 round-trippers in his decade in the majors, and once connected for eight homers in four straight games. He led or tied the National League in home runs seven straight years. Kiner finished up playing for the Cubs and later for Cleveland. He served as general manager of the San Diego club in the Pacific Coast League, is presently a member of the N.Y. Mets' broadcast- ing team. Kiner originated the phrase, "singles hitters drive Fords, home-run hitters drive Cadillacs."

ONE of the many things Hank Greenberg taught me when we were teammates and roommates with the Pirates in 1947 was that as long as I continued to hit home runs I'd continue to receive thrills.

How right Hank was. I've had many thrilling days in baseball, topped off by the contract I signed with the Pirates for 1950 and 1951 at $65,000 per season. They tell me that's the highest salary any National League player ever received. Quite a thrill for me at twenty-seven years of age.

I experienced many thrills in 1947 when I hit 51 home runs and again in 1949 when I reached 54. I can remember two days during 1947 when I hit three homers in one game, and each time Hank came over and shook my hand and I could tell by the glint in his eyes that he was just as happy as if he had done it.

Another reason these two separate afternoons gave me such a kick was that on both occasions I was playing at home, at Forbes Field, where the fans had been so loyal and patient and just plain wonderful to me.

In approaching what I consider my greatest baseball game, please allow me to tell a bit of the two afternoons I hit three home runs.

The first time it happened was on August 16. The third homer of the game was my 35th of the season. Ken Burkhardt of the Cardinals was the pitcher off whom I hit No. 1 and the other two came off of Ted Wilks, and John Grodzicki.

The next time I was fortunate enough to collect three in one game was on September 11. We were playing the Braves and I simply was "hot" again. I actually hit four homers that afternoon, three in the second game of a double-header, after getting one off Johnny Sain in the first game.

I nicked Bill Voiselle for the first two in the nightcap and the third one was off Walter Lanfranconi. The four that afternoon pushed me to 47 for the season and brought me within range of the magic figure of 50.

I was lucky enough to hit four more that month and ended the season with 51. I've always looked back upon the season of 1947 as the year that gave me the confidence to speak the same language of the home-run hitters before me.

Somehow you feel you belong when you hit 50 homers. It was quite a thrill and I believe I treasured the 50th home-run ball more than any up to that time. In fact, that ball went over the left field fence at Forbes Field and was later returned to me. I have it in my den at home.

But every time somebody talks home runs to me, my thoughts always go back to a September afternoon in 1948 at Wrigley Field, Chicago. It was on the 11th of September that year that I believe I enjoyed my greatest baseball game.

I've always had my heart set on playing for a pennant winner and I believed I'd get more kick out of being in a World Series than breaking Babe Ruth's record of 60 homers. It's something I've always dreamed of.

This helps set the stage for my greatest game because at that time the Pirates were in the midst of a winning streak and only three games behind the league leading Braves. We were on a long road trip that would eventually take us into the East and if we could stay close to the Braves, well, anything might happen.

We came into Chicago with a modest winning streak of five in a row and had won 10 of our last 14 games. I didn't feel right when I awakened that morning. I had the sniffles and a stomach-ache in the bargain.

I passed up breakfast and went right to the park. I thought perhaps a little exercise might straighten me out and, if I felt better, intended to send out for something to eat.

Manager Bill Meyer took a look at me and shook his head. I insisted I'd be okay and told him I'd make a stab at it. But as game time approached I was getting weaker and weaker and my stomach was acting up. I hadn't missed a game all year but it looked like the streak was a goner.

The game started without me and I went into the dressing room and filled myself with pills. I lay down on the rubbing table and the trainer worked on me.

He wasn't too hopeful.

We tuned in the game and the way things started out it didn't help me at all. The Cubs scored three runs in the second inning but we went ahead going into the sixth inning, 6 to 5. My cold and stomach-ache were improving and my temperature went down. But I had the miseries after we scored two runs in the sixth and the Cubs came back with five in their half to take over, 10 to 8.

Both teams were scoreless in the seventh but the Pirates organized a rally in the eighth and I had a hunch I might be needed. I grabbed my shoes, and was buttoning my shirt as I ran down the runway to the dugout.

By the time I had reached the bench we had scored one

THE BOX SCORE

PITTSBURGH · CHICAGO (N)

(September 11, 1948)

	A.B.	R.	H.	P.O.	A.		A.B.	R.	H.	P.O.	A.
Rojek, ss.	4	1	2	2	3	Verban, 2b.	6	1	2	2	0
Hopp, 1b.	5	1	0	9	4	Waitkus, lf.	5	1	1	0	0
Beard, cf.	5	0	0	1	0	Cavarretta, 1b.	3	3	1	8	1
F. Walker, rf.	4	2	4	2	0	Pafko, 3b.	5	1	3	2	0
West, lf.	4	1	2	1	0	Lowrey, cf.	5	1	2	3	0
Westlake, lf.	2	1	1	0	0	Nicholson, rf.	3	2	1	2	0
Murtaugh, 2b.	6	1	1	2	2	A. Walker, c.	2	0	0	2	0
Bockman, 3b.	5	1	2	4	2	c Schenz	0	1	0	0	0
Kluttz, c.	3	2	2	3	0	Chambers, p.	1	0	0	0	0
J. Riddle, c.	0	0	0	0	0	Borowy, p.	0	0	0	0	0
Fitzgerald, c.	1	1	0	1	1	McCall, p.	0	0	0	0	0
Chesne, p.	2	1	0	2	1	d Mauch	0	0	0	0	0
Higbe, p.	0	0	0	0	0	Smalley, ss.	5	2	3	6	2
a Gustine	1	0	0	0	0	Lade, p.	1	0	0	0	0
Queen, p.	0	0	0	0	0	Rush, p.	0	0	0	0	0
b Kiner	1	1	1	0	0	Chipman, p.	1	0	0	0	0
Singleton, p.	0	0	0	0	0	Dobernic, p.	0	0	0	0	0
E. Riddle, p.	0	0	0	0	1	Scheffing, c.	3	0	1	2	0
Totals	43	13	15	27	14	Totals	40	12	14	27	3

a Struck out for Higbe in 7th.
b Hit home run for Queen in 8th.
c Ran for A. Walker in 6th.
d Walked for McCall in 9th.

PITTSBURGH	0	0	2	3	1	2	0	5	0—13	
CHICAGO (N)	0	3	1	0	1	5	0	2	0—12	

Errors—Pafko, Smalley 2. Runs batted in—Nicholson, Smalley 2, West 3, Lowrey, Hopp, F. Walker 2, Rojek, Pafko 5, Scheffing, Waitkus, Kiner 4. Two base hits—Nicholson, Kluttz 2, Pafko. Home runs—Smalley, West, Pafko, Kiner. Stolen bases—Verban, Waitkus. Double plays—Verban, Smalley and Cavarretta; Rojek, Murtaugh and Hopp. Left on base—Pittsburgh 11, Chicago 7. Bases on balls—Lade 3, Chesnes 3, Rush 2, Dobernic 1, Higbe 1, Chambers 1, McCall 1, E. Riddle 2. Strikeouts—Lade 1, Chesnes 2, Dobernic 1, Chambers 1, Queen 1, Borowy 1, E. Riddle 1. Hits off—Lade 6 in 3, Rush 0 in 1-3, Chipman 3 in 1 2-3, Dobernic 1 in 1, Chesnes 9 in 5, Higbe 2 in 1, Chambers 3 in 1 1-3, Borowy 1 in 2-3, McCall 1 in 1, Queen 1 in 1, Singleton 2 in 1, E. Riddle 0 in 1. Wild pitch—Chesnes. Winning pitcher—Queen. Losing pitcher—Chambers. Umpires—Conlan, Stewart, Henline. Time—2:50. Attendance—17,095.

run and had the bases filled. The Cubs were in the process of changing pitchers when Meyer saw me.

"Can you make it?" he asked me.

"I can give it one good swing," I told him.

"That's all we need," he replied. "Go up and hit for Mel Queen (our pitcher) and take just one swing but make it a good one."

Hank Borowy was on the mound for the Cubs and I stalled as I went to bat to gather my strength. My legs were weak, my stomach was doing flip flops, and my eyes were watery and I recall I stepped out of the box two or three times to wipe my eyes.

The count ran to three and two and I hadn't even swung at a ball. Borowy and the Cubs knew I had been sick and I guess Hank figured he'd try and slip one by me. This was the one I was waiting for.

I connected with Borowy's curve and with a little wind to help out, the ball sailed over the left field fence for a grand slam. I jogged around the bases and kept right on going into the clubhouse.

We won the game, 13 to 12, and I can honestly say this was my greatest baseball game. It was the first home run I had hit that season in Wrigley Field. It was also the first grand slam homer for me since the third home run of my career, more than two years before in 1946. I had gone 109 homers without the thrill of a grand slam.

This one was doubly sweet because it gave us our sixth straight victory and our eleventh in the last fifteen games. It kept us within three games of the Braves, although we later ran out of gas and dropped from the running.

I celebrated My Greatest Baseball Game by returning to the hotel immediately and a physician was called. My temperature showed 101 and he ordered me to stay in bed. Then I had my first food of the day, soft-boiled eggs, toast and tea. That's all I had to eat. But it sure tasted good!

CONNIE MACK

as told to John P. Carmichael

Born Cornelius Alexander McGillicuddy on December 23, 1862, in Brookfield, Massachusetts, Connie Mack is baseball's longest living tribute to the game of baseball. Connie was a catcher in the nineteenth century before he became manager of Philadelphia's first team in the American League in 1901. In 50 years as the A's mentor Mack had nine pennant winners and five world's championship teams before retiring as field *leader at the close of the 1950 season. Mr. Mack died in 1956 after the Athletics franchise was sold to Kansas City.*

I'VE been fortunate enough to have seen some great baseball in my days. It is wonderful to remember pitchers like Matty and Walsh and Waddell and Johnson and Dean and Grove for more than 40 years. But to me the most thrilling World Series ever played was between the Cubs and Athletics in 1929 and I'll never forget the performance of Howard Ehmke. You see, Howard and I sort of put a fast one over on everybody and an old man likes to enjoy a chuckle at the expense of a younger generation. Only the two of us knew, two weeks ahead of time, that he was going to pitch the opening game, October 8.

We were leaving on the final western trip of the regular season when I called Howard up to my office in Philadelphia.

We had the pennant pretty well in hand by then and so did the Cubs, so we could make plans. Ehmke came in and sat down and I watched him for a few minutes while we just chatted and finally I said: "Howard, there comes a time in everybody's life when he has to make a change. It looks like you and I finally must part."

Well, he didn't say a word for the longest time, it seemed, just twiddled his hat and then he looked right at me and said: "All right, Mr. Mack, if that's the way it has to be. You've been fine to me and I haven't been much help to you this year. Lucky you haven't needed me. But I've been up a long time and I've always had an ambition to pitch in a World Series . . . anywhere, even for only an inning. Honestly, I believe there's one more good game left in this arm . . ." and he held it up to me like a prize fighter showing his muscle.

I couldn't help smiling. Howard of course, had no way of knowing what I thought of him. Really he was one of the most artistic pitchers of all time. He was bothered with a sore arm most of his major league career, but he had a great head on him and studied hitters. He might have been a fine pitcher. So I asked him: "You mean you think you could work a World Series game?" He told me: "Yes, Mr. Mack. I feel it." Then I explained what I had in mind. "So do I," I said. "I only wanted to see how you felt about it. Now you stay home this trip. The Cubs are coming in. Sit up in the stands and watch them. Make your own notes on how they hit. You're pitching the first game but don't tell anybody. I don't want it known."

After he'd gone I sat thinking about Howard. Maybe he never realized how close he came to not pitching at all. If he hadn't talked the way he did . . . if he'd said, for instance: "I realize I'm all through . . . my arm is gone" and accepted what he thought was dismissal, I wouldn't have worked him even though I had no intention of letting him go anyway.

Finally the big day came around in Wrigley Field. Funny

part of it was that none of my players nor even the news-papermen, bothered to ask me who'd start. They all took it for granted it would be Grove, or maybe Earnshaw. Since then people have asked me why I didn't start Grove, but that's a secret. I can't tell, but there was a reason. Anyway we were in the clubhouse before the game and somebody asked Grove if he was working and I heard him say: "The old man didn't say nothin' to me." Mose probably figured it was Earnshaw. When we got outside, they all threw the ball around. Ehmke must have had a sudden doubt that his dream was coming true because he came up to me on the bench and whispered. "Is it still me, Mr. Mack?" I said. "It's still you . . ." and he was smiling as he walked away.

When it came time for the rival pitcher to warm up, Ehmke, naturally, took off his jacket and started to throw. I made sure I was where I could look along our bench and you could see mouths pop open. Grove was looking at Earnshaw and George was looking at Mose. Al Simmons was sitting next to me and he couldn't stop himself in time. "Are you gonna pitch him?" he asked in disbelief. I kept a straight face and looked very severely at him and said: "Yes, I am Al. Is that all right with you?" You could sense him pulling him-self out of his surprised state and he replied quickly: "If you say so, it's all right with me, Mr. Mack."

Voices were muttering down the dugout. Phrases like "the old man must be nuts" and "hell, the guy's only finished two games all year" trailed off for fear I'd hear 'em. But I heard. I've often wondered what they'd thought of me if we'd been beaten with Grove and Earnshaw and Walberg on the bench. Bob Quinn, who was president of the Red Sox then, was in a box behind our dugout and he said he almost swooned when he saw Ehmke peel off his coat. I suppose the fans and you gentlemen of the press thought old Connie was in his dotage at last. But I was certain about Howard, although if he'd had any trouble early I would have had Grove in the bull pen. We didn't want to lose.

It was beautiful to watch. I don't suppose these old eyes ever strained themselves over any game as much as that one. Ehmke was smart. He was just fast enough to be sneaky, just slow enough to get hitters like Wilson and Hornsby and Cuyler, who like to take their cuts, off stride. If you recall, he pitched off his right hip, real close to his shirt. He kept the ball hidden until just before he let it go. The Cubs never got a good look at it and, when they did, it was coming out of those shirts in the old bleachers. Charley Root was fast himself and by the end of the sixth inning neither team had scored. Then Jimmy Foxx hit over Wilson's head, into the stands, and we led 1–0.

THE BOX SCORE
(October 8, 1929)

ATHLETICS	A.B.	R.	H.	P.	A.	CUBS	A.B.	R.	H.	P.	A.
Bishop, 2b.	4	0	0	1	1	McMillan, 3b.	4	0	1	1	2
Haas, cf.	3	0	0	1	0	English, ss.	4	0	2	1	3
Cochrane, c.	3	1	1	14	1	Hornsby, 2b.	4	0	0	1	3
Simmons, lf.	4	1	0	2	0	Wilson, cf.	4	0	0	3	0
Foxx, 1b.	4	1	2	4	0	Cuyler, rf.	4	1	1	1	0
Miller, rf.	4	0	1	3	0	Stephenson, lf.	4	0	2	4	0
Dykes, 3b.	4	0	1	1	1	Grimm, 1b.	2	0	2	8	0
Boley, ss.	4	0	0	1	0	Taylor, c.	2	0	0	6	0
Ehmke, p.	4	0	1	0	2	Gonzales, c.	0	0	0	2	0
						Root, p.	2	0	0	0	0
						Bush, p.	0	0	0	0	2
						Heathcote	1	0	0	0	0
						Hartnett	1	0	0	0	0
						Blair	1	0	0	0	0
						Tolson	1	0	0	0	0
Totals	34	3	6	27	5	Totals	34	1	8	27	10

Heathcote batted for Taylor in 7th.
Hartnett batted for Root in 7th.
Blair batted for Gonzales in 9th.
Tolson batted for Bush in 9th.

ATHLETICS	0 0 0 0 0 0 1 0 2—3
CUBS	0 0 0 0 0 0 0 0 1—1

Errors—Dykes, English (2). Home run—Foxx. Two-base hit—English. Sacrifice hit—Grimm. Struck out—By Ehmke 13, Root 5. Bases on balls—Off Ehmke 1, Root 2.

Jimmy touched home plate and came back to the bench
and Ehmke said: "Thanks, Jim" and I knew he'd made up
his mind maybe that was all the runs he'd get and it would
have to do. Only in the third had Howard been in a jam
when McMillan singled and English doubled with one out
and Hornsby and Wilson were up. Some of my players looked
at me as if to say: "Better get somebody warmed up . . .
here's where Ehmke goes," but he stood there calm and un-
hurried and struck out the two men on seven pitches. You
could tell the crowd had caught the melodrama of what was
going on; I don't believe I ever felt as happy in my life as
when he fanned Hornsby and Wilson. Very few pitchers
would have done as well in such a tense situation. He justified my faith in him right there.

In the seventh, after Foxx's hit, Cuyler and Stephenson
each singled and Grimm sacrificed. Joe McCarthy decided on
pinch hitters. He had Cliff Heathcote hit for Zach Taylor
and Simmons took care of a short fly for the second out. Then
Gabby Hartnett batted for Root and I was tempted to have
Howard put him on and take a chance on the next man, but
I said to myself:

"No. This is his game. He asked for it and I gave it to
him."

He struck out Hartnett and we got two runs in the ninth
on fumbles by English. I relaxed a little then, but we weren't
quite out of the woods. The Cubs got the tying runs on bases
in the ninth, with two out and Charlie Tolson up to pinch-
hit.

If Ehmke fanned him, he'd break the strikeout record for
world series play set by Ed Walsh against the Cubs in 1906
when he fanned 12. Howard already had struck out Hornsby,
Wilson, Cuyler and Root twice each. It happened. Tolson
went down swinging, too, for Howard's 13th strikeout and
the battle was over.

MICKEY MANTLE

as told to Dan Daniel

Mickey Mantle (named after Hall of Famer, Mickey Cochrane) was born at Spavinaw, Oklahoma, October 20, 1931, came up with the Yankees in the spring of 1951 at age 19, and has remained to become one of the superstars of this, or any other, era. He is one of seven sluggers to crash 400 or more homers in his career. He was the Most Valuable of the Yankees in the last decade, topping such performers as Whitey Ford, Yogi Berra, Gil McDougald and Roger Maris. The $1,200 given him by super-scout Tom Greenwade to sign with the Yankee organization remains *one of the all-time bargains. Mickey has two brothers who played briefly in the lower echelons of the Yankee farm system.*

FOR A ball player with batting aspirations, the day that stands out in his recollection is the one that saw him hit his first home run in the major leagues.

For me, that day was Tuesday, May 1, 1951, and the scene was Comiskey Park in Chicago.

We were opening our first invasion of the West. The White

Sox had given some evidences of the great form with which they were to run up 14 straight victories, and establish themselves in first place.

It was a hot, sunny afternoon. We had played a dozen games, and I had done little to justify Casey Stengel's having kept me, instead of shipping me to Kansas City, or back with Harry Craft, my manager at Independence and Joplin, who was running the Yankee farm at Beaumont.

In fact, as we faced lefthander Bob Cain in that game at Comiskey Park, my batting average had dropped to a shabby .222, and there had been stories in the New York sports pages about Casey's plan to bench me against lefthanders, and make a lefthanded batter out of me, exclusively.

The experts had dug up the fact that against lefthanded pitching my average was something like .150.

However, on the trip from New York to Chicago, Stengel changed his mind. He kept me in the lineup against Cain and that gave me a terrific lift. Within a week I was up at the .303 level.

In any event, as we opened at Comiskey Park I felt that my first American League home run was long overdue. I had hit eight during the training season, and had led the writers to believe that I might continue that pace for the Yankees.

Well, game followed game, and those pitchers showed me tricks I never knew men could do with a baseball.

They pulled the string when I figured they would fast ball me. They threw speed when I expected soft stuff. They hurled sinkers and sliders, screwballs and knucklers, curves and fast balls, in a bewildering style that really had me dazed.

However, I knew I could hit, and I never lost my confidence. Sure, I got down. I was sore at myself, and I felt sorry for Stengel, who had gone out on a limb to give me my chance.

In my first appearance against Cain, who was to shut us out later in the season, after the Yankees had played 109 games without having been prevented from scoring, I lifted a fly to second baseman Nelson Fox.

In the second inning, I got on base through an error by third sacker Orestes Minoso and in the fourth I drove in a run with a long fly to center fielder Jimmy Busby.

In the fifth inning, Yogi Berra got to Cain for a homer. That gave me notions. But Cain wasn't to pitch to me again that afternoon.

When I came to bat in the sixth, Vic Raschi was on second with one out, and righthander Randy Gumpert, former Yankee, was the Chicago pitcher.

His first delivery to me was a fast ball, just right. I drove it into the right center seats, just off the center field bleachers. The press box called it a 440 foot drive. It went on a line. My first homer in the majors.

There was a small delegation of service men, guests of the Chicago club, where my thrill hit landed. One of those soldiers got the ball. He was a pleasant faced Negro lad.

I wanted that ball and asked Arthur E. (Red) Patterson, public relations man of the Yankees, to go after it.

Red chased out to that right center pavilion and offered the GI five dollars for the ball. He gave Patterson a big smile, and a very definite "No, nothing doin'."

Patterson is one of those men who do not give up. He kept after the soldier, and finally the GI hollered, "Man, what I want most right now is for you to let me alone. I will pay you $5 to bother me no more."

Finally even the persistent Red had to admit defeat. But he still did not give up. He went down into the Yankee bullpen, just under the soldier's seat and told catcher Ralph Houk to get that ball for me.

Houk went to work on the soldier in a gentle way. He impressed on him the fact that I was just a rookie, that I wanted that ball more than anything else in the world, and what a shame it would be if I had to leave the park without this souvenir of my first batting feat in the American League.

Charley Silvera, who was in the bullpen with Houk, said

that night, "I never knew Ralph could operate so neatly as a persuader. He had all of us out there close to tears. The GI got so sentimental, he forgot to ask for the five that Patterson wanted to give him for the ball."

The Major delivered the ball to me in the clubhouse after we had beaten the White Sox by 8 to 3. I lost no time shipping the ball to Miss Merlyn Johnson, Picher, Okla.

I had a much bigger day against the White Sox in the Stadium on June 19, when we split a doubleheader with them. I hit a home run in each game, got four hits for ten bases, drove in four runs, stole a base, took a walk, but,—went out on strikes twice.

In the first game, I drove a three and two pitch off Lou Kretlow into the right center bleachers with two on. I got two singles later on in that contest, which we won by 11 to 9.

In the nightcap, won by Chicago, 5 to 4, I got to Joe Dobson for my sixth home run with the Yankees.

It was a very satisfying drive because it brought my runs driven in total to 42, and helped me to maintain the club leadership in that detail, which they tell me is very important.

At the close of this big day, one of the New York writers told me that I had made 14 hits, three of them homers, as many more doubles, and one triple, against Chicago pitching in nine games, and was going at a .389 clip in competition with Paul Richards' hurlers.

May 1, which brought my first big league homer, was my day of days. But I got just as big a thrill on the morning of May 17.

As you know, all major league clubs have to get down to the 25 player limit within 30 days after the opening of the season. May 16 was cutting down day, and as it dawned, I was batting .301 and had driven in 21 runs, but I still wasn't sure that I would survive the pruning of the roster. The Yankees were quite a few over the limit, and I figured I might get a ticket to Kansas City.

A lot of us, on all sixteen clubs in the major leagues, were afraid that day. Some were to suffer similar fears through June 15, the trading deadline.

Anyway, on the 16th of May I got my third homer, against Dick Rozek, of Cleveland, in the Stadium, lifting my average to .308 in an 11 to 3 victory. I also got a single and a pass and stole a base. But if I had been ticketed for Kansas City, my achievements that afternoon would not have saved me.

I got up very early the next morning and scanned the sports pages. Mickey Mantle still was with the Yankees, and still had that No. 6 locker in the Yankee clubhouse, and I am not ashamed to admit that Mantle cried for joy.

The emergence of Mickey Mantle as a star of the first magnitude on the heels of Joe DiMaggio's retirement has enabled the Yankees to offer an unbroken lure at the box office for almost three decades, a source of envy to all other major league clubs. Mantle, although beset by injuries, has managed to rise above them, has been a member of ten championship clubs, and was the League's Most Valuable player in 1956, 1957, and 1962.

In 1956 he won the coveted "Triple Crown," indicating supremacy in batting average (.353), homers (52), and runs batted in (130). Only a half-dozen others have accomplished this feat.

Mantle now lives in Dallas, is involved in a wide variety of ventures, has become a proficient golfer. His chief complaint is that Mickey Jr. shows a lack of interest in the weekly batting averages.

MARTIN MARION

as told to Lyall Smith

Baseball has known fewer finer fielding shortstops than Martin Whitford Marion of the St. Louis Cardinals. Born December 1, 1917, in Richburg, South Carolina, "The Octopus" was at his peak from 1940 through 1946. Marion started to slip only when recurring back and knee ailments curtailed his efficiency. Shortstop on four Cardinal pennant winners, Marion later managed the Cardinals, Browns and White Sox.

IT WAS a cocky bunch of Cardinals that went into that big barn of a Yankee Stadium on October 7 in the 1942 World Series. We'd found out by this time that we could whip the Yanks. We were on the long end of a 3–1 score in series games by now, but we wanted to do one thing. And that was to beat big Red Ruffing.

We knew we could lick him even though he'd won the opener down in St. Louis. He had us nibbling out of his hands for eight innings before we finally got over our chills and teed off on him to knock him out in the last of the ninth. But even though we chased him, Red won that game 7 to 4 and we still wanted to whip him all the way.

We knew he was going to face us in the fifth game when we went out to the park and even though we were anxious to pick on him we still had a few misgivings. For the day was one of those dark, dreary ones in New York with low misty clouds sailing in off the ocean.

Captain Terry Moore was standing at the window when I went into the locker room under the stands to dress for the game. He was staring out at the dull skies. "That Ruffing will be hard to hit today," he murmured. "If that fast one is working he'll be tough."

There's no fooling about our being chesty that day.

None of us was superstitious except Moore and he was really worried. I remember I walked into the dugout with Kurowski and we started talking about what we were going to do with the $6,000 that went to the winners.

"Holy smokes," moaned Terry. "Don't talk like that, you guys. We haven't won it yet." He really was fretting.

Well, we started the game. Jimmy Brown opened with a walk but Ruffing fooled Moore on a third strike and Slaughter banged into a double play. That was the first one we had hit into all through the series and Enos was really talking to himself when he went into the outfield.

It didn't take the Yanks long to score, for Phil Rizzuto, their little shortstop, slammed one of Johnny's fast balls into the stands the first time up and boom . . . just like that we were behind 1 to 0.

We pecked away at Ruffing in the second when Walker Cooper got a single, and then picked up another hit in the third on a liner by Jimmy Brown.

Came the fourth and Slaughter put us back in the game

with a homer off Ruffing that tied it up. We felt better but didn't have long to feel that way for Rolfe opened up the last half of the same inning with a bunt down to Beazley.

Johnny was too anxious and after fielding the ball badly he threw wild to first and Red went on down to second. He got around to third on a long fly by Roy Cullenbine and Joe Di-Maggio then socked a single to left on the first pitch to put the Yanks in front again 2–1. It looked bad for awhile when powerful Charlie Keller, toughest looking player I ever saw at the plate, hit another one of Beazley's slow curves for another single to put D. Mag on third. But Gordon fanned and I threw out Bill Dickey.

We got our fourth hit in the fifth when Beazley broke his bat on a single but nothing came of it and we still trailed as the Yanks came up in their half. Gerry Priddy opened with a smash through the box but I was playing him in the right spot and threw him out on a close play. But Ruffing beat out a tap to Beazley and when Johnny Hopp made a low throw to me on a grounder by Rizzuto I couldn't hold the ball and they had men on second and first. We got jittery for a minute and Jimmy Brown kicked Rolfe's roller to load the bases.

Then Beazley really bore down. He made Cullenbine pop out to me and Kurowski came up with DiMaggio's hot grounder to step on third for the out.

Up we came again. Moore hit Ruffing's first pitch for a single and Slaughter, who really was hungry that day, got another hit on the first pitch. We started whooping it up then and Ruffing looked a little rattled. He got Musial on an infield pop but Walker Cooper socked a fly down the foul line and although Cullenbine caught it, Terry came ripping in from third to score and tie it all up again.

That made it 2–2 and it stayed that way through the next two innings. Up came the ninth inning. Cooper was the first batter and he brought us off the bench when he reached out those long arms of his and poked a slow curve into right-center. Southworth gave Johnny Hopp the bunt sign and he laid down a beauty to put Walker on second. That brought up Kurowski.

Ruffing stood out there for a few short seconds that seemed like ages while he looked down at Whitey in the batter's box. He'd fanned him three times in that first game of the series, probably was trying to figure what he threw him those times. He got one strike and one ball on Kurowski and then served him another one. Whitey swung and he really hit it.

"There it goes," screamed Moore. "There it goes." Right into the stands and we had two more runs. We nearly killed Whitey when he crossed the plate. I remember tackling him and we mobbed him until he begged for us to let him go.

Then we sobered down in a hurry for we still knew the Yanks had a punch in those bats of theirs. And they proved it. Joe Gordon led off with a single and we started to worry. Dickey up. He hit a bouncer down to Brown at second, the kind that Jimmy had gobbled up all year easy-like. But he muffed this one and Bill was safe at first and Gordon was on second. We stopped to talk things over again with Cooper walking slowly out to the mound to talk to us.

He talked to Beazley for a while and then looked at me. "Watch it, Marty," he said. "We might try something."

That's all he said but I nodded. I knew. Priddy was at bat and we knew he was going to try to bunt those runners along. Walker called for a high fast one and Beazley sent one down a mile a minute that was right across Priddy's eyes. Quick as I could I cut behind Gordon who had about a 10-foot lead off second base. I dove for the bag and just as I hit it the ball got there too.

Cooper had reared back and thrown it with all the power he had in his big wide shoulders. And that was plenty. It came to me waist high just as I hit the bag. Gordon was on his way back to second and crashed into me. But I held the ball. He rolled over and I went at Umpire George Barr.

I just about jumped out of my shoes. "You're out," he bellowed. We'd picked him off!

THE BOX SCORE
(October 5, 1942)

ST. LOUIS (N. L.)

	A.B.	R.	H.	P.	A.
Brown, 2b.	3	0	2	3	4
T. Moore, cf.	3	1	1	3	0
Slaughter, rf.	4	1	2	2	0
Musial, lf.	4	0	0	2	0
W. Cooper, c.	4	1	2	2	1
Hopp, 1b.	3	0	0	9	2
Kurowski, 3b.	4	1	1	1	1
Marion, ss.	4	0	0	3	5
Beazley, p.	4	0	1	2	0
Totals	33	4	9	27	13

NEW YORK (A. L.)

	A.B.	R.	H.	P.	A.
Rizzuto, ss.	4	1	2	7	1
Rolfe, 3b.	4	1	1	1	0
Cullenbine, rf.	4	0	0	3	0
DiMaggio, cf.	4	0	1	3	0
Keller, lf.	4	0	1	1	0
Gordon, 2b.	4	0	1	3	3
Dickey, c.	4	0	0	4	0
Stainback	0	0	0	0	0
Priddy, 1b.	3	0	0	5	1
Ruffing, p.	3	0	1	0	1
Selkirk	1	0	0	0	0
Totals	35	2	7	27	6

Stainback ran for Dickey in 9th.
Selkirk batted for Ruffing in 9th.

CARDINALS	0 0 0 1 0 1 0 0 2—4
YANKEES	1 0 0 1 0 0 0 0 0—2

Errors—Brown (2), Hopp, Beazley, Priddy. Home runs—Rizzuto, Slaughter, Kurowski. Runs batted in—Rizzuto, Slaughter, DiMaggio, W. Cooper, Kurowski (2). Sacrifice hits—T. Moore, Hopp. Double plays—Gordon to Rizzuto to Priddy, Hopp to Marion to Brown. Bases on balls—Off Ruffing 1 (Brown), off Beazley 1 (Priddy). Struck out—By Beazley 2 (Gordon, Ruffing), by Ruffing 3 (Beazley (2), T. Moore). Earned runs—St. Louis 4, New York 2. Left on bases—St. Louis 5, New York 7. Umpires—Magerkurth (N. L.) at plate; Summers (A. L.) first base; Barr (N. L.) second base; Hubbard (A. L.) third base. Time of game—1:58.

Priddy popped out to Brown and Jimmy came right back to make up his earlier boots by throwing out George Selkirk who hit for Ruffing.

That gave us the World Series. We beat Red Ruffing. We smashed a Yankee hold on the world championship. And my day was complete. I was in the right spot at the right time for a throw.

A throw that I knew was coming just because Walker Cooper, best catcher I ever saw, told me we might try something.

PEPPER MARTIN

as told to John P. Carmichael

Only when John Leonard "Pepper" Martin, born February 29, 1904, in Temple, Oklahoma, came to the St. Louis Cardinals did the storied Gas House Gang begin its fabled existence. This strong-armed, dashing and wild-eyed chunk of a man typified the frenzied play of Cardinal teams of the early and middle 30's. Pepper's 1931 spirited performance, when he belted 12 hits in 24 times at bat against the Philadelphia Athletics in the World Series for a percentage of .500, is still the high-water batting mark compiled by an individual for a seven-game series. Playing his last game in 1944, Martin took to scout-ing, coaching and managing, and presently is a manager in the minors.

(" 'Pepper' Martin always could run," said Roy Moore, a Houston (Tex.) teammate back in 1929. "He used to scoot alongside a bunch of rabbits and every so often he'd reach for one and heft it for size. If it scaled a little thin, Martin'd put it down again; if it felt nice and fat, he'd drop it in his bag.")

I'M NOT a dignified man myself (said Martin) but when I look back over the World Series between the Cardinals and Ath-

142

letics of 1931, I always remember how the fans booed President Herbert Hoover in the first game at Philadelphia.

They cheered me; me, a rookie from Oklahoma who could run a little, and booed the President of the United States.

It just didn't seem right and I sure felt sorry for Mr. Hoover and I was kinda put out with the fans because, after all, being President of the United States is a pretty big job and should command respect.

My biggest day, of course, was right in this series but I ain't sure whether it was October 2, when "Wild Bill" Hallahan beat the A's 2–0 or when I spoiled George Earnshaw's no-hit game or even when I batted in four runs . . . and got a homer to boot . . . in the fifth game.

You know I was a pretty lucky fellow that year. I don't think the Cardinals were gonna play me regular at all in '31, even though I'd hit .363 at Rochester, so finally one day I got hold of Branch Rickey and I said:

"Look, Mr. Rickey, I'm a little tired chasin' up and down these minor leagues and if you can't use me here, why don't you trade me so I can play every day?"

Well, ol' Uncle Branch looked at me through those glasses and chewed on his cigar and finally said that he'd see. So I did all right, but I sure never looked for no series hero role and, anyway, my stealing five bases wasn't because I wanted to show off or anything.

No, we decided to run whenever we could against Catcher "Mickey" Cochrane because he wouldn't be looking for it and "Gabby" Street (Cardinal Manager) told both George Watkins and I to "limber up" right from taw.

"I don't know how much hittin' we'll get off Grove and Earnshaw," said Gabby, "so we better not waste time on the bases. Let's run everything out."

We lost the first game to Grove, but Hallahan gave up only three hits in the next game and we won, 2–0. I scored both runs. I came up in the second inning and hit a single in front of Al Simmons in left. Now Al could throw pretty good but

I figured he wouldn't expect me to try for second, so I kept right on going. As I hit second in a cloud of dust I turned my head around to look at Simmons and he was standin' there lookin' at me as much as to say: "Oh, a smart busher, huh."

I took a quick glance at our bench and Street looked sort of happy, so just as Earnshaw threw the next pitch to Jim Wilson, I lit out for third.

Cochrane almost threw the ball into left field tryin' to get me and I was safe again. Wilson flied and I scored easily. Then in the seventh I singled again and Wilson was up once more and I stole on the first pitch. I took third when Wilson grounded out.

Street decided to put the squeeze-play on, figuring Earnshaw was pretty apt to "get" Charley, so he told Charley to lay one down. I was all set and slid under Cochrane while Earnshaw was trying to field the bunt.

It's a good thing we did a little runnin' that day, because we weren't hitting. I bet Earnshaw got good and mad at me before the series was over, 'cause four days later he'd a had a no-hitter in the fourth game if I hadn't got both blows off him.

But I guess I'll have to take the fifth game as my biggest day. I got two singles and a home run and drove in four men. That made it 12 hits for me in five games and if I'd only got one more I'd a broken a series mark, but they horse-collared me in the last two games. It's probably just as well things didn't go on because my sombrero mightn't a fit me after all the luck I had.

The day we beat 'em 5–1 we started out with a run in the first inning. Sparky Adams singled past third to open the game, but he pulled a leg muscle turning first base and Andy High replaced him. This turned out to be a good move because, after Watkins flied, Frankie Frisch singled and High went to third. Adams wouldn't have been able to make it. I got a long fly and High scored.

In the fourth inning both Jim Bottomley and I singled, but

THE BOX SCORE
(October 7, 1931)

ST. LOUIS	A.B.	R.	H.	P.	A.	PHILADELPHIA	A.B.	R.	H.	P.	A.
Adams, 3b.	1	0	1	0	0	Bishop, 2b.	2	0	0	3	2
High, 3b.	4	1	0	2	3	McNair, 2b.	2	0	0	1	1
Watkins, rf.	3	1	0	3	0	Haas, cf.	2	0	0	2	0
Frisch, 2b.	4	1	2	6	1	Moore, lf.	2	0	1	1	0
Martin, cf.	4	1	3	0	0	Cochrane, c.	4	0	1	3	2
Hafey, lf.	4	0	1	1	0	Simmons, lf.-cf.	4	1	3	5	0
Bottomley, 1b.	4	1	2	7	1	Foxx, 1b.	3	0	0	8	1
Wilson, c.	4	0	2	7	0	Miller, rf.	4	0	0	2	0
Gelbert, ss.	4	0	1	1	2	Dykes, 3b.	4	0	1	0	1
Hallahan, p.	4	0	0	0	0	Williams, ss.	4	0	1	2	5
						Hoyt, p.	2	0	0	0	0
						Walberg, p.	0	0	0	0	0
						Heving	1	0	0	0	0
						Rommel, p.	0	0	0	0	0
						Boley	1	0	0	0	0
Totals	36	5	12	27	7	Totals	35	1	9	27	12

Heving batted for Walberg in 8th.
Boley batted for Rommel in 9th.

ST. LOUIS	1	0	0	0	0	2	0	1	1—5
PHILADELPHIA	0	0	0	0	0	0	1	0	0—1

Runs batted in—Martin (4), Gelbert, Miller. Two-base hits—Frisch, Simmons. Home run—Martin. Left on bases—St. Louis 6, Philadelphia 8. Double plays—Bishop to Foxx, Gelbert to Bottomley to Wilson. Stolen base—Watkins. Struck out—By Hallahan 4, Hoyt 1, Walberg 2. Bases on balls—Off Hallahan 1, Walberg 1. Hits—Off Hoyt, 7 in 6 innings; Walberg, 2 in 2; Rommel, 3 in 1. Losing pitcher—Hoyt. Umpires—Klem (N.), Nallin (A.), Stark (N.) and McGowan (A.). Time—1:56.

Wilson lined into a double play. We were still in front, but only by one run, so we didn't feel too safe and ol' Sarge (Street) kept tellin' us on the bench: "Let's get some power at the plate. This ain't Earnshaw or Grove today."

We finally sewed up the game in the sixth. Frisch doubled to left with one gone and I was up again. I think Hoyt got a little careless with me . . . or maybe he figured I'd try to get Frisch to third by laying one down . . . because he put a pitch right down the middle and took a couple of steps as if to field the ball.

It looked so good I couldn't help swinging and the ball went into the left-field stands for a homer . . . my first in my first World Series.

Frisch waited for me at the plate and held out his hand. "If you'd a bunted that ball and made me run, I'd a died between third and home," he said. "That's the way to hit . . . so old man Frisch can walk home."

Well, that's about all. I got a single in the ninth to score Watkins and then I tried to steal another base, but this time Cochrane nailed me easy. But we'd won the game . . . that was the main thing.

You remember, of course, my vaudeville engagement after the series ended. Hell, I couldn't stand that. I'm a ballplayer, not an actor so I just quit after a couple of weeks.

I couldn't go on takin' a man's money under false pretenses.

CHRISTY MATHEWSON

as told by Lloyd Lewis

One of the first college graduates in the hurly-burly era of baseball, Christopher "Big Six" Mathewson, born August 12, 1880, in Factoryville, Pennsylvania, was also the first of its great pitchers. Christy was with the New York Giants from 1900 through 1916, moving on to Cincinnati as manager of the Reds in 1917. In 17 active seasons, Matty won 373 games and compiled the highest lifetime pitching percentage of

any National League pitcher. A victim of tuberculosis, while in the prime of life, Matty died on October 7, 1925.

WHEN the bleacher gates at Shibe Park in Philadelphia were thrown open on the morning of October 24, 1911, I was in the mob that went whooping toward the front seats. I got one, partly because the right-field crowd was smaller than the one in left. Most Philadelphians wanted to sit close to their worshiped Athletics, for the World Series at that moment stood two games to one for Connie Mack against John Mc-Graw, and Philadelphia was loud and passionate in the confidence that now they would get revenge for the bitter dose —4 games to 1—three shutouts the Giants had given them six years before.

Me, I wanted to get as close to the Giants as possible, and found a place at the rail close to the empty chairs which would that afternoon become the Giants' bull pen. My whole adolescence had been devoted, so far as baseball went—and it went a long way to an Indiana farm boy—to the Giants and to their kingly pitcher, the great, the incomparable Christy Mathewson. I hadn't had the courage to cut classes in the nearby college and go to the first game of the series at Shibe Park. But today I had. Things were desperate. Up in New York's Polo Grounds to start this, the World Series, Mathewson had won—2 to 1—giving but five hits and demonstrating that with 12 years of herculean toil behind him he was practically as invincible as when in 1905 he had shut out these same Athletics three times.

It had looked like 1905 over again; then in the second game, the A's long, lean yokel third baseman J. Franklin Baker had suddenly and incredibly knocked a home run off Rube Marquard, the Giants' amazing young pitcher. Baker, who had hit only 9 homers all season, had tagged the 22-year-old Giant and two runs had come in—and the final had stood 3–1.

The papers which I read, as the morning wore on, were still full of that home run and its aftermath.

From the start of the series the newspapers had been publishing syndicated articles signed by Giant and Athletic stars —the real start of the "ghost writers" whose spurious trade flourished so long but which the better papers in time eliminated. And in the article signed by Mathewson the day after Marquard's disaster it had been said that Rube had lost the game by failing to obey orders. The article rebuked the boy for throwing Baker the high outside pitch he liked, instead of the low fast one he didn't like and which McGraw had ordered.

The rebuke had been a sensation which grew in the third game when Baker had hit another homer off Mathewson himself, and had been the main wrecker of the great man's long sway over the A's. Up to the ninth inning of that third game Matty had kept command. Always when the Athletics had got men on bases he had turned on his magic. As he went to the bench at the end of the eighth, New York had risen and given him a tremendous ovation, for in 44 innings of World Series play, 1905 and 1911, he had allowed the Mackmen exactly one run—and the A's were hitters, indeed. Their season's average for 1911 had been .297.

Then in the ninth, Eddie Collins had gone out, and only two men had stood between Matty and his fifth series victory over his victims. Up had come Baker with the American League fans begging him to do to Matty what he had done to Marquard—and, incredible as it seemed, he did.

As home runs go, it hadn't been much more than a long fly that sailed into the convenient right-field stand at the Polo Grounds, but it went far enough to tie the score and give Baker a nickname for life—"Home Run" Baker.

Snodgrass, the Giants' center fielder, one of the smartest and greatest of base runners, had ripped Baker's trousers almost off him, sliding into third in the first of the 10th inning. With McGraw snarling, railing, jeering from the coaching line, the Giants made no secret of their hatred of Baker. To them he was merely a lucky lout, a greenhorn who had by sheer accident homered off the two top pitchers of the season.

But Baker had hit again, a scratch single in the eleventh which had been part of the making of the run which had won, and Marquard in his "ghosted" article had quipped at Mathewson's advice.

All that was in everybody's mind—and mine, as on October 24 the fourth game came up. The papers had had time to chew the sensation over and over, for it had rained for a week after the third game and now, with seven days' rest, Mathewson was to try again—this time in Shibe Park.

The long delay hadn't cooled excitement. The press box was still as crowded as at the opening game. This was the first World Series to be handled in the modern publicity fashion —the first to have as many as 50 telegraphers on the job—the first to wire the game play-by-play to points as distant as

Havana, Cuba—the first to which newspapers in the Far West and South sent their own writers. And though the A's now had a lead of two games to one, the threat of the Giants was still great enough to keep fever high.

It was a little after 1 o'clock when my long vigil ended. Onto the field came the Giants with their immemorial swagger, chips still on their shoulders—the cocky, ornery, defiant men of Muggsy McGraw—the rip-roaring demons who had that season of 1911 set a record of 347 stolen bases—a record which would stand for another 31 years without any other club ever coming nearer to it than the Senators' 288 in 1913.

And here at long last they were. I knew them from their pictures as, clad in dangerous black, they came strutting across toward their dugout. McGraw had dressed his men in black, back in 1905 when he had humbled the Athletics, and he was playing hunches now.

Muggsy was first—stocky, hard-eyed. Behind him came slim, handsome Snodgrass, the great base-stealer who was a genius at getting hit by pitched balls and in scaring infielders with his flashing spikes. Then came swart, ominous Larry Doyle; lantern-jawed Art Fletcher; Buck Herzog, whose nose curved like a scimitar; lithe little Josh Devore; burly Otis Crandall; flat-faced mahogany-colored Chief Meyers, the full-blooded Indian; Fred Merkle, all muscles even in his jaws, a lion-heart living down the most awful bonehead blunder ever made in baseball.

There came Marquard, 6 feet 3, his sharp face wreathed in a smile—his head tilting to the left at the top of a long wry neck—Marquard the meteoric. At 19 years of age he had been bought at a record price from Indianapolis and had immediately flopped two straight years for McGraw, becoming the nationally goatish "$11,000 lemon." Then this 1911, he had flamed out, won 24 games and become the "$11,000 beauty."

As the Giants began to toss the ball around, I couldn't see my hero, the Mathewson whom I had come to see, the great one who from the time I was 9 I had pretended I was, playing ball in the Indiana cow pasture, throwing his famous "fade-away" which, for me, never came off. Then, suddenly, there he was, warming up and growling "Who am I working for, the Giants or the photographers," as the cameramen, not 20 feet from my popeyed head, begged him for poses.

I was let down for a minute. He didn't speak like a demi-god, but as I stared, he looked it, all the same. He held his head high, and his eye with slow, lordly contempt swept the Athletics as they warmed up across the field. He was 31, all bone and muscle and princely poise. Surely he would get those Athletics today and put the Giants back in the running. Surely his unique "fadeaway," the curve that broke back-ward, his speed, his snapping curve, his fabulous brain couldn't be stopped. It had been luck that had beaten him in the last game. Now he'd get them.

My eye never left him till the bell rang and he strode, hard but easy, with the swing of the aristocrat, into the dugout and little Josh Devore went up to hit.

Josh singled, Doyle tripled, Snodgrass scored Larry with a long fly. Black figures were flying everywhere. The big copper-colored Chief Bender on Mack's mound was wob-bling, and when the side was finally out he practically ran for the dugout. Later, we learned, he had run in to cut out band-ages from his ribs, from an old injury. After that he was to be unworkable.

Up came the Athletics. Matty, as though in princely dis-dain, fanned the first two men. The third man, Eddie Collins, singled. Here came Baker, his sun-tanned face tense, his bat flailing—the air thick with one word from 25,000 throats, "Homer! Homer!"

Matty studied him as a scientist contemplates a beetle, then struck him out! What I yelled, I don't know. All I re-member is standing there bellowing and paying no heed to the wadded newspapers the Athletic fans around me threw. It was wonderful.

On the fourth, Baker came up to start it and doubled. Dannie Murphy doubled, Harry Davis doubled. Ira Thomas hit a sacrifice fly—three runs. It couldn't be. Up came Baker again in the fifth with Collins on first and another double boomed across the diamond. I saw Snodgrass eventually stop it, but he didn't really have it in his glove at all. It had stuck in my gullet.

Right in front of me an unthinkable thing happened. Hooks Wiltse, the Southpaw, began warming up for the Giants. Was Matty knocked out? Another figure rose from the bull pen. Rube Marquard. He didn't warm up, he only strolled up and down, a great sardonic grin on his face. The fans around me were screaming at him, "You're even with Matty now, Rube! He won't tell you what to pitch anymore!" etc., etc. Rube smirked at them.

Matty got by without more scores, but in the seventh with a man on third Christy walked Baker and Shibe Park's walls waved in a cyclone of "boos." I wished I was dead.

The eighth. A pinch hitter went up for Mathewson. I was sorry I hadn't died in the seventh. Finally it was all over.

I walked out through 25,000 of the most loathsome individuals ever created—all jeering at Mathewson, all howling Baker's virtues. I dragged my feet this way and that trying to escape the currents of fans. At the end of a dolorous mile I stopped at a saloon. I had never had a drink. Now was the time.

"Beer," I said, in the voice of Poe's raven.

"You ain't 21," the bartender rasped. Then he took a second look, saw that I was 100 years old, and splashed a great stein in front of me.

I took one swallow. It was bitter, just as bitter as everything else in the world. I laid down a nickel and walked out. Every step of the way downtown I kept telling myself that in my coffin, some day, there'd be only room for one thing besides myself—my hatred of the Athletics.

But what I started out to tell was about my greatest day in

baseball. That came three years later, October 9, 1914, when
the lowly despised Boston Braves wallowed, humbled, tram-
pled, laughed at the lofty Athletics to the tune of 7 to 1. I
came out of Shibe Park, spent hours hunting that same
saloon, but I couldn't find it. It had to be that one. What I
wanted to do was to walk in all alone—find nobody else in
there—order two beers and when the bartender looked in-
quiringly at the extra one, say to him in a condescending
voice, "Oh, that? That's for Mathewson."

STAN MUSIAL

as told to Bob Broeg

Stan Musial's story is one of the glamorous highlights of the game of baseball. A sore-armed pitching prospect in Class D., discouraged and ready to give up, he was persuaded to try his hitting talents and two years later he was in the majors for a career granted few men in any calling. In 1963 Musial celebrated his twenty-fifth year in organized ball. Honored as no other player in history, Musial still looks and acts much as he did when he came to the big leagues from his home town, Donora, Pa. in the late '30s. His records fill an entire page in the record book; he has won Most Valuable Player honors in the National League three times, has led the loop in hitting seven times.

THE flag atop the right field foul pole at Braves Field was starched due east. The wind, for once, was blowing out toward the Charles River, which fringes the outfield, instead of coming in like a gale toward home plate. And a St. Louis writer traveling with the Cardinals nudged me on the dugout steps, pointed and grinned. But I just shook my head.

Ordinarily my bats would have jumped for joy in the dug-out rack, and I would have looked forward eagerly to taking advantage of the friendly elements, but for two reasons I wasn't happy that chilly afternoon in late September, 1948.

For one thing, we had our backs against the wall because one more victory for the Braves would clinch Boston's first National League pennant since 1914. For another, both my wrists were swollen, sore and throbbing, and batting normally as pleasant as digging into a thick steak, seemed a distasteful and painful chore.

Three days earlier in Brooklyn I had hurt my left wrist playing one of the greatest defensive games of my career. In center field at Ebbets Field, where I've always hit the hardest and most consistently, I raced back to the wall for an "unconscious" gloved catch and charged in for two somersaulting snatches, the second of which saved the bacon in the eighth inning. It was on that play, tumbling over after lunging to pluck the ball off the grass, that I jammed the wrist of my throwing hand.

The left wrist began to hurt at once, but I forgot it temporarily in the good-natured by-play of the clubhouse afterward. Chiding me because I had failed that day for one of the rare times to get one or more blows at Brooklyn, Captain Terry Moore, the old defensive master whose big shoes I was trying to fill in center, punched me in the ribs in the shower and said, "If you only could hit, you might make the team."

The next day we moved over to the Polo Grounds to play the Giants a double-header, and there one of the New York pitchers—names aren't important where accidents are concerned—let a fast ball get away from him, and the ball hit me on the right wrist. Man, that hurts right now.

So into Boston we went for the last stand, and overnight that right wrist began to ache as much as the left. The first day the Braves just about hammered the last nail in our coffin, sweeping a double-header, and I hardly could swing a bat, getting just two hits in both games. I was mighty blue then, as I've mentioned, because I had looked forward to playing on my fifth pennant-winning team—no, you never get tired of winning—and, too, the best season of my career was being hurt by my inability to take a good grip, swing and tee off.

By the time the wind blew toward the right field bleachers that late September afternoon, I had given up my slightest hopes of hitting .400, though I eventually finished with .376, the highest to lead the National League in more than ten years, and I already was assured of finishing first in every offensive department except home runs, a title I lost by one. There was one record, however, that still interested me.

Back in 1922 the one and only Ty Cobb had four outstanding days in each of which he came up with five hits, and that mark had remained unchallenged ever since. Fred Lindstrom and Lefty O'Doul had come closest in the National League with three five-hit days in one season, and I had tied our league's record as early as July 23—and right in Boston, too.

Earlier I had five-hit games in Cincinnati and Brooklyn, and in that July night game at Braves Field I got a chance to tie the N. L. mark and win a ball game at the same time. I had connected safely four times when, one run behind in the ninth inning, we filled the bases with two out and me on deck. As I started up to the plate, Billy Southworth changed pitchers, switching from a right-hander to southpaw Clyde Shoun.

During the delay while Shoun came in to warm up, I started back to the visitors' dugout to change bats and at the steps leading down to the bench, arms folded as usual, Manager Eddie Dyer met me. Unsmiling, Dyer said, "I'm sorry, kid, but I'm afraid I'll have to send up a hitter for you."

I had started back toward the plate and did a double-take on that one, whirling to find Dyer and the whole bench laughing at the rib. Then I hit Shoun's first pitch right past him into center field for my fifth base hit in a row, scoring two runs and winning the game.

But that was July 23, this was September 22, and in between another five-hit day or night had eluded me. It's tough to get five hits even when you're feeling like a million. You have to be hitting good, but you need some breaks, too, because you can't walk and you can't lose any hits on tough luck. I remember a game earlier that season at Pittsburgh, always my toughest park to hit in. I had "4 for 4" going into the ninth inning when I sent a hot line drive right back at he box, and Bob Chesnes, a good fielding pitcher, reached out and grabbed it.

Now we were through with batting practice, of which I had taken little because the wrists hurt so much. Then I decided to rip off the adhesive tape that seemed so binding it eliminated the little snap I had left. And with Warren Spahn, Boston's great left-hander, due to pitch the Boston "pennant clincher," I made up my mind to try to hit to left field. The pain was too intense when I tried to pull a ball. Besides, I couldn't snap the wrists the way I ought to when going for right field.

The first time up I looped a single to short left field. Spahn, fortunately, was pitching me away, and fortunately, too, he wasn't having one of his good days. In the third inning he put the ball outside again, and high, and I belted a double over the left fielder's head. That was Warren's last inning, incidentally, and when I came up in the fourth the Boston pitcher was Charley (Red) Barrett.

The talkative Barrett, one of baseball's best jockeys, had been giving us the needle from the Boston dugout. As an old former teammate he was digging in the spurs, reminding us what he would do with the big World Series share we'd miss. And now he was out there in a relief role, a "cute" pitcher, as we call his kind—not fast enough to break an egg most of the time, but sneaky enough to slip one past you now and then, and a cagey thrower with plenty of control.

Nibbling at the corner, Red just missed with his first two pitches. Then, behind on the ball-and-strike count, he figured that I would be looking for his "fast" ball or slider. Instead, he served up a change of pace, but it wasn't a good one. The slow one was high, it hung and didn't fool me, and quickly I said "to heck with the wrists" and swung for the right field fence. The wind I previously hadn't been able to use helped now, and the ball sailed into the bleachers for my 38th home run.

By the time I batted in the sixth, the third Boston pitcher was Shoun, and I was paying the piper for the full cut I had taken against Barrett. The wrists seemed on fire, and I poked a pitch on the ground between third base and shortstop, just past Al Dark's outstretched glove. That made it four hits in a row, and because we had a big lead and Boston's flag-wrapping appeared certain to have to wait another day at least, I began thinking about the record seriously.

One more chance, I wanted, and it came against Al Lyons, a wild right-hander Southworth seldom used. Lyons threw and was wild. Ball one. He pitched again. Ball two. My heart began to sink as I feared a walk that would deprive me of the last chance I wanted. The players on our bench and in the bullpen were on their feet, pulling for me and needling Lyons to get the ball over, and I made up my mind that while any other time I'd take a pass if it was for the good of the ball club, I'd swing this time at anything, and to blazes with the wrists or where I hit the ball.

The next pitch was close enough, though to this day I couldn't tell you whether it was in the strike zone. I swung, pulling the pitch, and sent a sharp ground ball toward right field. For a fraction of a second, as I dropped the bat and started for first base, I wondered numbly whether the ball would get through, but then I saw it—white against the green grass—bouncing along in the outfield.

Five for five, a fourth time, tying Cobb's old major league record!

THE BOX SCORE

St. Louis (N)   Boston (N)

(September 22, 1948)

	A.B.	R.	H.	P.O.	A.		A.B.	R.	H.	P.O.	A.
Schoendienst, 2b.	5	1	1	2	1	Holmes, rf.	3	0	1	1	0
Marion, ss.	5	0	1	2	6	Dark, ss.	4	0	0	2	2
Musial, rf., lf.	5	3	5	4	0	M. McCormick, cf.	4	0	0	4	1
Slaughter, lf.	2	1	1	0	0	Elliott, 3b.	4	0	0	1	1
Northey, rf.	2	0	1	0	0	F. McCormick, 1b.	4	0	0	8	2
Dusak, rf.	0	0	0	1	0	Conatser, cf.	4	1	2	3	0
Jones, 1b.	5	1	2	12	0	Masi, c.	4	0	2	4	0
Moore, cf.	5	0	1	2	0	Sisti, 2b.	4	0	0	2	0
Lang, 3b.	5	1	3	0	3	Spahn, p.	0	0	0	0	1
Rice, c.	4	0	1	4	0	a Sturgeon	1	1	1	0	0
Brazle, p.	4	1	1	0	4	Barrett, p.	0	0	0	0	0
						Hogue, p.	0	0	0	0	0
						b Ryan	1	0	0	0	0
						Shoun, p.	0	0	0	0	1
						Lyons, p.	1	0	0	2	1
Totals	42	8	17	27	14	Totals	34	2	6	27	9

a Tripled for Spahn in 3rd.
b Popped out for Hogue in 5th.

St. Louis (N)   0 1 2 4 0 1 0 0 0—8
Boston (N)   0 0 1 0 0 0 1 0 0—2

Errors—Musial, Jones, Holmes. Runs batted in—Rice, Slaughter, Jones, Marion, Musial 2, Northey, Dark, Masi. Two base hits—Musial, Lang 2, Schoendienst, Northey, Conatser, Masi. Three base hit—Sturgeon. Home run —Musial. Double play—Hogue, Elliott and F. McCormick. Left on base—St. Louis 9, Boston 6. Bases on balls—Brazle 1, Barrett 1, Hogue 1. Strikeouts— Brazle 4, Spahn 1, Barrett 1, Shoun 1. Hits off—Spahn 6 in 3, Barrett 4 in 2-3, Hogue 2 in 1 1-3, Shoun 3 in 2, Lyons 2 in 2. Wild pitch—Shoun. Losing pitcher—Spahn. Umpires—Robb, Pinelli and Gore. Time—1:54. Attendance —10,937.

Musial's big-league career spans several generations of ball players. He probably would have difficulty remembering the various managers for whom he played, all of whom received one hundred per cent effort from Stan the Man. Men he played with in the '40s are now receiving baseball pensions, others have entered the Hall of Fame, others are no longer on the scene.

Musial has managed to move serenely through the years, getting his hits, smashing his homers, which totaled 463 after the 1962 campaign. He is sixth on the all-time list in this respect, and first among the active players.

An amazing face of Musial's career as he pushes toward the mid-forties is his enthusiasm for the game. "I like to play as much today as the day I first started," he says. "If I didn't I wouldn't be doing it."

Since Stan the Man has several million dollars cushioning him against any financial bumps or misadventures there is only one course open: you have to believe him.

MEL OTT

as told to John P. Carmichael

Stumpy Melvin Thomas Ott, born March 1, 1909, in Gretna, Louisiana, spent all his major league life with the New York Giants. In 22 active years, Master Mel cracked 511 homers and drove in 1860 runs, top National League records. Ott also managed the Giants for six years before joining the club's scouting staff. In 1951 he went to the minors for the first time, when he assumed the field leadership of the Oakland club of the Pacific Coast League. He died in 1958.

CAN a fellow change his mind? You know for quite a few years I always remembered the day in 1926 that I reported to the Giants in Sarasota, when I was 16 years old, as my greatest thrill; when I first saw John McGraw and heard him say: "Go to the outfield, young man." I wondered afterward how I even had the courage to say a word . . . why didn't I just nod my head and run quick. Instead I heard myself: "But I'm a catcher, Mr. McGraw," and he didn't even seem to be looking at me when he came back:

"That's all right, Bresnahan always thought he was a pitcher, too!"

Can I change my mind again? Up to the night of August 7, 1940, in the Polo Grounds, whenever anybody asked me my greatest day it was that afternoon in Washington in 1933 when I hit the home run that gave us the World Series; when I saw ol' Dolph Luque break a curve off so sharp to Joe Kuhel for the strike which gave us the championship that Gus Mancusco had to dig it out of the dirt. But since August 7, 1940, I know what it means to have an outstanding day to remember. That was Mel Ott night with 53,000 fans in the stands.

All the things that I'd done in baseball for myself just seemed swallowed up in what the fans were doing for me that evening. I'll always be grateful to Mr. Stoneham for picking a regularly scheduled Brooklyn-Giant game for my night, because neither he nor myself wanted to use me to get people out . . . to swell the crowd. The Dodgers and Giants at night would draw anyhow, anytime, so nobody could say we were building up a gate.

I told my wife, before I left for the park, that she'd be lucky if I didn't fall down going after a ball or strike-out with the winning run on third and disgrace her, because I was as nervous as a cat. I've been knocked down and got up again and never thought a thing about it, but I knew there'd be speeches and gifts and I was as tense inside as could be. It's a little embarrassing at that, even though you know the fans mean it and you feel pretty proud. People had been contributing dimes and nickels and more to the committee and my wife knew in advance what I was going to get and she was tickled to death with the gifts. I didn't blame her after I saw 'em. In the clubhouse the boys were calling me the grand old man of the Giants. . . . I was 31 . . . and prophesying that Freddy Fitzsimmons, who was gonna pitch for Brooklyn, would fan me all night long. That's usually the way.

Well, finally we were around the plate and there were flowers all over and then came the gifts. You know what I got? Honestly, it was enough to make a guy choke up. I got a set of flat silver, 208 pieces, a coffee and tea set imported from England, a silver water pitcher, a complete set of golf clubs and bag (they were from the players) a couple of plaques and a gold card of membership in the Baseball Writers Association of America. Carl Hubbell presented the clubs, only it should have been the other way 'round. I ought to have been up there saying those things about him and the rest of the gang.

It was a relief to get the game started. Just as I walked to the plate the first time, a guy with a foghorn voice from upstairs bellowed: "You were a nice guy a little while ago, Ott, but you're a bum beginning now." He must have been a Dodger rooter and, after all, they were only five games behind the Reds at the time. Ol' Hub was pitching for us and you couldn't ask for a more perfect setup for the customers . . . Hubbell against Fitzsimmons who used to be one of us. For Hub to win meant more to me than anything else, but I wasn't much help to him . . . only one hit in five times up and I made the last out in the ninth after Brooklyn had won, 8–4, but even a homer then wouldn't have helped us.

They got five runs in the seventh and the only thing I did at all was in the fifth when Camilli hit one four country miles. I could see the ball going straight for the Giant bull pen and I just ran automatically and finally jumped at the last minute and it stuck in my glove. It made me feel good because at the time we were leading 4–3 and at least our fans got a chance to yell. Funny about a game like that; chances are most of the folks came out to see two great rivals play, but they'd sort of included me in the celebration.

While we were changing pitchers in the seventh I looked around those stands with fans yelling and laughing and I thought what an ungrateful guy a ballplayer could be who didn't just give everything he had all the time to people who only asked just that and were willing to even make a hero out of him. I never was what you'd call colorful, meaning I just tried to play hard and hit and give my best. You either have a flair for color or you don't and Bill Terry used to kid me lots and say:

"Why don't you do something . . . go get drunk . . . disappear for a few days . . . roll over and catch a ball . . . come into the plate on your hands?"

But that wouldn't have been me and he knew it, too. One time I got a job in a New Orleans clothing store. Didn't have to do a thing but hang around from about 11 A.M. until 3 in the afternoon and I was being overpaid. How could I earn it? Nobody came in to buy suits from the fellow . . . they just wanted to talk baseball. He didn't get any good out of it, so I quit.

Well, to get back to my biggest day, you'd think that I'd gotten everything a fellow could get in one night, but when the game was over and we were going home, there still was more to come. Way back when I first started to play ball, I went with a semipro club in Patterson, Miss. It was owned by a lumberman named Harry Williams, who wanted a camp team and it was Williams who sent me up to McGraw. They were old friends and so I've always had him to thank for my chance. Williams later married Marguerite Clark, the movie actress.

So I got home, with all my presents, and you can imagine how my wife acted over the silver and things and there was a special delivery letter for me. It was from Miss Clark. Williams had died about six years before. The letter said:

"Do you mind if I add a little something to the gifts which all Giant fans are proud and happy to contribute? If Harry were alive, he would want me to do this I know. It would have made him very happy."

It arrived the next day . . . a salad set to match our silver.

PEE WEE REESE

as told to Harold Rosenthal

Harold H. (Pee Wee) Reese, the Dodgers' all-time short-stop, played in more World Series (seven) than any other Dodger. The "Pee Wee" nick-name came from his pro-ficiency shooting marbles, not his size. He enjoyed a major league career of almost two decades and finished up a coach with his old Dodgers in new Los Angeles before mov-ing on to a new career as a telecaster with Dizzy Dean on

Game-of-the-Week. Reese lives in Louisville, where he first broke into organized ball.

ALL OF my World Series games and All-Star appearances did not provide me with my biggest baseball thrill. It came that September day in Boston when we clinched the 1941 Na-tional League pennant in the greatest game ever. It's almost a quarter of a century ago but I can remember it as though it happened yesterday.

That was my first full year, 1941. I wasn't writing any let-ters home to Louisville on the way I was taking the big leagues apart. Matter of fact, I wasn't. I was booting them at shortstop where I had replaced Leo Durocher and the best I could manage at the plate for the season was a measly .229. I was finding that big league pitch a little different from the ones I saw in the American Association.

You'll remember that Brooklyn bought me from Louisville after the 1939 season. My first year with the big club I got to play about half the season. I shared the job with Durocher who had become the Brooklyn manager the year before.

I had my troubles right from the day I reported. For one thing the fellow at the gate took one look at me when I told him I was Pee Wee Reese reporting for spring training and gave me a "G'wan kid, who are you trying to fool?" Then I hurt my leg during the season, got conked on the head as well.

I was all better at the start of the 1941 season and expected a big year. I read all those nice things that were written about me during the winter, began to believe I was as good as they said I was.

I had Pete Coscarart and Billy Herman at my left at second base and Cookie Lavagetto playing on my right at third base. You remember Cookie. He's the fellow who got the pinch hit in the 1947 World Series, the hit that won the game for us, and spoiled Bill Bevens' no-hitter.

Pete and Cookie were good glove men and I tried hard to keep up with them. Maybe I was trying a little too hard like most kids will do. I started to bobble a couple. That tightened me up and after that you know what happened. I started to kick them all over the lot in every inning of every game, or so it seemed.

I felt as though I had ten thumbs, all with hangnails. I can't remember the number of games I kicked away, but I have a distinct recollection of booting one away in Philadelphia one day just when Freddie Fitzsimmons, our knuckleballer, had it all wrapped up. I remember that I felt so badly about it that I sat in front of my locker and cried until Durocher came over and forced me to dress. He said if I sat there much longer the whole team would miss the train back to New York.

Maybe the choice of my roommate was a little unfortunate too. Don't get me wrong. Pete Reiser is one of the greatest fellows I've ever met but he was in the middle of the best year of his life and he had only one topic to talk about, baseball. They say a ballplayer should eat, drink, sleep and talk baseball, but how about a ballplayer when he's in a slump? Do you think it's right medicine for him to rehash all his day's errors during the night and listen to how the other fellow has been knocking the ball out of the lot? I never did get to give the other routine a tryout. With Pete that year you either talked baseball or you didn't talk. He wound up as the League's batting champion with a .343.

Toward the end of the season the club began to get just as desperate as I was. Everyone was asking Durocher when he was going to stop fooling around and get in back there and play shortstop. He gave them all the "folded-arms treatment" and told them "Pee Wee is the shortstop on this club, not me."

Somehow I got through the first three weeks in September without bleeding to death out there on the field and we got up to the pennant-clinching game in Boston. We had our best man going for us, Whitlow Wyatt, and he didn't fail us. He shut out the Braves, 6–0, with a five-hitter and won his twenty-second game of the year.

Wyatt pitched a great game for us. He gave Boston three hits going into the eighth. Carvel Rowell made the fourth but what might have turned into a serious rally was stopped when Herman made a spectacular diving stop on a grounder hit by Frank Demaree. Herman shook himself up so badly in the process he had to be taken out of the game.

Paul Waner got another hit, I remember, in the ninth, but it was the last, and it didn't mean anything. What meant a lot to us was that scoreboard telling us how the Cards were doing with Pittsburgh. The Pirates had to win for us to clinch the pennant that afternoon. They did, and Brooklyn had its first pennant in twenty-one years.

We had a big party on the train coming back and Cookie Lavagetto started things by snipping off my tie. After a while no one in the dining room had a tie on, and they started on each other's shirts. I guess mine was the first to be ripped off. We never saw a dining-car check that night. When we got to New York it seemed that everyone in the city was down at Grand Central to meet us. Every one that is except Larry MacPhail, who was president of the Dodgers at the time.

MacPhail, the way I got it, had planned to get on board

THE BOX SCORE

BROOKLYN   BOSTON (N)

(September 25, 1941)

	A.B.	R.	H.	P.O.	A.		A.B.	R.	H.	P.O.	A.
Walker, rf.	5	1	3	3	0	Sisti, 3b.	3	0	0	1	4
Herman, 2b.	4	0	0	2	2	Dudra, 3b.	1	0	0	0	0
Cocarart, 2b.	1	0	0	0	1	Cooney, cf.	1	0	0	0	0
Reiser, cf.	3	1	2	2	0	Moore, cf.	3	0	0	0	0
Camilli, 1b.	4	1	0	10	0	Hassett, 1b.	4	0	0	9	2
Medwick, lf.	4	0	1	1	0	Waner, rf.	3	0	1	1	0
Lavagetto, 3b.	2	1	0	2	4	West, lf.	4	0	2	3	0
Reese, ss.	3	0	1	2	3	Miller, ss.	3	0	0	2	4
Owen, c.	4	1	1	5	1	Roberge, 2b.	0	0	0	1	0
Wyatt, p.	4	1	1	0	0	Rowell, 2b.	3	0	2	2	3
						Berres, c.	2	0	0	5	2
						a Demarree	1	0	0	0	0
						Johnson, p.	0	0	0	1	0
						Earley, p.	2	0	0	1	3
						Masi, c.	1	0	0	1	0
Totals	34	6	9	27	11	Totals	31	0	5	27	18

a Batted for Berres in 8th.

BROOKLYN	1	1	1	0	0	0	2	1	0—6
BOSTON (N)	0	0	0	0	0	0	0	0	0—0

Errors—Rowell 2, Miller. Runs batted in—Medwick, Reiser 2. Two base hit —West. Home run—Reiser. Stolen base—Owen. Double plays—Herman, Reese and Camilli; Hassett, Miller and Hassett; Miller, Rowell and Hassett; Johnson, Miller and Hassett. Left on base—Brooklyn 7, Boston 5. Bases on balls —Wyatt 5, Earley 5, Johnson 1. Strikeouts—None. Hits off—Earley 8 in 8, Johnson 1 in 1. Losing pitcher—Earley. Umpires—Reardon, Goetz and Stewart. Time—2:03. Attendance—10,098.

the train at the 125th Street station, but it didn't stop there and came on right into Grand Central. He blamed Durocher for the train not stopping and fired him on the spot although he hired him back the next day.

Durocher's standing by me helped me through a bad year but about the only thing that saved me was the game that clinched the pennant for us. I remember there was a lot of laughing, yelling, crying and shirt-ripping in our clubhouse. I guess I laughed as loud, yelled as loud and cried just as hysterically as anyone in the place. And I'll bet that I meant all three as sincerely as any of the other Dodgers.

PHIL RIZZUTO

as told to Ben Epstein

Phil (Scooter) Rizzuto, All-Star with the Yankees for a decade and a half, still carries on as a Yankee broadcaster. He was one of the most graceful shortstops ever to brighten the major-league picture, and for several years his bat played a surprisingly effective role in the American League race. His high water mark was in 1950 when he won Most Valuable Player honors, hitting .324. Rizzuto was one of *the most skillful bunters ever to play in the majors, and one of the smallest (5'6") to wear the Yankee pinstripes.*

WITH the Yankees, it's a thrill a day—that's the story. Singling out my biggest is entirely too confusing. And picking out my top personal whopper by the year is practically impossible.

But if you want me to simmer it down, I guess I'd nominate August 28, 1949, in Chicago. I knew that date would get you to wondering. Off hand, it means nothing and, as far as I know, it's not the birthday of a president. Yet, in my book, it's the long, long afternoon that won us the pennant and please don't remind me that we had to knock off the Red Sox to clinch it on the very last day of the season.

On that August 28—I love repeating that date—we beat the White Sox in a double-header. We headed for Comiskey Park that morning only a game and one-half out and grabbing both ends was a must. That's the day it looked as if we had lost Henrich and Johnny Mize for the season. Remember Henrich busted up his back in the opener and Mize all but lost a shoulder in the first inning of the nightcap. Henrich and Mize, of course, came back to kill 'em in the Series. However, let's not run away from the subject.

It's the opener I am asking you to slip into your sights. What a job the Sox did to our pitchers. They knocked 'em out in this order: Fred Sanford, Clarence Buxton, Clarence Marshall, Joe Page, Vic Raschi, the winner and Ed Lopat, who finally deadened 'em in the ninth. All this added up left us going into the top half of the last inning on the short end of 7 to 2. For eight innings, Mickey Haefner, then fresh from Washington, was doing a pretty good job on us and remind me to tell you how a left-handed knuckle ball looks some time.

Then it happened. George Stirnweiss batted for Raschi and singled. DiMag lined one into the left-field stands and we were back in the ball game. Somehow I knew it. I guess you get that way after being a Yankee for awhile. Mize doubled, Hank Bauer singled, there were a couple of walks, Billy Johnson singled. Max Surkont went in and out and the next thing I knew I was looking at left-handed Billy Pierce and there was Cliff Mapes over there on first base and the winning run.

And while Frankie Crosetti and Bill Dickey were pep-talking me (I'll guarantee it wasn't necessary) from their respective third and first base coaching slots, I wound up waiting for the big one. The count was 3 and 2 and don't let me forget to tell you it was two away. I guessed a curve. That's what it was—just where I wanted it and I took a cut. The ball sailed over second into center and Mapes, who can run faster than any guy for his size I know, just took off. And when George Metkovich overran the ball slightly, Cliff scored with the bananas and I reached second where I was left stranded but dancing.

That hit has been dancing in my head ever since. I felt that I had done my share in a six-run rally that converted us from a gang of tired old gaffers into a go-gettum outfit. There's nothing that a timely win can't cure, especially when you're fighting for the flag and all the good things that go with it. After that win I was confident that nothing could stop us. It whipped the same feeling into the entire squad and the terrible blows suffered by Henrich and Mize seemed to make us more determined than ever. Maybe I'm daffy but that's the way it hit me.

Confidentially, I like to brag about my hitting. I guess it's because I'm not as big as the next guy. And when a bantamweight like myself gets hold of one—well, that's the cream in my coffee. Later that year I hit two homers against the Browns in the Stadium. To tell you the truth, nobody could hold me after that. I tied that one to another homer memory. That's when I grandslammed also in Chicago (odd, that I'm always kicking up in Comiskey Park, isn't it?) for old Bobo Newsom in July of 1947. That's the first game Bobo had pitched since he joined us and it enabled us to keep on going until we had won 19 straight, tying the American League record.

Naturally, it's nice to recall the time I was named the No. 1 Minor League Player of the Year in 1940 when I played at Kansas City; when I tied the major league record by participating in most double plays by a shortstop, five, on August 14, 1942 and a little of this and that—such as being honored by the New York baseball writers in the winter of 1950—but, as of now, I must go for my base hit in Chicago on August 28, 1949.

THE BOX SCORE

NEW YORK (A)					CHICAGO (A)				

(August 28, 1949)

	A.B.	R.	H.	P.O.	A.		A.B.	R.	H.	P.O.	A.
Coleman, 2b.	1	0	0	6	4	Philley, rf.	3	1	2	1	0
Rizzuto, ss.	5	0	3	0	5	Kress, 1b.	2	0	1	4	0
Henrich, rf.	1	0	0	0	0	e Zernial	1	0	0	0	0
Mapes, rf.	3	1	0	1	0	Souchock, 1b.	2	0	0	8	0
c Stirnweiss	2	1	1	0	0	Appling, ss.	2	0	1	0	4
Lopat, p.	0	0	0	0	0	Hancock, ss.	1	0	0	0	0
DiMaggio, cf.	4	2	2	3	0	Michaels, 2b.	3	0	0	3	3
Mize, 1b.	4	1	2	9	0	Metkovich, cf.	5	0	0	2	0
Bauer, lf, rf.	5	1	2	2	0	Ostrowski, lf.	5	2	2	0	0
Johnson, 3b.	3	1	1	1	2	Malone, c.	4	2	1	6	0
Silvera, c.	5	0	2	4	1	Baker, 3b.	4	2	2	3	2
d Berra	0	1	0	0	0	Haefner, p.	2	0	1	0	3
Niarhos, c.	0	0	0	0	0	Surkont, p.	0	0	0	0	0
Sanford, p.	0	0	0	0	0	Pierce, p.	0	0	0	0	0
Buxton, p.	1	0	0	0	1						
a Lindell	1	0	0	0	0						
Marshall, p.	0	0	0	0	0						
Page, p.	1	0	0	1	0						
b Brown	1	0	0	0	0						
Raschi, p.	0	0	0	0	0						
Woodling, lf.	1	0	0	0	0						
Totals	38	8	13	27	13	Totals	34	7	10	27	12

a Fouled out for Buxton in 4th.
b Grounded out for Page in 8th.
c Singled for Mapes in 9th.
d Ran for Silvera in 9th.
e Lined out for Kress in 4th.

NEW YORK	0 0 0	1 0 0	1 0 6—8
CHICAGO (A)	1 1 0	2 0 0	0 3 0—7

Errors—Coleman, Haefner, Metkovich. Runs batted in—Metkovich, Rizzuto 2, Philley 2, Zernial, Bauer, Souchock, DiMaggio 2, Silvera 2. Two base hits—Ostrowski, Mize, Kress. Three base hit—Ostrowski. Home run—DiMaggio. Stolen bases—Malone, Philley. Sacrifices—Haefner 2. Double plays—Rizzuto, Coleman and Mize; Appling, Michaels and Souchock. Left on base—New York 12, Chicago 10. Bases on balls—Haefner 5, Buxton 2, Marshall 2, Page 1, Raschi 2, Surkont 1. Strikeouts—Haefner 4, Buxton 1, Marshall 1, Page 2. Hits off—Sanford 2 in 0, Buxton 2 in 3, Page 2 in 3 2-3, Haefner 11 in 8, Marshall 2 in 1 1-3, Raschi 2 in 1, Surkont 1 in 0, Lopat 0 in 1, Pierce 1 in 1. Hit by pitcher—Haefner (Johnson, Rizzuto, Mize). Winning pitcher—Raschi. Losing pitcher—Surkont. Umpires—Boyer, Paparella, Hubbard, Berry. Time—3:07.

It's always something when you're a Yankee and one never knows what's around the next base in baseball. In my case, I can truthfully say it's produced nothing but happiness and a good living for my wonderful wife and kids.

JACKIE ROBINSON

as told to Harold Rosenthal

A controversial, exciting figure on and off the playing field, Jackie Robinson became the first Negro to enter baseball's Hall of Fame in 1962. His entire ten years in the majors were spent in the service of the Dodgers, and he also was the first Negro to win Most Valuable Player honors (1949).

Robinson excelled in all phases of baseball: running, hitting and fielding. In college, Robinson was an All-American halfback for the University of California, at Los Angeles.

He is now an executive in a well known food and restaurant chain.

MY GREATEST thrill in baseball didn't come from any ball I hit, from any base I stole or from any play I made. It came when I heard the national anthem played just before the start of the 1947 World Series, my first World Series.

They lined us Dodgers up along the third base line and

put the Yankees along the first base line. Then they played
The Star-Spangled Banner and the flag went up out there on
the Yankee Stadium flagpole in center field. I don't remember much else about this particular game except that we lost
it. But what happened before the game gave me the biggest
thrill in my life.

But I guess the game that gave me the most satisfaction,
and was about the greatest I played in was that one in Shibe
Park on August 10, 1949. It was the night I hit the homer off
Jim Konstanty. It was the first time I ever got a hit off him.
The homer I got won the ball game.

I remember there was a lot of talk about whether Konstanty should have pitched to me or not. There were two out
and one man on and first base was open at the time. The
score was tied and Konstanty went ahead and pitched to me
instead of walking me like a lot of people thought he should
have. I think he did right. You don't walk a man intentionally when he's never gotten a hit off you.

We hadn't been going too good against the Phillies. The
night before I had picked up a bad bruise on my left heel
during a double steal. We had run on Ken Trinkle, the old
Giant relief pitcher, and when Gene Hermanski went down
to second base, I took off for home. I beat the throw by
plenty, so that I didn't even have to slide. Maybe it would
have been better if I had gone down in the dirt because when
I ran across the plate instead I took a long, funny kind of a
tagging step and came down hard on my heel.

Right away I knew I had done something to it because it
hurt like blazes. I didn't get much sleep that night and the
next day I could hardly put my foot down on the ground. I
stayed in there, though, and that night I got a hit in my
second trip to the plate off Ken Heintzelman.

In the game I want to tell you about, we got out in front in
the first few innings, thanks to the way Carl Furillo was bang-
ing the ball, but around the sixth or seventh they came up
and tied it. Then they used a pinch hitter for Heintzelman

and when the ninth inning came around it was Konstanty, a fellow who looked good against us all year.

It looked like another good night for Konstanty. Pee Wee Reese and Billy Cox were the first two batters and he got them on infield rollers. Then Furillo banged a single into left field, and went to second on Konstanty's bad pick-off throw, if I remember right. That gave me a shot at him.

I don't remember whether it was eight, nine or ten times I had tried to get a hit off Konstanty during the season and couldn't. But that night it was different. I think it was one ball and one strike and then he let me have my best kind of pitch, one just over the letters on my shirt.

THE BOX SCORE

BROOKLYN — PHILADELPHIA (N)
(*August 10, 1949*)

	A.B.	R.	H.	P.O.	A.		A.B.	R.	H.	P.O.	A.
Reese, ss.	5	0	1	3	3	Ashburn, cf.	3	2	2	0	0
Cox, 3b.	4	0	1	1	1	Hamner, ss.	3	1	1	1	3
Furillo, rf.	5	2	3	4	0	Nicholson, rf.	3	1	0	3	0
Robinson, 2b.	3	2	2	2	6	Ennis, lf.	3	0	1	3	1
Hodges, 1b.	4	1	1	6	2	Jones, 3b.	4	0	0	1	5
Edwards, c.	4	1	1	3	0	Goliat, 1b.	3	0	0	8	0
Brown, lf.	3	1	1	1	0	Konstanty, p.	1	0	0	0	0
Hermanski, lf.	1	0	0	1	0	Lopata, c.	4	1	1	5	1
Olmo, cf.	3	0	0	4	0	Miller, 2b.	2	0	0	2	1
Snider, cf.	1	0	1	0	0	Sisler, 1b.	2	0	0	4	0
Branca, p.	3	0	1	1	0	Heintzelman, p.	2	0	1	0	1
Banta, p.	1	0	0	1	0	Blattner, 2b.	2	0	0	0	1
Totals	37	7	12	27	12	Totals	32	5	6	27	13

BROOKLYN	0	0	0	4	1	0	0	0	2—7		
PHILADELPHIA (N)	0	0	3	0	0	0	2	0	0—5		

Errors—Hamner, Brown, Konstanty. Runs batted in—Ennis 3, Ashburn, Hamner, Edwards 2, Brown 2, Furillo, Robinson 2. Two base hits—Ashburn, Furillo, Lopata, Ennis. Home runs—Brown, Robinson. Stolen base—Robinson. Double plays—Heintzelman, Hamner and Goliat; Reese, Robinson and Hodges. Left on base—Brooklyn 7, Philadelphia 4. Bases on balls—Heintzelman 2, Branca 4. Strikeouts—Heintzelman 2, Branca 3, Konstanty 1. Hits off—Branca 6 in 6 2-3, Banta 0 in 2 1-3, Heintzelman 9 in 7, Konstanty 3 in 2. Hit by pitcher —Heintzelman (Robinson). Winning pitcher—Banta. Losing pitcher—Konstanty. Umpires—Stewart, Conlan and Warneke. Time—2:13. Attendance—16,426.

I swung, and the next thing I knew, the ball was gone, right into the seats, way out in left field. That's a pretty good carry in Shibe Park. I was glad it was a homer instead of any other kind of hit. My foot was aching so badly I could hardly put any weight on it. I don't know what I'd have done if I had to run at top speed or try to slide.

Konstanty then struck out Hodges, the next batter but the two runs in that inning gave us the ball game, because the Phillies couldn't do anything in their half of the ninth. I never got another hit off Konstanty after that but the way things turned out I didn't mind it too much.

Jackie Robinson had a great many thrills coming after those early years. And he provided thrills to the customers with his base running, his ability to inspire the Dodgers to come from behind in the late segments of a game. One season he stole home five times.

Robinson's appearance opened major-league careers to Negroes, and when he hung up his playing equipment after 1956, all clubs in the majors had Negroes on their rosters. Ironically, it was another Negro, Jim Gilliam, who forced Robinson off his second base position and had him finish his career as a third-baseman, outfielder. Robinson made the Hall of Fame the first year he was eligible, with the writers putting ability over all other considerations.

MUDDY RUEL

as told to Lloyd Lewis

Herold "Muddy" Ruel, born February 29, 1896, in St. Louis, Missouri, caught 20 years in the American League and gained a wide and enviable reputation as a tolerant and shrewd handler of pitchers. He played with the championship Washington Senators of 1924 and 1925 in addition to serving limited terms with the Yankees, Browns, Red Sox, Tigers and White Sox.

After several front-office stints Ruel retired in the mid-'50s.

I HAVE either been playing ball, coaching or scouting for big league clubs since 1915, but in that time, which is now almost one-half a century, I never saw a day in baseball like that of October 10, 1924, in Griffith Stadium, Washington.

It was the seventh game of the World Series between the Senators and the Giants and my 156th of the year. I had caught 149 for Washington in the pennant fight, and although we only had a mediocre ball club we had won it by keeping the team together, that way, day after day, same lineup—Goose Goslin and Sam Rice playing 154 games in the outfield, Joe Judge 140 on first, Peckinpaugh 155 at short,

179

Bucky Harris 143 at second—a tough, determined ball club, paced by the boy-manager, Harris, who would get hit by pitched balls to get to first and who would knock fielders out of his way to get to second.

The series had started on high, with the Senators' immortal Walter Johnson smothered by telegrams, letters, handshakes, sentimental publicity because this was his first pennant—his first World Series. The great man had never been on a flag winner before, and the whole country seemed to be whooping for him but betting on the Giants.

Even the Giants, looking at us with tolerance and amused confidence, spoke well of the great Walter. They could afford to. They figured the series was in the bag. They had in the outfield the really terrific Ross Youngs, a .355 hitter, and Meusel, another .300 man; Hack Wilson, a murderous freshmen hitter, and George "Highpockets" Kelly with an average of .323 and 21 home runs to his credit that season. When southpaws worked against the Giants, Kelly went back to first, his old post, but against right-handers McGraw used a kid named Bill Terry on the bag, a pitcher whom he was converting into a slugger. Great kids the Giants had, an 18-year-older, name of Freddie Lindstrom, on third; a sophomore, aged 20, name of Travis Jackson, on short, and nobody but Frankie Frisch, aged 24, on second.

The whole club had hit .300 for the season, had pulled a pitching staff of Nehf, Bentley, McQuillan, Ryan, Jess Barnes and Jonnard through to a flag. They had Hughie Jennings, the "ee-yah" coach, on third, and McGraw scowling from the bench—an awesome club, but not to us. We Senators were tough, too.

The pressure should have been terrific on us, for the City of Washington was wild with its first flag. Even President Coolidge came out to the first game to root, in his own restrained way, for Walter Johnson.

Walter was in the evening of his career, 37 years old, and getting so he'd tire in the late innings, and I'd seen that fast one coming in a shade slower than in other years. The Giants had licked him the first game, tagged him for 14 hits, 4–3 in 12 innings.

The big, swarthy kid, Bill Terry, got three for five off Walter that day and Art Nehf, Ross Youngs and Kelly had hammered out two runs in the 12th inning to win.

But old Tom Zachary—he wasn't old, just looked so sage and crafty and cunning that he'd been called "Old Tom" from his second year—he stepped out and beat the Giants 4–3 in the second game.

The third game we lost 6–4, but Mogridge had pulled us back in the fourth game by holding the Giants to six hits and four runs while we got seven runs across. Johnson tried again in the fifth game and lost. The kid Terry was still hammering him—had four hits in seven times up off Walter in two games. And Lindstrom hit Walter that day as if he owned him—four for five.

That looked like curtains for us, but Old Tom Zachary didn't think so, and pitching slow and tormentingly, beat the Giants in the sixth game 2–1, to square it at three all. That brought us up to the payoff, October 10—and Washington was wilder than ever.

We talked before the game and figured we had to get Terry out of there, so Harris announced Curley Ogden, a second-string right-hander to start. That meant McGraw would start Terry, who was a left-hand hitter, on first and use Long George Kelly in the outfield.

It worked, and after Ogden had pitched to two batters, Harris took him out and sent Mogridge, a southpaw, who held them till the sixth, when they tired him out by waiting for walks. With two on and Terry up, McGraw jerked his young first baseman and sent in Meusel.

We had done it! We had got Terry out of the game, and Kelly would now go to first, but we were still in trouble and Harris sent Mogridge off the hill and brought in Fred Marberry, the greatest relief pitcher I ever saw. He was a second-

year man, 24 years old, and a character. On the mound he'd
grab at the ball, paw the ground with his spikes, fume, fret,
wave his big shoes in the batter's face and blaze a fast one
through. But the Giants weren't bothered by his big feet
that inning and, helped by errors by Judge and Oscar
Bluege, they scored three.

In the eighth Liebold doubled for us and I was up. I
hadn't made a hit in the whole series, and I could feel the
crowd sigh as I came to the plate. I singled. Then with two
out Harris bounced a sharp one a little to Lindstrom's left.
It hopped over Freddie's head and, coming in behind
Liebold, I scored the tying run.

The yell from the crowd wasn't any louder or longer,
however, than a few minutes later when Walter Johnson
came out to pitch the ninth. Washington was crazy for him
to get even for the two lacings the Giants had given him.

He had to face the top of the Giants' batting order, with
Lindstrom, his kid Nemesis, leading off. He got Freddie, but
that dad-gummed Frisch hit a triple to center. The ball
seemed never to stop rolling and I was crazy for fear Frisch
would come clear home. With him on third, Ross Youngs
came up. He'd crouch at the plate and poise himself like
lightning about to strike, his eyes boring in on the pitcher,
tense as a violin string. I'll never forget that big white bat
of his hanging over my head as I crouched behind the plate.
We walked him.

Kelly up, with everybody thinking about those 21 homers
of his. Walter threw. Strike one. Youngs went with the pitch
to second and Frisch was ready to break for home if I threw.
I bluffed it, hoping to trap Frankie. That one run on third
was important for it could win for them. Two runs were
no worse, so I let Youngs steal. But Frisch was thinking right
along with me and wouldn't be betrayed. He knew, too, that
if I did throw to second Harris would run in and cut it off
and throw home, and nobody in the history of baseball ever
could make that play better than Bucky. So Frisch stuck to

the bag and we went back to work on Kelly. Walter threw twice more, and I can see yet that ball streaking in through Kelly's swing for "Strike Three."

That left Meusel up, two down. Johnson got him to ground out.

We got Barnes out of there in our half of the ninth, but Hughie McQuillan kept us from scoring and he and Johnson kept the plate free till the last of the 12th. Johnson fanned Kelly again in the 11th after Groh had singled and Youngs had walked once more—fanned Kelly and Frisch, too—with the stands a real inferno of noise.

Miller started our 12th going out at first. I hit a high foul over the plate and everybody said, "Two outs," but Hank Gowdy, the Giants' catcher, stepped on his mask, stumbled, dropped the ball, and on the next pitch, like a sinner forgiven, a lifer pardoned, I doubled—my second hit of the whole series.

Walter hit sharp to Jackson's right and I made as if to run past Travis, then turned and scuttled back to second. Jackson fumbled the ball. Two on, one out. The fans were really giving tongue now. They couldn't believe things like this happened.

McNeely up. He bounced one sharply but straight to Lindstrom, who was about 12 feet from third base. Running hard, I figured all I could do on a sure out like that would be to throw myself to the left, into the diamond in front of Freddie and try to get him to try and tag me instead of throwing to first. I saw Freddie hold his hands ready at his chest for the ball, then I saw him jump up. The ball had hit a pebble and bounced away over his head. I swerved back into the base line, tagged third and came home with the winning run. Meusel had no chance to get me. It was over. We were in!

BABE RUTH

as told to John P. Carmichael

George Herman Ruth left the playground of a Baltimore orphanage to become the greatest home run hitter of all time and baseball's most flamboyant figure. He was born in Baltimore, February 6, 1895. Ruth hit 714 homers in league play, 15 in world series competition, and his 1927 total of 60 is still the top mark for a 154-game season. Ruth entered the major leagues as a pitcher with the Boston Red Sox in 1915, and established a record for the most consecutive scoreless innings pitched in world series play with 29⅔ before turning his unlimited talents to the outfield. He scaled Olympian heights with the New York Yankees, 1920–1934, and played his last season in 1935 with the Boston Braves. The Babe died in New York, August 16, 1948.

NOBODY but a blankety-blank fool would-a done what I did that day. When I think of what-a idiot I'd a been if I'd struck out and I could-a, too, just as well as not because I was mad and I'd made up my mind to swing at the next pitch if I could reach it with a bat. Boy, when I think of the good breaks in my life . . . that was one of 'em!

Aw, everybody knows that game; the day I hit the homer off ol' Charlie Root there in Wrigley Field, the day, October 1, the third game of that 1932 World Series. But right now I want to settle all arguments: I didn't exactly point to any spot, like the flagpole. Anyway, I didn't mean to. I just sorta waved at the whole fence, but that was foolish enough. All I wanted to do was give that thing a ride . . . outta the park . . . anywhere.

I used to pop off a lot about hittin' homers, but mostly among us Yankees. Combs and Fletcher and Crosetti and all of 'em used to holler at me when I'd pick up a bat in a close game: "Come on, Babe, hit one." 'Member Herb Pennock? He was a great pitcher, believe me. He told me once: "Babe, I get the biggest thrill of my life whenever I see you hit a home run. It's just like watchin' a circus act." So I'd often kid 'em back and say: "O.K., you bums . . . I'll hit one." Sometimes I did; sometimes I didn't . . . but what the heck, it was fun.

One day we were playin' in Chicago against the White Sox and Mark Roth, our secretary, was worryin' about holdin' the train because we were in extra innings. He was fidgetin' around behind the dugout, lookin' at his watch and I saw him when I went up to hit in the 15th. "All right, quit worrying," I told him. "I'll get this over with right now." Mike Cvengros was pitchin' and I hit one outta the park. We made the train easy. It was fun.

I'd had a lot of trouble in '32 and we weren't any cinches to win that pennant, either, 'cause old Mose Grove was tryin' to keep the Athletics up there for their fourth straight flag and sometime in June I pulled a muscle in my right leg chasin' a fly ball. I was on the bench about three weeks and when I started to play again I had to wear a rubber bandage from my hip to my knee. You know, the ole Babe wasn't getting any younger and Foxx was ahead of me in homers. I was 11 behind him early in September and never did catch up. I wouldn't get one good ball a series to swing at. I remember one whole week when I'll bet I was walked four times in every game.

I always had three ambitions: I wanted to play 20 years in the big leagues. I wanted to play in 10 World Series, and I wanted to hit 700 home runs. Well, '32 was one away from my 20th year and that series with the Cubs was No. 10 and I finally wound up with 729 home runs, countin' World Series games, so I can't kick. But then along in September I had to quit the club and go home because my stomach was kickin' up and the docs found out my appendix was inflamed and maybe I'd have to have it out. No, sir, I wouldn't let 'em . . . not till after the season anyway.

The World Series didn't last long, but it was a honey. That Malone and that Grimes didn't talk like any Sunday school guys, and their trainer . . . yeah, Andy Lotshaw . . . he got smart in the first game at New York, too. That's what started me off. I popped up once in that one, and he was on their bench wavin' a towel at me and hollerin': "If I had you, I'd hitch you to a wagon, you pot-belly." I didn't mind no ballplayers yellin' at me, but the trainer cuttin' in . . . that made me sore. As long as they started in on me, we let 'em have it. We went after 'em and maybe we gave 'em more than they could take 'cause they looked beat before they went off the field.

We didn't have to do much the first game at home. Guy Bush walked everybody around the bases. You look it up and I'll betcha 10 bases on balls scored for us. Anyway, we got into Chicago for the third game, that's where those Cubs decided to really get on us. They were in front of their home folks and I guess they thought they better act tough.

We were givin' them (the Cubs) hell about how cheap they were to Mark Koenig only votin' him a half-share in the series and they were callin' me big belly and balloon-head, but I think we had 'em madder by givin' them that ol' lump-in-the-throat sign . . . you know, the thumb and finger at the windpipe. That's like callin' a guy yellow. Then in the very first inning I got a hold of one with two on and parked it in the stands for a three-run lead and that shut 'em up pretty well. But they came back with some runs and we were tied 4 to 4 going into the fifth frame. You know another thing I think of in that game was the play Jurges made on Joe Sewell in that fifth . . . just ahead of me. I was out there waitin' to hit, so I could see it good and he made a helluva pickup, way back on the grass, and "shot" Joe out by a half-step. I didn't know whether they were gonna get on me any more or not when I got to the box, but I saw a lemon rolling out to the plate and I looked over and there was Malone and Grimes with their thumbs in their ears wiggling their fingers at me.

I told Hartnett: "If that bum (Root) throws me in here, I'll hit it over the fence again," and I'll say for Gabby, he didn't answer, but those other guys were standing up in the dugout, cocky because they'd got four runs back and everybody hollerin'. So I just changed my mind. I took two strikes and after each one I held up my finger and said: "That's one" and "that's two." Ask Gabby . . . he could hear me. Then's when I waved to the fence!

No, I didn't point to any spot, but as long as I'd called the first two strikes on myself, I hadda go through with it. It was damned foolishness, sure, but I just felt like doing it and I felt pretty sure Root would put one close enough for me to cut at, because I was showin' him up. What the hell, he hadda take a chance as well as I did or walk me?

Gosh, that was a great feelin' . . . gettin' a hold of that ball and I knew it was going someplace . . . yes sir, you can feel it in your hands when you've laid wood on one. How that mob howled. Me? I just laughed . . . laughed to myself going around the bases and thinking: "You lucky bum . . . lucky, lucky" and I looked at poor Charlie (Root) watchin' me and then I saw Art Fletcher (Yankee coach) at third wavin' his cap and behind him I could see the Cubs and I just stopped on third and laughed out loud and slapped my

THE BOX SCORE
(*October 1, 1932*)

NEW YORK	A.B.	R.	H.	P.	A.	CHICAGO	A.B.	R.	H.	P.	A.
Combs, cf.	5	1	0	1	0	Herman, 2b.	4	1	0	1	2
Sewell, 3b.	2	1	0	2	2	English, 3b.	4	0	0	0	3
Ruth, lf.	4	2	2	2	0	Cuyler, rf.	4	1	3	1	0
Gehrig, 1b.	5	2	2	13	1	Stephenson, lf.	4	0	1	1	0
Lazzeri, 2b.	4	1	0	3	4	Moore, cf.	3	1	0	3	0
Dickey, c.	4	0	1	2	1	Grimm, 1b.	4	0	1	8	0
Chapman, rf.	4	0	2	0	0	Hartnett, c.	4	1	1	10	1
Crosetti, ss.	4	0	1	4	4	Jurges, ss.	4	1	3	3	3
Pipgras, p.	5	0	0	0	0	Root, p.	2	0	0	0	0
Pennock, p.	0	0	0	0	1	Malone, p.	0	0	0	0	0
						May, p.	0	0	0	0	0
						Tinning, p.	0	0	0	0	0
						Gudat	1	0	0	0	0
						Koenig	0	0	0	0	0
						Hemsley	1	0	0	0	0
Totals	37	7	8	27	13	Totals	35	5	9	27	9

Gudat batted for Malone in 7th.
Koenig batted for Tinning in 9th.
Hemsley batted for Koenig in 9th.

NEW YORK   3 0 1 0 2 0 0 0 1—7
CHICAGO   1 0 2 1 0 0 0 0 1—5

Errors—Lazzeri, Herman, Hartnett, Jurges (2). Runs batted in—Ruth (4), Gehrig (2), Cuyler (2), Grimm, Chapman, Hartnett. Two-base hits—Chapman, Cuyler, Jurges, Grimm. Home runs—Ruth (2), Gehrig (2), Cuyler, Hartnett. Stolen base—Jurges. Double plays—Sewell to Lazzeri to Gehrig, Herman to Jurges to Grimm. Struck out—By Root, 4; by Malone, 4; by May, 1; by Tinning, 1; by Pipgras, 1; by Pennock, 1. Bases on balls—Off Root, 3; off Malone, 4; off Pipgras, 3. Hit by pitched ball—By May, 1. Hits—Off Root, 6 in 4 1-3 innings; off Malone, 1 in 2 2-3 innings; off May 1 in 1 2-3 innings; off Tinning, 0 in 2-3 innings; off Pipgras, 9 in 8 innings; off Pennock, 0 in 1 inning. Winning pitcher—Pipgras. Losing pitcher—Root. Umpires—Van Graflan (A. L.), Magerkurth (N. L.), Dineen (A. L.), and Klem (N. L.). Time—2:11. Attendance—49,986.

knees and yelled: "Squeeze-the-Eagle-Club" so they'd know I was referrin' to Koenig and for special to Malone I called him "meat-head" and asked when he was gonna pitch.

Yeah, it was silly. I was a blankety-blank fool. But I got away with it and after Gehrig homered, behind me, their backs were broken. That was a day to talk about.

AL SIMMONS

as told to John P. Carmichael

Born May 22, 1903, in Milwaukee, Wisconsin, as Aloysius Szymanski, the name soon changed but never the batting stance. Al Simmons first began his 20-year outfielding career with the Philadelphia Athletics, and despite a most unorthodox method of batting which earned him the title of Bucketfoot, Al drove in more than 100 runs for more consecutive seasons— nine—than any other player in baseball history. He spent his last playing days in the American League with the Chicago White Sox. Simmons returned to his beloved A's as a third-base coach before transferring to Cleveland, in the same capacity. Here illness in 1951 caused his retirement. He died in 1956.

WHEN that 1930 season was over and we had won our second straight pennant I understand Clark Griffith told Connie Mack: "I went back and checked up on Al Simmons this year. He hit 14 home runs in the eighth and ninth innings and every one figured in the ball game. We were never the same after he licked us in that double-header." So Connie gave me a three-year contract for $100,000, which he didn't intend to do at all. But that's more like the end, not the beginning, of this particular day. . . . Memorial Day, 1930!

The Senators were in town for morning and afternoon games. They were leading the league by four games and we were second. What's more, they wanted to make so sure of knocking us off twice and really getting a strangle hold on first place that they'd sent Pitchers Ad Liska and "Bump" Hadley into town 48 hours ahead of the team to get fully rested for the big day. Liska worked the opener against "Lefty" Grove, but we weren't worried, because Mose never had lost a morning game in his career . . . that's a fact . . . and he always asked to pitch them.

Well, we were brand-new world champions, of course, and we had a good crowd on hand, but we weren't doing so well near the end of the affair. Liska was one of those semi-underhand pitchers with a little of this and that and not much of anything, but he had us off stride and was ahead 6–3 into the ninth with two out, nobody on base and Grove up. Naturally Grove didn't hit. Connie sent Spencer Harris up to swing for him and he got a single. Then Dibs Williams hit safely and old man Simmons was on the spot. I'd already gone four for the collar and those Philly fans could be tough every so often. Some of 'em were yelling "Three out" and: "How about another pinch hitter?" and I was thinking, "Boy, we better win that second game," when Liska cut loose.

The ball was right in there and didn't break and I really swung. It landed in the left-field seats, the score was tied and the customers were all for me now. We couldn't do anything more and went into extra innings. I got a double in the 11th, but we didn't score. I singled in the 13th and didn't get home. In the 15th I hit another two-bagger . . . four straight hits, mind you, after going out easily four times in a row. Jimmie Foxx came up and hit a twisting roller down the third-base line . . . topped the ball. He beat it out by a half step and on the play I went to third and rounded the bag as if I might try to score. I got caught in a run-down. Well, there I was, scrambling around and cursing myself for blowing a chance to get the game over, but finally I dove for third and was safe. Just as I lit I felt something go haywire in my right knee.

Standing on the bag I could feel it swelling up under my uniform and by the time "Boob" McNair singled and I scored the winning run it was becoming stiff. We went inside and got the clothes off and the damn thing was twice its normal size. Connie Mack couldn't believe his eyes. "How did you do it?" he kept asking. I didn't know myself . . . didn't hit anything but the ground. He put in a call for Dr. Carnett, our club physician. I can't remember his first name . . . and he's dead now . . . but he was one of the outstanding doctors in the East and a great ball fan. He came in and ordered cold compresses on it.

"You've broken a blood vessel," be said, "but it'll be all right."

We didn't have so much time between games, because that opener had taken too long, so there was nothing to do but sit around and order a little lunch. The outgoing crowd was all mixed up with the incoming customers and, of course, a lot of those who figured to see only the morning game were so het up that they turned right around outside the gates and bought their way back in again. Meanwhile the swelling in my knee was going down, but it hurt and finally Mr. Mack said to Carnett: "He can't play any more today, I suppose," and Doc said no. "You'll probably want to take him to a hospital," said Connie and Carnett agreed.

"But not today," he said. "I came out here to see a double-header and I'm going to see it. You . . ." and he addressed Mr. Mack . . . "can put him back in a uniform and let him sit on the bench. He can't run, but he might come in handy as a pinch hitter. What's more . . . if a spot comes up, I want him in there, too. I'll take care of the knee later, but at the moment I'm a rabid fan and assistant manager."

Out we went for the second game and the fans were in a great state when they saw Harris going to left instead of me. Only a few knew anything had happened and they

THE BOX SCORE
(May 30, 1930)

WASHINGTON	A.B.	R.	H.	P.	A.	PHILADELPHIA	A.B.	R.	H.	P.	A.
Loepp, cf.	4	0	1	1	0	Bishop, 2b.	4	1	0	2	3
Goslin, lf.	6	0	0	3	0	Haas, cf.	5	0	0	8	0
Judge, 1b.	5	1	0	13	0	Cochrane, c.	3	1	1	6	0
Meyer, 2b.	6	1	1	3	0	Perkins, c.	0	0	0	1	0
Cronin, ss.	5	2	1	1	6	Williams	0	1	0	0	0
Bluege, 3b.	5	1	2	2	3	Quinn, p.	2	0	0	0	3
Ruel, c.	4	1	2	7	1	Simmons, lf.	7	3	3	3	0
Liska, p.	4	0	1	0	3	Foxx, 1b.	7	0	6	12	1
Marberry, p.	1	0	0	0	0	Miller, rf.	3	0	0	4	0
West, cf.	1	0	0	4	0	Dykes, 3b.	6	0	0	0	2
Rice, rf.	6	0	1	4	0	Boley, ss.	2	0	0	1	1
						McNair, ss.	3	0	2	1	1
						Grove, p.	2	0	0	0	2
						Harris	1	1	1	0	0
						Schang, c.	2	0	0	1	0
Totals	47	6	9	*38	13	Totals	47	7	13	39	13

* Two out when winning run scored.

Williams batted for Perkins in 9th.
Cramer batted for Boley in 8th.
Harris batted for Grove in 9th.

WASHINGTON	0 1 0 0 0 4 0 1 0 0 0 0 0 0—6
PHILADELPHIA	2 0 1 0 0 0 0 0 3 0 0 0 1—7

Errors—Ruel, Cochrane, Boley. Two-base hits—Foxx (2), Simmons. Three-base hits—Foxx, Ruel. Home runs—Cochrane, Simmons. Stolen base—Cronin. Sacrifices—Haas (2), Grove. Double plays—Foxx to McNair. Bases on balls—Liska, 7; Marberry, 3; Grove, 4. Struck out—Liska, 3; Marberry, 3; Grove, 6; Quinn, 1. Hits—Liska, 7 in 8 2-3 innings; Marberry, 6 in 4; Grove, 9 in 9; Quinn, none in 4.

couldn't understand why I was benched after driving in three runs and scoring the last one. I think George Earnshaw was going for us and Hadley for them and he got off just as good as Liska had in the first game. Came the seventh inning and we were behind 7–3. We sent up a pinch-hitter for Joe Boley and he got on and then there was a base on balls and a hit and the bags were loaded. Suddenly I saw Connie look down the line and crook that finger at me.

"Looks like this is the time and the place," he said. "This is what Dr. Carnett meant and you know what he said. Walk around the bases if you can."

I picked out a bat and there I was for the second time in the same day in the clutch. Hadley told me afterwards: "I never wanted a place to put somebody so much in all my life, but we were full up." He seemed to take a long time and finally pitched and it was outside for a ball. He tried another in the same spot and I let it go. Then he changed up on me and tried for a strike.

My bat caught it just right . . . where you know that even if the ball is caught, you've hit it solid. This one came down in the left-field stands, too, and the score was 7–7. I hobbled around the bases and got back to the bench and Connie was sitting up straight, his eyes bright like a bird's, and he said: "My, that was fine, Al!" We won in the ninth and down came Carnett and lugged me off to the hospital.

GEORGE SISLER

as told to Lyall Smith

George Sisler, born March 23, 1893, in Manchester, Ohio, was one of baseball's top stars. His .420 average in 1922 is still the highest seasonal batting figure in the American League. A powerful and timely batter, skillful fielder and cunning base stealer, Sisler was truly outstanding in all departments. Pitcher, first baseman, outfielder and left-handed throwing second baseman, George achieved his finest seasons with the St. Louis Browns from 1915 through 1927. Associated with Branch Rickey, his discoverer, since closing out his active playing career in 1930, Sisler is now a talent man for the Pittsburgh Pirates.

EVERY American kid has a baseball idol. Mine was Walter Johnson, the "Big Train." Come to think about it, Walter still is my idea of the real baseball player. He was graceful. He had rhythm and when he heaved that ball in to the plate he threw with his whole body just so easy-like that you'd think the ball was flowing off his arm and hand.

I was just a husky kid in Akron (Ohio) High School back around 1910–11 when Johnson began making a name for himself with the Senators and I was so crazy about the man that I'd read every line and keep every picture of him I could get my hands on.

Naturally, admiring Johnson as I did, I decided to be a pitcher and even though I wound up as a first baseman my biggest day in baseball was a hot muggy afternoon in St. Louis when I pitched against him and beat him. Never knew that, did you? Most fans don't. But it's right. Me, a kid just out of the University of Michigan beat the great Walter Johnson. It was on August 29, 1915, my first year as a baseball player, the first time I ever was in a game against the man who I thought was the greatest pitcher in the world.

I guess I was a pretty fair pitcher myself at Central High in Akron. I had a strong left arm and I could throw them in there all day long and never have an ache or pain. Anyway, I got a lot of publicity in my last year in high school and when I was still a student I signed up to play with Akron.

I didn't know at the time I signed that contract I was stepping into a rumpus that went on and on until it finally involved the National Baseball Commission, the owners of two big league clubs and Judge Landis.

I was only 17 years old when I wrote my name on the slip of paper that made me property of Akron, a club in the Ohio-Pennsylvania League and a farm club of Columbus in the Association. After I signed it I got scared and didn't even tell my dad or anybody 'cause I knew my folks wanted me to go on to college and I figured they'd be sore if they knew I wanted to be a ball player.

In a way, that's what saved me, I guess. For by not telling my dad he never had a chance to okay my signature and in that way the contract didn't hold. The way it worked out Akron sold me to Columbus and Columbus sold me to Pittsburgh and all the time I was still in high school and hadn't even reported to the team I signed with! Wasn't even legally signed the way it turned out.

They wanted me to join the club when I graduated from high school but I was all set to go to Michigan so I said "no" and went up to Ann Arbor. Well, to make a long story short the story came out in the open there and when the whole thing was over I had been made a free agent by the old National Commission and signed up with Branch Rickey who at that time was manager of the St. Louis Browns.

I pitched three years of varsity ball up at Michigan and when I graduated on June 10, 1915, Rickey wired me to join the Browns in Chicago. Now, all this time I was up at school I still had my sights set on Walter Johnson. When he pitched his 56 consecutive scoreless innings in 1912 I was as proud as though I'd done it myself. After all, I felt as though I had adopted him. He was my hero. He won 36 games and lost only seven in 1913 and he came back the next season to win 28 more and lose 18. He was really getting the headlines in those days and I was keeping all of them in my scrapbook.

Well, then I left Michigan in 1915 and came down to Chicago where I officially became a professional ballplayer. I hit town one morning and that same day we were getting beat pretty bad so Rickey called me over to the dugout.

"George," he said, "I know you just got in town and that you don't know any of the players and you're probably tired and nervous. But I want to see what you have in that left arm of yours. Let's see what you can do in these last three innings."

I gulped hard a couple of times, muttered something that sounded like "thanks" and went out and pitched those last three innings. Did pretty good, too. I gave up one hit but the Sox didn't get any runs so I figured that I was all right.

Next day, though, I was out warming up and meeting more of the Browns when Rickey came over to me. He was carrying a first baseman's glove. "Here," he said. "Put this on and get over there on first base."

Nothing much happened between the time I joined the club in June until long about the last part of August. Rickey would pitch me one day, stick me in the outfield the next and then put me over on first the next three or four. I was hitting pretty good and by the time we got back to St. Louis the sports writers were saying some nice things about me.

They were saying it chiefly because of my hitting. I'd only won two-three games up to then. I still remember the first one. I beat Cleveland and struck out nine men. Some clothing store gave me a pair of white flannels for winning and I was right proud of them.

As I was saying, we got back to St. Louis late in August. Early one week I picked up a paper and saw that a St. Louis writer, Billy Murphy, had written a story about Washington coming to town the following Sunday and that Walter Johnson was going to pitch.

I was still a Johnson fan and Murphy knew it, for when I got halfway through the story I found out that he had me pitching against Johnson on the big day, Sunday, August 29.

That was the first I knew about it and I figured it was the first Manager Rickey knew about it, for here it was only Tuesday and Murphy had the pitchers all lined up for the following Sunday.

Well, he knew what he was talking about, because after the Saturday game Rickey stuck his head in the locker room and told me I was going to pitch against Johnson the next day. I went back to my hotel that night but I couldn't eat. I was really nervous. I went to bed but I couldn't sleep. At 4:00 A.M. I was tossing and rolling around and finally got up and just sat there, waiting for daylight and the big game.

I managed to stick it out, got some breakfast in me and was out at Sportsman's Park before the gates opened. It was one of those typical August days in St. Louis and when game time finally rolled around it was so hot that the sweat ran down your face even when you were standing in the shadow of the stands.

All the time I was warming up I'd steal a look over at Johnson in the Washington bull pen. When he'd stretch 'way out and throw in a fast ball I'd try to do the same thing. Even when I went over to the dugout just before the game started I was still watching him as he signed autographs and laughed with the photographers and writers.

Well, the game finally started and I tried to be calm. First man to face me was Moeller, Washington's left fielder. I didn't waste any time and stuck three fast ones in there to strike him out. Eddie Foster was up next and he singled to right field. Charley Milan singled to right center and I was really scared. I could see Mr. Rickey leaning out of the dugout watching me real close so I kept them high to Shanks and got him to fly out to Walker in center field. He hit it back pretty far though and Foster, a fast man, started out for third base. Walker made a perfect peg into the infield but Johnny Lavan, our shortstop, fumbled the relay and Foster kept right on going to score. That was all they got in that inning, but I wasn't feeling too sure when I came in to the bench. I figured we weren't going to get many runs off Johnson and I knew I couldn't be giving up many runs myself.

Then Johnson went out to face us and I really got a thrill out of watching him pitch. He struck out the first two Brownies and made Del Pratt fly to short center. Then I had to go out again and I got by all right. In the second inning, Walker led off with a single to center field and Baby Doll Jacobson dumped a bunt in front of the plate. Otto Williams, Washington catcher, scooped it up and threw it 10 feet over the first baseman's head. Walker already was around second and he came in and scored while the Baby Doll reached third.

I think I actually felt sorry for Johnson. I knew just how he felt because after all, the same thing had happened to me in the first inning. Del Howard was next up for us and he singled Jacobson home to give us two runs and give me a 2–1 lead.

Well, that was all the scoring for the day, although I gave up five more hits over the route. Johnson got one in the first

THE BOX SCORE
(August 29, 1915)

WASHINGTON	R.	H.	P.	A.	ST. LOUIS	R.	H.	P.	A.
Moeller, lf.	0	0	2	0	Shotton, lf.	0	0	0	0
Foster, 2b.	1	2	3	3	Austin, 3b.	0	2	2	1
C. Milan, cf.	0	1	0	0	Pratt, 2b.	0	0	4	3
Shanks, 3b.-rf.	0	1	0	2	Walker, cf.	1	1	4	0
Gandil, 1b.	0	1	6	3	Jacobson, rf.	1	1	1	0
Johnson, p.	0	1	1	1	Howard, 1b.	0	1	9	1
Williams, c.	0	0	6	3	Lavan, ss.	0	0	3	5
McBride, ss.	0	0	5	1	Severeid, c.	0	1	4	1
Acosta, rf.	0	0	1	0	Sisler, p.	0	1	0	1
Morgan, 3b.	0	0	0	0					
H. Milan, rf.	0	0	0	0					
Totals	1	6	24	13		2	7	27	12

WASHINGTON	1	0	0	0	0	0	0	0	0—1
ST. LOUIS	0	2	0	0	0	0	0	0	*—2

Errors—Williams, Lavan (2). Sacrifice hits—Williams, Pratt, Lavan, Johnson, Moeller. Double plays—Lavan to Howard (2); Severeid to Austin. Bases on balls—Off Sisler, 2. Hit by pitched ball—Acosta by Sisler; Sisler by Johnson. Struck out—By Johnson, 6; Sisler, 3.

of the fifth, a blooper over second. I was up in the last of the same inning and I'll be darned if I didn't get the same kind. So he and I were even up anyway. We each hit one man, too.

There wasn't much more to the game. Only one man reached third on me after the first inning and only two got that far on Johnson.

When I got the last man out in the first of the ninth and went off the field I looked down at the Washington bench hoping to get another look at Johnson. But he already had ducked down to the locker room.

I don't know what I expected to do if I had seen him. For a minute I thought maybe I'd go over and shake his hand and tell him that I was sorry I beat him but I guess that was just the silly idea of a young kid who had just come face to face with his idol and beaten him.

ENOS SLAUGHTER

as told to Lyall Smith

Enos Slaughter enjoyed two careers in the majors, one with the Cardinals, the other with the Yankees. These covered a span of more than two decades. One of Slaughter's most proud possessions is the gold lifetime pass which signifies 20 years of major-league service.

Slaughter's name was synonymous with "hustle," a habit he picked up to survive in the Cardinal farm chain before World War II.

He was still running at the age of 40.

His batting eye helped, too, because he finished up with a lifetime .300 average, and 169 homers.

MAYBE it doesn't sound just right to say it, but we Cards never were scared of the Yankees. After all, we beat them in the '42 spring series in Florida six games out of nine and showed them we were just as tough as they were. Maybe even tougher.

We'd lost the first two spring games and I remember that third one real well. Somebody hit a home run for us. I think it was Mort Cooper, and Marv Breuer, pitching for the

Yanks, was real mad. Jimmy Brown was up and Marv threw right at his head once. Jimmy got up, brushed himself off and then went down again in a hurry as Marv threw for his head again. He would have beaned him if Jimmy's bat hadn't turned it away from his temple. We really went after them then, got into a big fight and beat them the next six out of seven.

Before the World Series started in October, 1942 we figured we could lick 'em again, even after that 7-4 score in the first game when they beat us to the punch. After that ninth inning when we got going for four runs we knew we had them and the day of the second game in the clubhouse we all said: "We can handle these fellows. We can score on them." So we went out and did it.

Remember how we jumped off to a two-run lead in the first inning and then got another in the seventh? All this time Johnny Beazley was bearing down hard and never had a lot of trouble. In the fourth though, Keller just about took off Beazley's head with a single over the mound. Joe Gordon slammed a liner at Kurowski, who stuck up a glove, grabbed it and almost doubled Keller off first. Dickey was up next and he swung on one of Johnny's curve balls for a single to me on the ground.

As I raced over to get it I figured Keller would go for third sure. Anybody would go from first on a single that was taking more than one bounce into far right. I hoped to get the ball clean and be able to fire it across to Kurowski on third for a close play, anyway.

This throw to third was one I'd practiced ever since I came up to the Cards in 1938. My arm was wild in those days and the word had gone around the league: "Run on Slaughter. Take an extra base on him." So I'd practiced mornings and off days, anytime I could get somebody to hit fungoes to me and a bat boy to stand on third for a target.

I had improved, but I wondered as I grabbed up the ball off the grass if I could deliver now, when the chips were down. I didn't see anything but Kurowski waiting on the bag as I threw, but as the ball left my hand I saw Keller's back, about 15 to 20 feet past second, splitting himself going for third. I looked back and saw the ball going right to Kurowski on the bag. It was going to be a strike!

Then I saw Art Fletcher, the Yank coach, right behind the bag wave his arms and jump and waggle that long jaw of his, and I saw Keller stop, turn and hustle back to second. At that, he didn't much more than make it for Kurowski fired the ball to second fast.

I was still thinking about having made the play right, when Hassett flied out to me, deep, to end the inning.

That Keller, though, homered in the eighth to tie the score at 3–3. When we batted in the last half of the inning I was up with two outs and nobody on. Ernie Bonham was pitching for the Yanks and he was tough on me so far. I hadn't hit the whole game and was as mad as one of them Carolina fighting roosters.

Ernie got the first one in for a strike and then wasted two low outside ones trying to make me bite. I waited though and on his next pitch I slapped a liner down over Hassett's head and it rolled clear down the right-field line for a double. I slid into second ahead of Cullenbine's peg but got up when I saw Rizzuto muff the throw in. I went down to third and slid again but it wasn't necessary. Musial was up next and he got one of those poky singles of his out over second and I came in with the run that eventually won for us.

But my big thrill came in the first of the ninth on that throw I made on Hassett's single which caught Stainback sliding into third with what could a been the tying run.

That big Dickey started out the Yanks' ninth with a smash that was too hot for Jimmy Brown to hold and then Mc-Carthy sent out Tucker Stainback to run for Bill. Buddy Hassett came up. He let a couple of Beazley's streakers go by and then swung on one that they told me afterwards was outside. It was a grounder that went down toward Johnny Hopp at first. Johnny went over fast as he could, but when he got to the spot the ball already was through and rolling out toward me.

Now I kinda had a hunch Hassett was going to hit one out my way and I was coming in just about as soon as he swung. We outfielders don't have any way to know what our pitchers are throwing some special batter, but I recalled how before the game we were talking about keeping them outside to Buddy. Anyway, I was charging in as fast as I could run when I saw that roller get through between Hopp and Brown. Here was lightning hitting twice at me in the same place. Could I do it again? Could I throw another strike to third?

I picked the ball up on the run and without ever knowing where Stainback was by now—I knew he must be well on his way to third though—I let one go. Well, you know what happened. They told me afterwards and the newspaper fellows had it in their stories that the throw was my greatest one. I saw it go across that infield and get to Kurowski while Stainback, a fast man, was still five feet away.

Guess it was a pippin at that for the ball came in to Kurowski right at his knees and he was waiting there when Stainback came charging into the bag. Umpire Magerkurth was right there on the play and Stainback was out. That made it two out for the Yanks and that big run, the tying one, had been cut down. The next fellow up was Ruffing, who came in to hit for Bonham and he boosted one out to me that went about as high as a Georgia pine and I got under easy. That was the ball game and we were all even with the champs.

Some fellows like to say that throw of mine was one that cut the hearts out of the Yankees. Said it made them more cautious when they were running the bases after that but I don't know. That throw was my best though and I guess it meant the biggest baseball thrill in my life.

I got another big one though in the last game of the series in New York when we put the clincher on the title and beat the Yanks 4–2. I was first man up in the fourth and got a homer off Ruffing that tied the game. I can remember just as plain as I'm sitting here how I hit his first pitch for a homer. It's funny, too, because I generally wait a pitcher out for a while to see what he's going to try on me. But that first one was too good to pass up. Old Red wound up and tried to fog one right past me about waist high. I got a good toe hold and belted it with all I had. It came down in the bleachers.

Looking back a little more though, I guess I'd have to take one day in Philly as my best hitting day. About 18 fellows came up from my home town of Roxboro, N. C., to see me play. It was in 1939 and none of them had ever seen me in the big time before. I used to play second base with those fellows down in the tobacco country and boy, I was really hoping to go some.

Well, I ended up with a good day. It was a double-header and when it was all over I had five hits out of eight times up, including two doubles, a triple, a single and a home run with the bases loaded.

WARREN SPAHN

as told to Bob Ajemian

Greatest left-handed winner in the history of the National League, Warren Spahn is listed among the ten top winners of all time. For more than a decade he has been the mainstay of the Braves' mound staff, has a 400-game lifetime career as his goal. He holds the major league record for most seasons as a 20-or-more winner, and holds the National League record for home runs by pitchers. Over the years he has even been used as a pinch-swinger in tight spots.

BROOKLYN needed one game to clinch the pennant. I needed that same game to reach 20 wins. It was a day late in September, Ebbets Field was jam-packed as I walked out to the mound, and if you want to know why this was my greatest game, listen to me.

I had 16 wins the day we left Boston for our last Western trip of the 1947 season. Sixteen wins, ten losses, and the string was running out.

I've been on a pennant winner since then, the 1948 team; I've pitched in a World Series, but even now in looking back, winning that 20th game in 1947 was the greatest challenge and thrill I've received out of baseball.

It was early in September when the Braves began their final trip of the year. On the train I figured out how many starts I'd probably have left. If Billy (Southworth) kept working me in my regular turn, I counted on five more.

Johnny Sain was chasing his 20th win just like I was. Of course, he had won 20 the year before. He was ahead of me now, about one or two games. I think he had 18 when we left Boston. He finished up with 21 for the season, I remember that.

The difference between winning 19 games and winning 20 for a pitcher is bigger than anyone out of baseball realizes. It's the same for hitters. Someone who hits .300 looks back on the guy who batted .295 and says "tough luck buddy."

Twenty games is the magic figure for pitchers; .300 is the magic figure for batters. It pays off in salary and reputation. And those are the two things that keep a ballplayer in business.

Well, the first town we hit was Cincinnati. I was as ready as I'll ever be. We won, 3 to 0. I was strong, had plenty of stuff.

The last out was a fly to Tommy Holmes in right field. He came running in afterwards, handed me the ball and said:

"That's 17, Spahnny. You're off now."

My next chance came in St. Louis. Again I was pretty hot. We beat the Cards, 5 to 0, another shutout. I grabbed the game ball and tucked it away. Things felt pretty good that night.

The 19th victory, four days later, was against Chicago in Wrigley Field. We won, 1 to 0, my third shutout in a row. I was finally in that slot, one before 20. The pressure was really on now, and I could feel it.

I wanted to ask Billy how many more starts I'd get, but I decided against it. The Braves had recalled some kid pitchers from the minors, and I figured they would be looking them over. But Billy came through for me.

He told me I was going to pitch against the Dodgers on September 21. I told myself:

"It will be your last chance. Don't count on any more. This is the one you'll have to win. They've got too many kids they want to test."

My wife, Lorene, flew down from Boston to be with me. She had been writing to me all the time while we were on the road, and I knew she was going through the same feeling I was.

The night before the game, we sat in our room together in the Hotel Commodore. I said to her:

"Brooklyn needs only one win to clinch the pennant. Every Dodger fan in New York will probably want to be there to-morrow to see them do it. Branca's going to pitch, did you see the paper? He's won 21 already."

"Let's not talk about the game," she said to me. Lorene was as nervous as I was.

But the payoff came the next afternoon just before the game. If anything could have upset the applecart, this would have been it.

Lorene and I allowed plenty of time to get to the ball park. We took the subway from the Commodore, hoping, of course to get off in Brooklyn. Instead we were let off in the Battery. The subway only went as far as the bridge that day and stopped.

We hurried out to a cab and headed for the Brooklyn Bridge. The going was slow, the lights seemed to be against us all the way. Lorene didn't say a word, but I could see she was getting jumpy. All I could think about was getting there on time.

After a long ride, we finally got near the ball park. What a mob. The place was sold out completely. Everybody had turned out to see Brooklyn clinch the pennant.

They had the whole place roped off to prevent people with no tickets from getting anywhere near the ball field.

And I had no ticket. We don't need them at the players' entrance. But the players' entrance was 100 yards away, past a crowd of people, a rope, and some tough-looking policemen.

My wife and I barged through, got to the rope, and were pushed back by a cop.

"But I'm a ballplayer," I started to argue. He gave me a quick answer and a half-shove back.

"So am I," he said. "An' we're gonna do all our playin' right out here. Now get on with you and don't be disturbin' me."

"But I'm with the Boston club and I have to pitch today," I said to him. "I'm late already."

"Listen buddy, I'm from Brooklyn and so are you. Now get movin'."

He was starting to get mad, I could see that. If I had said anything else, there's no telling what he might have done.

This is where my wife stepped in. She went right under the rope and after him. If it hadn't been for her, Brooklyn might have clinched the pennant that day, and I might never have—well let me tell you.

The next thing I heard was:

"Pardin' me madam, but how was I to know you were Mrs. Spahn." We were ushered over to the entrance.

But I had even more trouble when I finally walked onto the mound.

It wasn't the capacity crowd that bothered me, even though they were yelling like the mischief. It was a strong wind coming out of New York harbor and blowing from the first base side of the plate out toward left field—a sort of crosswind.

It made my curve ball break just too wide of the plate. It took me only two batters to find out. I tried using my change-up, and that kept coming in too low. The wind was too strong.

I'm a control pitcher. That's my strength, and if my control is off, I might as well throw underhand. I had walked only nine batters in the last 77 innings I had pitched before this game.

In the first four innings that afternoon, five Dodgers got bases on balls.

The first inning was rough. I loaded the bases, with walks to Stanky and Reese and an error on Bruce Edwards' grounder. Two men were out and Dixie Walker was the hitter.

I got him to ground to Connie Ryan at second.

In the second inning, with men on first and third, two men out, I struck out Jackie Robinson.

In the third inning with Reese on third base, two out, I got Walker on a change up. He popped a short fly to 'Bama Rowell in left field.

I felt good. And I kept telling myself:

"This has got to be the one. You won't get another chance after today."

It seemed to be paying off.

In our half of the fourth, Torgy (Earl Torgeson) doubled and Dick Culler scored him with a single.

In their fourth, Don Lund, a rookie outfielder, was the first batter. The wind was still bothering me. I walked him. Then Spider Jorgenson smashed a ball between first and second. It looked like a hit.

Torgy raced over and made a dive for the ball. He turned a somersault in the air, no kidding a complete somersault. And he came up sitting on the ground.

He threw the ball over to me from his sitting position. I raced across the first base bag. I could feel Jorgenson's foot hit the bag after mine.

But Scotty Robb—some name for an ump, huh?—called him safe. It upset me a lot because I felt we had made the play. Especially after Torgy's stop.

Branca then tried to sacrifice. He popped a bunt foul a few feet outside the third base line. Bob Elliott, you know how big he is, sprinted over from third the same as I did from the mound.

I reached out for the ball, felt it in my glove, then collided with Bob.

They told me in the dugout afterwards we both started spinning like tops. Elliott did a full spin and fell right on his back. He crashed down on his head. I spun a couple of times, but kept my balance, and also luckily kept the ball.

The first thing I saw when my eyes stopped blinking was Elliott. He was lying flat on the ground. The next thing I saw was Lund. He was trying to sneak from second to third after the catch. And the third thing I saw was Phil Masi, our catcher, streaking down to cover third.

I was off balance, but threw to Masi anyway. It was about knee-high and to the far side of the bag. Phil tumbled to his knees, reached out beyond the bag for the ball and grabbed it. He put it on Lund for the double play.

Everything was happening.

We got two more in the fifth when Masi doubled two runners in.

I had a three-run lead to work with. The pressure was off. Someone told me after the game I had made 86 pitches in the first four innings. I made only 18 in the next two.

In the seventh, Stanky and Reese singled with two out. I walked Carl Furillo to load the bases and you should have heard the crowd yell when Edwards stepped into the box.

He was late on a fast ball and popped to Ryan at second.

The walk to Furillo was the last one I gave. I was used to the wind a little more by now and fooled around with some pitches.

My wife was sitting right in back of the Braves' dugout. I hadn't dared to look at her before the seventh. When Edwards popped up, I glanced at her before walking into the dugout. She had a big smile; I think she realized how confident I felt by then.

We won, 4 to 0. The Dodgers only got six hits, Reese got

three of them. It was my fourth shutout in a row, my 20th
win of the season.

Every guy on that team shook my hand after the game.
Even the fans who had come looking for a Dodger pennant
that afternoon gave me a big hand as I walked off the field. It
was the biggest game of my life.

*   *   *   *   *

It's funny how certain things which happen in baseball
will always stick with a guy, especially a pitcher who must
learn to accept both victories and defeats as the inevitable in
approximately 35 or 40 games. Yet there are always one or
two contests which can never slip from a fellow's memory.
And so it is that for as long as I'm capable of remembering
clearly and vividly, never will I forget a lazy, sunshiny spring
day, again at Ebbets Field, in 1951, when I pitched—and lost
—one of my greatest games.

The season was only five days old and I had already
dropped my first start, a toughie to the Giants, when I took
the mound to face the Dodgers that Monday afternoon. April
23rd was the date, a forever memorable one since it also was
my twenty-ninth birthday, but sixteen innings and three
hours and fifty-three minutes later I realized that Brooklyn
wasn't going to allow me to celebrate.

Joe Hatten was my pitching opponent at the outset, and
he gave up the first run—and the only one we were to score
in sixteen innings—in the third inning. My catcher, Ray
Mueller, slashed a line drive into left field, good for two
bases, and Buddy Kerr's single moved him to third base.
Then I topped a roller down the first-base line, and Ray just
did beat Gil Hodges' toss to the plate for our lone tally.

The first four innings were easy enough for me, and I still
had a run lead until that big Hodges came up in the fifth
and blasted one deep into those friendly left-field seats. From
then on the game belonged to the pitchers.

As the zeros plopped out on the scoreboard inning after

inning I honestly felt I could go on until we were forced to catch our train for the next town. The Dodgers weren't giving me too much trouble, but our boys weren't exactly wearing the ball out either, and the Brooklyn pitchers—there were three of them that day—were just as stubborn about staying out in the sun.

For years left-handers were regarded as erratic individuals, to be babied, perhaps, and looked upon with a certain indulgence at least. Certainly they were not expected to perform with the consistency of right-handers.

From the fifth to the fifteenth innings I turned in ten scoreless frames, but never did get the eleventh.

The sixteenth stanza started harmlessly enough. I retired Pee Wee Reese on a foul fly, but then Billy Cox rifled an honest single to left and moved to second when pitcher King sacrificed. So there were two out, the winning run on second and pinch-hitter Eddie Miksis at the plate, still not too ominous a situation. And when Miksis banged a grounder at Gene Mauch, who had replaced Sid Gordon at third base. Our outfielders started to throw away their gloves and come in for their licks in the seventeenth inning. But there were to be no more innings played that day! The usually sure-fingered Mauch bobbled the bounder and now the Dodgers had their winning run on third and a man on first.

Before the next Brooklyn batter, Carl Furillo, a right-handed swinger, got to the plate, Billy Southworth dashed out of the dugout with those brisk steps of his and was at my side suggesting that I pass Furillo in order to pitch to the lefty-hitting Duke Snider. I knew Billy's counsel was sound and in keeping with the pitching percentages, but I was a trifle leery of walking Furillo to load the bases, and then maybe being forced to come in with a "fat" pitch to Snider if I got behind on the count. So I pitched to Furillo, but carefully, and then with a two-two count on him Carl blasted a real beauty to the top of the scoreboard for the game-winning blow.

THE BOX SCORE

BOSTON (N)   BROOKLYN

(September 21, 1947)

	A.B.	R.	H.	P.O.	A.		A.B.	R.	H.	P.O.	A.
Holmes, rf.	5	1	3	5	0	Stanky, 2b.	4	0	1	1	2
Hopp, cf.	3	0	0	2	0	Robinson, 1b.	5	0	0	6	1
Rowell, lf.	4	1	1	3	0	Reese, ss.	5	0	3	0	2
Elliott, 3b.	5	0	0	0	11	Furillo, cf.	2	0	0	2	0
Torgeson, 1b.	3	2	1	4	0	Edwards, c.	3	0	0	9	0
Masi, c.	4	0	1	6	0	Bragan, c.	0	0	0	2	0
Ryan, 2b.	4	0	0	2	2	Walker, rf.	4	0	0	1	0
Culler, ss.	4	0	2	4	2	Lund, lf.	2	0	0	6	0
Spahn, p.	2	0	0	1	1	Jorgensen, 3b.	4	0	2	0	2
						Branca, p.	2	0	0	0	0
						a Lavagetto	1	0	0	0	0
						Hatten, p.	0	0	0	0	1
						b Miksis	1	0	0	0	0
						Behrman, p.	0	0	0	0	0
Totals	34	4	8	27	16	Totals	35	0	6	27	8

a Flied out for Branca in 7th.
b Popped out for Hatten in 8th.

BOSTON (N)	0 0 0	1 2 0	1 0 0—4
BROOKLYN	0 0 0	0 0 0	0 0 0—0

Error—Rowell. Runs batted in—Culler, Masi 2. Two base hits—Reese, Torgeson, Masi. Sacrifice—Hopp. Double play—Spahn and Masi. Left on base —Boston 10, Brooklyn 12. Bases on balls—Spahn 6, Branca 5, Hatten 1. Strike-outs—Spahn 5, Branca 7, Hatten 1, Behrman 1. Hits off—Branca 8 in 7, Hatten 0 in 1, Behrman 0 in 1. Wild pitch—Spahn. Losing pitcher—Branca. Umpires —Pinelli, Robb, Gore. Time—2:35. Attendance—34,123.

Warren Spahn changed all that. His big-league career which actually started in 1947, has had very few peaks or bottoming outs. He has fanned more than 100 batters for sixteen straight seasons, a record. He pitched in 246 or more innings for sixteen straight years, another unmatched mark.

He never has started less than 32 times a season, has led the National League in complete games eight times. All in all, Spahn adds up to the highest-paid pitcher in history, a World Series performer, and a man with a bright future at the age of 42.

TRIS SPEAKER

as told to Francis J. Powers

Tristam Speaker moves in exclusive company. He's the third man in baseball's all-time, all-star outfield. Born August 4, 1888, in Hubbard City, Texas, the "Grey Eagle" was baseball's finest defensive outfielder, and only Cobb before him ever established a higher league lifetime batting average. The silver-thatched Speaker glittered for 20 years, starting with the Red Sox before moving on to Cleveland, where he managed for eight years. Tris keeps active as a tutor for the Indians during the spring training period and as a Texas oil man the year-round.

I'LL always think of the 1912 season as one of the greatest in major league history. That's natural for it was in 1912 that I first played with a pennant winner and world's championship team, and there are no greater thrills for a young player. Our Boston Red Sox, managed by Jake Stahl, a former University of Illinois star, won the American League pennant while the New York Giants were the winners on the National League side.

There were a couple of great teams. The Red Sox won 105 games that season for a league record that stood until the Yankees won 110 in 1926. And the Giants came home with

103 victories and no other National League winner since touched that total until the Cardinals won 106 in 1942. Joe Wood won 34 games for us, almost one-third of our total and 10 of them were shutouts.

Many a time I have heard "Smoke" say in our clubhouse meetings, "get me two runs today and we'll win this one." Woody won 16 in a row and beat Walter Johnson after the Big Train had won a similar string and no one has beaten those marks although they have been tied. We had Duffy Lewis and Harry Hooper in the outfield and there never were any better, Larry Gardner at third, Heinie Wagner at short and Buck O'Brien and Hugh Bedient on the pitching staff, just to mention some of our stars.

While Wood (and Johnson) made pitching history in the American League that summer Rube Marquard was writing an unequaled chapter in the National. The gangling, wry-necked left-hander won 19 straight and no one has come along to wipe out that performance. Those Giants were a hard hitting, fast running team with the likes of Josh Devore, Red Murray, Buck Herzog, Chief Meyers and Fred Merkle and had great pitchers in Christy Mathewson, Marquard, Jeff Tesreau and Red Ames.

In the opening game of the World Series Woody beat Tesreau, 4 to 3. I guess maybe John McGraw figured "Smoke" would beat any of his pitchers so he held Marquard and Mathewson back; although Tesreau was a great pitcher. The second game went 11 innings to a six-all tie with Matty pitching for the Giants and Bedient, Ray Collins and Charlie Hall, who died a few weeks ago, working for Boston. In the third game the Giants made it all even with Marquard getting a 2–1 decision over O'Brien. Then Wood and Bedient beat Tesreau and Mathewson in terrific 3–1 and 2–1 duels and we were ahead three games to one and it looked as if the series was about finished.

But the Giants weren't through by any means. In the sixth game, Marquard beat O'Brien and Collins and in the seventh, the Giants took a toe hold and pounded Wood out of the box and kept on hammering O'Brien and Collins to win 11–4. So the series went into its eighth game on October 16 and that's where I had my biggest day.

McGraw called on Christy Mathewson with the chips down and that was natural for Matty still was in his prime; his fadeaway was tough to hit and he knew every angle of the pitching business. Since Wood already had worked three games, and had been beaten the day before Stahl couldn't send him back, so he started Bedient.

The game quickly took the form of a magnificent pitcher's battle and I don't think that Matty ever was much better than that autumn afternoon. He turned us back with machinelike precision for six innings and by that time the one run the Giants had scored in the third began to look awful big. I got a double into right field in the first inning but through six innings that was about our only scoring chance. The Giants got their run when Devore walked, advanced on two outs and scored when "Red" Murray hit a long double. That the Giants weren't another run to the good in the fifth was due to one of the greatest catches I ever saw. Larry Doyle hit a terrific drive to right that appeared headed for a home run but Harry Hooper cut it off with a running, leaping catch that was easily the outstanding play of the series.

Boston tied the score in the seventh due to confusion among the Giants. Stahl hit a Texas leaguer toward left and it fell safe when Murray, Fred Snodgrass and Art Fletcher couldn't agree on who was to make the catch. Wagner walked and then Stahl sent Olaf Hendrickson up to bat for Bedient. Now Hendrickson was one of the greatest pinch hitters ever in the game; like Moose McCormick of the Giants. He was one of those rare fellows who could go up cold and hit any sort of pitching. Matty worked hard on Hendrickson but the Swede belted a long double that scored Stahl. Then Joe Wood came in to pitch for us.

The score still was one-one going into the 10th and the
Giants tried their best to put the game away in their half.
Murray doubled again and he was the tough man for us all
through the series and raced home on Merkle's single. So
there we were behind again with the last chance coming up.

Once more the breaks and big breaks went our way. Clyde
Engle batted for Woody and reached second when Snod-
grass muffed his fly in center field. Hooper flied out and
Yerkes worked Matty for a pass. And I was the next batter.

It looked as if I was out when I cut one of Matty's fade-
aways and lifted a high foul between the plate and first base.
The ball was drifting toward first and would have been an

THE BOX SCORE
(October 16, 1912)

NEW YORK	A.B.	R.	H.	P.	A.	BOSTON	A.B.	R.	H.	P.	A.
Devore, rf.	3	1	1	3	1	Hooper, rf.	5	0	0	3	0
Doyle, 2b.	5	0	0	1	5	Yerkes, 2b.	4	1	1	0	3
Snodgrass, cf.	4	0	1	4	1	Speaker, cf.	4	0	2	2	0
Murray, lf.	5	1	2	3	0	Lewis, lf.	4	0	0	1	0
Merkle, 1b.	5	0	1	10	0	Gardner, 3b.	3	0	1	1	4
Herzog, 3b.	5	0	2	2	1	Stahl, 1b.	4	1	2	15	0
Meyers, c.	3	0	0	4	1	Wagner, ss.	3	0	1	3	5
Fletcher, ss.	3	0	1	2	3	Cady, c.	4	0	0	5	3
McCormick	1	0	0	0	0	Bedient, p.	2	0	0	0	1
Mathewson, p.	4	0	1	0	3	Hendrickson	1	0	1	0	0
Shafer, ss.	0	0	0	0	0	Wood, p.	0	0	0	0	2
						Engle	1	1	0	0	0
Totals	38	2	9	*29	15	Totals	35	3	8	30	18

* Two out when winning run scored.   Hendrickson batted for Bedient in
McCormick batted for Fletcher in 9th.   7th.
Shafer went to shortstop in 10th.   Engle batted for Wood in 10th.

NEW YORK	0	0	1	0	0	0	0	0	0	1—2
BOSTON	0	0	0	0	0	0	1	0	0	2—3

Errors—Doyle, Snodgrass, Speaker, Gardner (2), Stahl, Wagner. Two-base
hits—Murray (2), Herzog, Gardner, Stahl, Hendrickson. Sacrifice hit—Meyers.
Sacrifice fly—Gardner. Stolen base—Devore. Struck out—By Mathewson, 4;
by Bedient, 2; by Wood, 2. Bases on balls—Off Mathewson, 5; off Bedient, 3;
off Wood, 1. Hits—Off Bedient, 6 in 7 innings; off Wood, 3 in 3 innings. Winning pitcher—Wood. Umpires—O'Loughlin (A. L.), Rigler (N. L.), Klem
(N. L.) and Evans (A. L.). Time—2:39. Attendance—17,034.

easy catch for Merkle. I was going to yell for Meyers to make the catch for I didn't think he could, but before I could open my mouth I heard Matty calling: "Meyers, Meyers."

Meyers chased the ball but it was going away from him and finally Merkle charged in but he was too late and couldn't hold the ball. Fred was blamed for not making the catch and the term "bonehead" was thrown at him again, recalling his failure to touch second base in 1908. I never thought Merkle deserved any blame at all. It was Matty who made the blunder in calling for Meyers to try for the catch.

That gave me a reprieve and I didn't miss the second chance. I got a good hold of a pitch for a single to right that scored Engle and the game was tied again. Then Matty walked Lewis, purposely, for Duffy always was a money hitter, filling the bases. With Gardner at bat the Giant infield played in close on the chance of cutting Yerkes off at the plate. But Gardner was another who did his best when the chips were on the table and crashed a long fly that sent Yerkes home with the deciding run.

I was in other World Series, but outside of the game between Cleveland and Brooklyn in 1920, when Bill Wambsganss made his unassisted triple play, I can't recall any when there was more drama and when there were more unusual incidents. It was a great thrill for me to manage the Cleveland Indians to the 1920 world's championship, with my mother looking on; but from strictly a playing angle, that single off Matty was my biggest moment.

CASEY STENGEL

as told to John P. Carmichael

"*Oldest man in uniform*" *is the proud boast of the septuagenarian Casey Stengel, a World Series manager whose five straight titles with the Yankees, 1949-53, should stand long after he is gone. An outfielder who never forgot anything he learned, Stengel suffered through a long managerial drought before coming to his career with the Yankees, a career which made him a national figure on and off the field. Fired by the Yankees after the 1960 season because he was "too old," Casey came back in 1962, af- ter writing his life story, to lead the New York Mets in their first year.*

Two ballplayers lolled on a bench one day in Kankakee, Ill., in 1910, watching the antics of a teammate in the outfield. The object of their gaze would haul down a fly ball, throw it into the infield, then sail his glove ahead of him on the grass, take a run and slide into the mitt. "He won't be with us long," observed one onlooker. "You mean he's going up?" asked the other. "No," replied the first, "there's an institution here to take care of guys like that . . . !"

I was only practicing three things at once (said Stengel) like running, throwing and sliding. And I fooled them, because two years later, in September, I got off a train in New York, a brand new suitcase in one hand and $95 in my pocket. The next day was my greatest in baseball. I was reporting to Brooklyn. Is that 30 years ago? I must be getting old.

The bag was Kid Eberfield's idea. He was back from the majors and playing with us at Montgomery, Ala., in the Southern League when Manager Johnny Dobbs gave me the offer to join the Dodgers. The Kid and Mrs. Eberfield came over to say good-by and good luck while I was packing. I had one of those cardboard valises . . . they'd last about 1,000 miles if you got good weather, but if you ever got caught in the rain with one, you'd suddenly find yourself walking along with just a handle in your hand.

Well, they told me I couldn't go to the big leagues with a thing like that and made me lay out $18 for a good one. I'd gone two and a half years to dental school and I was trying to save up enough tuition dough for another year. It cost about $150 plus more for instruments and I was short enough without buying a bag. "You won't come back," said Eberfield. "Never mind the money. Forget about being a dentist."

So I got to New York. It was in the evening and no use going to the park then, so I asked a cab-driver for a place to stay and he drove me to the Longacre Hotel at 47th st. I checked in and went down and sat in the lobby. I was afraid to go out, it was so dark, but finally I walked down to 46th st. and then hustled back, for fear I'd get lost. About 20 minutes later I went as far as 45th and back. I kept adding another block each trip and had been clear to 42d st. and returned by midnight when I decided to turn in. Next morning I started for the park. Brooklyn played then at the old Washington st. grounds at 5th av. and 3d and with the help of an elevated and a streetcar I made it. The gateman found out what I wanted and waved toward the clubhouse. "Go on down there," he said . . . and, as I walked away, he called after me: "You better be good."

I'll never forget walking into the locker room. There was a crap game going on in one corner. The only fellow who paid any attention to me was Zack Wheat. He introduced me around. Nobody shook hands. Some grunted. A few said hello. I walked over to the game and decided maybe I ought to get in good with the boys by participating in their sport, so I fished out $20 and asked if I could shoot. Somebody said: "Sure," and handed me the dice. I rolled 'em out. A hand reached for my 20 and a voice said: "Craps, busher," and I never even got the bones back. I was about to reach for more money when I felt a tap on my shoulder and there was Manager Bill Dahlen.

"Are you a crapshooter or a ballplayer, kid?" he asked. I told him I was a player and he said: "Well, get into a suit and on that field while you still have carfare." I hustled, believe me, and I've never touched dice since. I got to the bench and just sat there. I knew better than to pick up a bat and go to the plate. Eberfield told me what happened to rookies who tried that. Finally Dahlen came over and said: "Let's see you chase a few" and I ran like hell for the outfield. Behind the fence was a big building with fire escapes all down one side and guys in shirt sleeves were parked on the steps, passing around pails of beer and getting set for the game.

I never expected to play, but just as the umpires came out Dahlen told me to "get in center." Hub Northern, the regular center fielder, had been sick, and I guess they decided they might as well get me over with quick. My first time at bat we had a man on first and Dahlen gave me the bunt sign. The pitch wasn't good and I let it go by. Claude Hendrix, the league's leading pitcher was working for Pittsburgh and George Gibson catching. Hendrix threw another and I singled to right-center. When I got to the bench after the inning Dahlen stopped me. "Didn't you see the bunt sign?" he asked. I told him yes, but that down South we had the privilege of switching on the next pitch if we wanted to. "I don't want you to carry too much responsibility, kid," he said, "so I'll run the team and all you'll have to worry about is fielding and hitting." My ears were red when I got to center field.

Up on the fire escape the boys were having drinks on my hit and I could hear them speaking real favorably of me. I heard somebody holler and it was Wheat telling me to move back. Hans Wagner was at the plate. He larruped one and I went way back and grabbed it. In the dugout Wheat said: "Better play deeper for him." I thought of the catch I'd made and said to myself: "I can grab anything he can hit." Two innings later he came up again and Wheat waved me back, but I wouldn't go and wham! old Hans peeled one off. The ball went by me like a bee bee shot and he was roosting on third when I caught up with it.

I got three more hits right in a row. The first time Hendrix had fed me a fast ball, figuring why waste his best pitch, a spitter on a busher. He was pretty mad by the time I combed two blows off his spitter and another off his hook. Once when I was on first Dahlen gave me the steal sign and away I went. I beat Gibson's throw and Wagner just stood there, looking down at me. Never said a word. I stole two bases and when I came up the fifth time we'd knocked Hendrix out and a left-hander was pitching for the Bucs. Manager Fred Clark hollered at me: "All-right, phenom, let's see you cross over." I was feeling cocky enough to do it. . . . I stepped across the plate and stood hitting right-handed and damned if I didn't get a base on balls.

The Dodgers were playing the Cubs two days later when Stengel came to bat with nobody on. Cub Catcher Jimmy Archer looked up at him and said: "So you're the new Brooklyn star, huh? A base-stealer, too, huh? Well, I hope you get on and go down." Stengel got on and, with two out, Dahlen gave him the green light. "I was 20 feet from the bag when I saw Johnny Evers with the ball," said Casey. "I tried to slide around him, but no use. He really crowned me. As I lay there, he pulled up one pant leg. 'Oh, tryin' to spike me,' he growled, although I hadn't even touched him. 'I'll stick this ball down your throat if you ever try it again, busher!'"

Stengel's greatest day was over. His education had begun!

JOE TINKER

as told to Francis J. Powers

Joseph Bert Tinker, born July 27, 1880, in Muscotah, Kansas, was the party of the first part of baseball's most celebrated trio, "Tinker to Evers to Chance." A .300 batter but once during 15 years, Tinker's nuisance value with men on base was well-known and respected throughout the National League. A fine-fielding shortstop, Tinker managed Cincinnati and the Cubs for the last four years of his career. He died on July 2, 1948.

MY GREATEST day? You might know it was against the Giants. I think that goes for every Cub who played for "Husk" Chance in those years on Chicago's West Side. I know it did for Johnny Evers and Miner Brown and I'm sure it would for Chance if he still was alive. All of us have bright memories of World's Series against the White Sox and Tigers and Athletics.

But the games you play over and over, even after more than 30 years, were against the Giants and John McGraw. Chance and McGraw were born to battle on baseball fields.

If you didn't honestly and furiously hate the Giants, you weren't a real Cub.

I was in the famous game when Fred Merkle failed to touch second and then the playoff for the 1908 pennant when Chance and McGraw never were far from blows. I was in the lineup when we beat the Tigers in eight out of ten games in two World's Series.

But the game which gave me the greatest thrill was on Aug. 7, 1911. That was the one in which I made four hits and stole home on Christy Mathewson which is something a man tells his grandchildren or writes down in a book.

The Cubs, with four pennants and two world's championships in five seasons still were on top of the National League on that August day but closer to a complete collapse than any of us knew. The old lineup was breaking, Young Vic Saier had taken "Husk's" job at first; Heinie Zimmerman was on third in place of Harry Steinfeldt and Jimmy Archer had replaced Johnny Kling back of the plate.

I guess my memory of the game is made keener by the fact that two days before I'd had a terrific argument with Chance and had been suspended. On Saturday—that'd be Aug. 5 —we were playing Brooklyn and out in front 2–1 in the third. There was a strong wind blowing to left field and two were out and two on. The Dodger batter pumped one over my head. I went back and yelled to Jimmy Sheckard I'd take it. Well the wind blew the ball out and it dropped safe and two Dodgers scored.

By the seventh we were ahead again, 4–3, and once more the Dodgers had two on and two out. At that time the wind had changed and was coming in from left field. When the batter popped another one over my head. Sheck started in and I didn't move. The wind drove the ball back toward the infield but I thought Jimmy would get it and let it alone. Jimmy couldn't reach the ball and two more runs scored.

When I got back to the bench, Frank, his face red with

fury, snarled: "I'm damn sick and tired of you letting those flies drop."

I was just as mad because the Dodgers had scored, so I screamed right back, "I'm damn sick and tired of you yelling at me."

"Husk" told me to turn in my uniform and fined me $150.

Well, there was no game on Sunday and Charlie Murphy, he owned the Cubs, sent for me to come to his office. He said he wanted Frank and me to straighten things out and I said it would be all right with me.

Now Monday also was an open day but the Giants were coming through and McGraw had agreed to stop off and play a postponed game. So "Husk" agreed to reinstate me for that game. Chance was a great guy and a square manager. And smart.

Only two games out of first place and going into August the game looked like the spot for New York to pick up some ground. And McGraw had Matty ready to pitch. Chance countered with Brown, who always gave Matty a battle.

There was a good crowd at the old West Side Park to see Matty and Brownie. The game was in an uproar before it was one minute old. Brownie hit Josh Devore in the head with his first pitch and they had to carry the Giant left-fielder off the diamond.

McGraw sent Red Murray in to run for Devore and Brownie was nervous. He passed Larry Doyle, and Fred Snodgrass singled to fill the bases. It looked for a minute as if Brownie wasn't going to last. Then Sheck took Beals Becker's low liner so fast that Murray had to stay on third. Merkle slammed one hard at me and I could have forced Murray at the plate but I tossed the ball to Zim and he whipped it to Saier, and Snodgrass and Merkle were out by a mile.

Sheckard opened our half with a triple on Matty's first pitch. And then Matty guessed wrong when Schulte's bunt didn't roll foul. Archer hit to Matty, and Sheck was run

down but Schulte went all the way to third and then was
nailed at the plate, trying to score on Zim's roller. You ran
the bases and took the chances for Chance. Zim and Archer
tried a double steal but Meyers broke it up easily and we were
all square.

I was up second in the next inning and hit a single to left
and when Murray decided he'd throw to first, I went into
second and scored on Saier's double to put us one run ahead.

We got all tangled up in the fourth when the Giants tied
the score. Schulte fumbled Becker's liner and Beals went clear
to third and scored on Herzog's single. Then Brownie threw
over first and Buck reached second and we were shaky again.
But Meyers hit to me and I started a double play with young
Jack Doyle, who was subbing for Evers, on the pivot and we
got clear.

Then we got two runs in the fourth, but I forget the details,
for the big moments of my greatest day were coming.

THE BOX SCORE
(*August 7, 1911*)

CUBS	A.B.	R.	H.	P.	A.	GIANTS	A.B.	R.	H.	P.	A.
Sheckard, lf.	5	0	1	3	0	Devore, lf.	0	0	0	0	0
Schulte, rf.	4	0	1	3	0	Murray, lf.-rf.	4	1	1	2	0
Archer, c.	3	1	0	4	0	L. Doyle, 2b.	4	0	2	2	2
Zimmerman, 3b.	4	3	2	1	7	Snodgrass, cf.	5	2	3	2	0
J. Doyle, 2b.	3	1	0	1	2	Becker, rf.-lf.	4	2	2	1	0
Tinker, ss.	4	3	4	3	6	Merkle, 1b.	5	0	1	10	0
Saier, 1b.	4	0	1	12	0	Herzog, 3b.	5	0	2	1	2
Hoffman, cf.	4	0	1	0	0	Fletcher, ss.	4	1	2	0	4
Brown, p.	4	0	0	0	1	Meyers, c.	3	0	1	6	2
						Mathewson, p.	4	0	0	0	7
Totals	35	8	10	27	16	Totals	38	6	14	24	17

NEW YORK	0 0 0 1 0 0 1 2 2—6
CHICAGO	0 1 0 2 0 2 0 3 *—8

Errors—Schulte, Brown, Murray, Merkle, Fletcher. Two-base hits—Saier,
Tinker, Becker. Three-base hits—Sheckard, Zimmerman, Tinker, Murray.
Sacrifice hits—J. Doyle. Stolen bases—Tinker. Double plays—Tinker to Zim-
merman to Saier; Zimmerman to Tinker to Saier. Struck out—By Brown, 2;
Mathewson, 3. Base on balls—Off Brown, 3; Mathewson, 1. Hit by pitched ball
—By Brown (Devore).

In the sixth I hit off the left-field fence for a triple. It might have been a homer inside the park except that Zim got a slow start off first and I had to pull up at third. I guess maybe Matty thought I was winded and would rest awhile. But I broke on his next pitch and scored standing up.

Honestly, I believe that was one of the worst games Matty ever pitched. In the eighth, when Jack Doyle sacrificed Zim to third, Matty scooped the ball with his bare hand and when Bob Emslie called Heinie safe, Christy was so mad he almost stopped the game.

When I came up, Matty threw me one of those low, outside curves that almost sent me back to Kansas City before Frank made me change my batting style. I hit it for a long double to score Zim and Archer and that was the ball game. We won 8–6 and made 14 hits off Big Six.

And when we got back into the clubhouse, Chance came over to me with a big grin and said: "Damn it, I ought to suspend you every day."

JOHNNY VANDER MEER

as told to Gabriel Paul

John Samuel Vander Meer, born November 2, 1914, in Paterson, New Jersey, accomplished a feat unlikely to be repeated in big league baseball—he pitched two successive no-hit, no-run games for Cincinnati in 1938. Never more than a journeyman pitcher because of poor control and arm ailments, Vandy's achievement will stand as the game's most dramatic feat. Vander Meer was traded to the Cubs in 1950 after serving 11 years with the Reds. He has managed for a decade in the minors.

IT WOULD seem natural for me to name the second successive no-hitter I pitched in 1938 as my biggest day in baseball, and I'll have to explain why it isn't.

Those games were as much a surprise to me as to the baseball world. I wasn't keyed up to their meaning then. Before the no-hitter against Boston on June 11 that year I was just a rookie that nobody but Bill McKechnie knew, and after the June 15 repeat of the performance against Brooklyn I was still just a novelty, a kid who had done a freakish thing.

To understand my feelings at the time you've got to understand that I came up to the Reds that year after an unsuccessful season at Syracuse in the International League. I had won only five and lost eleven for the Chiefs. Nobody thought I was good but Bill McKechnie, manager of the Reds, who told me, when I arrived at spring training in Florida, that he was counting on me to be a regular. He said he believed I could make it.

He gave me hope, and then on the way north that spring in an exhibition series with the Boston Red Sox Lefty Grove gave me some tips on what I was doing wrong. I'll never be able to thank Lefty for his friendliness and smartness in putting his finger on my errors. McKechnie kept giving me great advice, too, all spring.

I'll never forget the day that spring we were at Lynchburg, Va. I was pitching batting practice and after a little while McKechnie, on the bench, began to yell: "He's got it! He's got it! That boy is going to make it!"

That helped more than I can say, and I got off to a pretty good start in the season, pitching a shutout against the Giants at the Polo Grounds on May 20. I had my confidence. I felt I could do it. Then, all at once, came those consecutive no-hitters.

But they came too fast. I was more confused than thrilled. All the publicity, the attention, the interviews, the photographs, were too much for me. They swept me off my feet too far to let me have time to think about the games themselves. There were too many people around me.

As I look back at it now those days are the haziest period of my life—sort of like a dream.

I might have been dreaming then, but I awoke the next season, 1939, when I won five and lost nine. I was sick that spring and never did seem to regain my stride. My confidence went, too. I wasn't much better in the spring of 1940. Bill McKechnie and Warren Giles talked to me about going to Indianapolis of the American Association to regain my confidence. I thought it was a swell idea. I knew that was what I needed. At the same time it made me realize just how quickly a fellow can fall from the pedestal.

My going to Indianapolis was the best thing that ever happened to me. I got off on the right foot there, won six and lost four, had an earned-run average of 2.40 and struck out 109 in 105 innings. That satisfied Giles and McKechnie, for they brought me back for the last stages of the 1940 pennant race.

The Reds were in first place. They were on their way to the pennant, but they hadn't clinched it. I was given an opportunity to start a game and won it. Then we went to Philadelphia September 17, needing only two victories to clinch the pennant. We won on the 17th, then McKechnie gave me another chance to work, on September 18—the day that is my biggest.

I was up against Hugh Mulcahy, one of the smartest and most determined of pitchers and awfully tough when he was in form. We saw right off that he was in form when the game started. Joe Marty, whom the Phils had got from the Cubs, was on a rampage that day, too, getting three hits. And Mulcahy was leveling off with his bat, as well as with his arm. We could get hits, but we couldn't get runs. Mulcahy would turn us back.

The Phils got me for two runs in the second inning, and it was the fifth before we got one run. I began to wonder if I was going to let the team down on the one game it needed to clinch the flag. It was life-and-death in my mind. I had to hang on to my "comeback." I had to win.

We finally tied it in the seventh 2–2, but in the 10th we got one to give us what we thought was the game, but the Phils in their half got one off me to even it up again. It was true I had blanked them the seven innings between the second and the 10th, and the team was all the time telling me how good I was going, but there it was, we'd been ahead and I'd let the Phils tie us.

Was I really a comeback or not? Could I clinch the flag or couldn't I?

I gave everything I had straight through the 11th and 12th innings and blanked them. But we didn't score either and the scoreboard still showed 3–3.

I was up in the 13th at bat and I figured now was the time. All of Mulcahy's pitches were good, but I kept swinging and somehow all at once whistled one into left center and ran faster than I ever had before, I suppose. I got to second. They sacrificed me to third. Then Mike McCormick hit an infield ball and I was held at third, too risky to chance a run in. Mike beat it out.

Ival Goodman was up. Twice he cracked the ball and I tore for home, only to be called back because the drive went foul. Then he got one fair, a short fly to the outfield and I tagged up and when McKechnie on the coasting line said, "Run, Johnny, run!" to give me the exact moment the ball settled into the fielder's glove, I sure ran. I took off in the hardest slide I ever made and looked up through the dust. The umpire was motioning "safe."

We were ahead.

McKechnie, cool always, looked at me and figured how much running I'd done that inning, and told me to sit it out, he'd send in Joe Beggs to pitch the last half. Joe got them 1-2-3 and the flag was ours.

HANS WAGNER

as told to Chet Smith

John Peter Wagner, the "Peerless Dutchman," was the first "great" in the National League. Born February 24, 1874, in Carnegie, Pennsylvania, Wagner was a huge, barrel-chested man with long arms and ham-like hands who was flushed out of a Pennsylvania coal mine to achieve an outstanding career as a superlative all-round player. Beginning with Louisville, Honus moved over to Pittsburgh where he played every position but catcher. During 21 years Wagner batted better than .300 in 17 seasons. Hans coached for the Pirates before illness forced him to retire. He died in 1955.

WHEN a fellow has played 2,785 games over a span of 21 years it's not the easiest thing in the world to pick out a single contest and say it was his best or that it gave him his biggest thrill. But I was never sharper than in the last game of the World Series our Pirates played with the Detroit Tigers of 1909, and I never walked off any field feeling happier.

It was the afternoon of October 16 and not only a big day for me but for all the sport fans, for on that same afternoon

Big Jack Johnson, heavyweight prize-fight champion, knocked out Stanley Ketchel in the 12th round of their battle in San Francisco to retain his crown.

I regard that final game with the Bengals as tops because it meant the end of a grand fight against a bunch of real fighters. I'm still willing to testify that the club of Hughie Jennings and Ty Cobb, of "Wahoo Sam" Crawford and Donie Bush, of Davy Jones and George Moriarity, was a holy terror. And it tickles my vanity to think the Pirates outbattled and defeated them.

Cobb stole two bases in the series, but I was lucky and got six. Cobb made six hits, I made eight.

Ask Ty what happened the day he stood on first and yelled at me, "Hey, Kraut Head, I'm comin' down on the next pitch." I told him to come ahead, and by golly, he did. But George Gibson, our catcher, laid the ball perfect, right in my glove and I stuck it on Ty as he came in. I guess I wasn't too easy about it, 'cause it took three stitches to sew up his lip. That was the kind of a series it was from start to finish. Fred Clarke, our manager, told us we'd better sharpen our spikes since the Tigers would be sure to, and we took him at his word. We were sorta rough, too, I guess.

Cobb surprised the Pirates by playing an unusually clean series, but some of the others weren't so careful.

The trouble started in the first game. Both sides had their jockeys warmed up. The Tigers let us have it and we gave it back to 'em with interest. There was a jawing match on nearly every pitch, and it was a good thing we had two of the greatest umpires who ever worked—Bill Klem and "Silk" O'Loughlin. They were young fellows then, but they knew their business and kept us in line. At least there weren't any riots.

In that first game, Fred Clarke hit a home run off Big George Mullin, who was Detroit's best pitcher that year. I followed Clarke at the plate, and I could see that Mullin was boiling, and anxious to get back at us. I always stood pretty far away from the plate, but this time took every inch I could, figuring Mullin would throw at me. I wasn't wrong. He laid his fast ball right in my ribs. Of course, you can't say a thing like that is deliberate, but our boys reckoned it was, and from that minute the rough-housing was on.

We came into the final game tied up at three apiece. It was played in Detroit, and the night before, the Tiger rooters hired two or three bands to play in front of our hotel and keep us awake, but Clarke fooled 'em by taking us all out to a tavern along the lake shore.

We knew our pitcher was going to be Babe Adams, the kid who had won two of our three victories. Babe was hardly old enough to shave, but Clarke had a hunch on him all along. I'll never forget the look on Adams' face when I told him Clarke wanted him to pitch the opener. He asked me if I wasn't fooling and I told him I wasn't and he hadn't better fool, either, when he got on the mound. What a job he did for us.

I guess I don't have to tell you what the feeling was that last day. "Wild Bill" Donovan, who started for the Tigers, lived up to his name and we got two runs off him in the second. Mullin came in to pitch in the fourth and couldn't find the plate, either. There were two walks and two singles, giving us two more. In the sixth I got my only hit, but it was a three-bagger that drove in Clarke and Tommy Leach, and I kept coming and crossed the plate when Davey Jones made a bad throw from the outfield. We certainly didn't need the run we picked up in the seventh, but it made us eight, and with Adams pitching perfect ball that was the score 8 to 0. But it's far from being the whole story.

On my hit Jones kicked the ball into the overflow crowd, trying to hold it to a double under the ground rules, but O'Loughlin saw him and wouldn't allow it. Another time there was a close play at first and the Tiger runner hit Bill Abstein, our first baseman, in the stomach with his fist. Abstein folded up and Ham Hyatt had to take his place.

THE BOX SCORE
(October 16, 1909)

PITTSBURGH	R.	H.	P.	A.	DETROIT	R.	H.	P.	A.
Byrne, 3b.	0	0	0	0	D. Jones, lf.	0	1	3	0
Hyatt, cf.	1	0	0	0	Bush, ss.	0	0	3	5
Leach, cf.-3b.	2	2	4	2	Cobb, rf.	0	0	1	0
Clarke, lf.	2	0	5	0	Moriarity, 3b.	0	1	1	0
Wagner, ss.	1	1	3	3	O'Leary, 3b.	0	0	1	1
Miller, 2b.	0	3	3	0	Delehanty, 2b.	0	2	2	3
Abstein, 1b.	1	1	10	0	Crawford, cf.	0	0	4	0
Wilson, rf.	1	0	0	0	T. Jones, 1b.	0	1	9	0
Gibson, c.	0	2	2	1	Schmidt, c.	0	1	3	1
Adams, p.	0	0	0	4	Donovan, p.	0	0	0	1
					Mullin, p.	0	0	0	2
Totals	8	9	27	10	Totals	0	6	27	13

PITTSBURGH	0 2 0 2 0 3 0 1 0—8
DETROIT	0 0 0 0 0 0 0 0 0—0

Error—D. Jones. Hits—Off Donovan, 2 in 3 innings. Three-base hit—Wagner. Two-base hits—Moriarity, Abstein, Leach, Gibson, Schmidt, Miller, Delehanty. Sacrifice hits—Leach. Stolen Bases—Clarke (2), Abstein, Miller. Hit by pitched ball—Byrne, Bush. Struck out—By Adams 1, Mullin 1. Base on balls—Off Adams 1, Donovan 6, Mullin 4. Double play—Bush to Schmidt to Bush. Umpires—O'Loughlin and Klem.

Another Tiger slid into second and cut Jack Miller on the head and leg. Bobby Byrne, our third baseman, banged into Moriarity so hard that Bobby had to leave the field with a broken ankle, and George, who concealed his injury until the next inning, went to the doctor to have 11 stitches put in his knee. Talk about "bean balls"—they were flying around everybody's head all afternoon.

ED WALSH

as told to Francis J. Powers

Only one twentieth century pitcher before him ever won more games in one season than Edward Arthur "Big Ed" Walsh. But you can't ignore a guy who racked up a total of 40 wins, and with a club that was known as the "Hitless Wonders," the Chicago White Sox of 1907. Born May 19, 1882, in Plains, Pennsylvania, Walsh was blessed with great strength and endurance, a blazing fast ball and uncanny control of an almost unhittable spitter. Coming into the big leagues in 1904, Walsh was the ace of the Chicago staff for 13 years, and won two games in the 1906 world series for the Pale Hose against the Chicago Cubs. He died in 1959.

DID you ever see Larry Lajoie bat? No. Then you missed something. I want to tell you that there was one of the greatest hitters—and fielders, too—ever in baseball. There's no telling the records he'd made if he'd hit against the lively ball. To tell you about my greatest day, I'll have to go back there to October, 1908, when I fanned Larry with the bases full and the White Sox chances for the pennant hanging on every pitch to the big Frenchman.

That was October 3, and the day after I had that great game with Addie Joss and he beat me 1 to 0 with a perfect game; no run—no hits—no man reached first. There was a great pitcher and a grand fellow, Addie. One of my closest friends and he'd been one of the best of all time only for his untimely death two years later. That game was a surprise to both of us for we were sitting on a tarpaulin talking about having some singing in the hotel that night, when Lajoie, who managed Cleveland, and Fielder Jones told us to warm up. A pitcher never knew when he'd work in those days.

I don't think there'll ever be another pennant race like there was in the American League that year. All summer four teams, the Sox, Cleveland, Detroit, and St. Louis, had been fighting and three of 'em still had a chance on this day. When Joss beat me the day before it left us two and one-half games behind the Tigers and two behind the Naps (as Cleveland was called in honor of Lajoie). We had only four games left to play.

It was a Saturday and the biggest crowd ever to see a game in Cleveland up to that date jammed around the park. Jones started Frank Smith for us and we got him three runs off Glenn Liebhardt and were leading by two going into the seventh. I was in the bull pen, ready for anything because, as I said, we had to win this one.

As I recall it George Perring, the shortstop, was first up for Cleveland and he went all the way to second when Patsy Dougherty muffed his fly in the sun. I began to warm up in a hurry. Nig Clarke batted for Liebhardt and fanned and things looked better. Smith would have been out of trouble only Tannehill fumbled Josh Clarke's grounder and couldn't make a play. Clarke stole second and that upset Smith and he walked Bill Bradley. I rushed to the box and the first batter I faced was Bill Hinchman. Bill wasn't a champion hitter but he was a tough man in a pinch. I knew his weakness was a spit ball on the inside corner so I told Sully (Billy Sullivan) we'd have to get in close on him. I did. My spitter nearly always broke down and I could put it about where I wanted. Bill got a piece of the ball and hit a fast grounder that Tannehill fielded with one hand and we forced Perring at the plate.

So, there were two out and Larry at bat. Now if the Frenchman had a weakness it was a fast ball, high and right through the middle. If you pitched inside to him, he'd tear a hand off the third baseman and if you pitched outside he'd knock down the second baseman. I tried him with a spit ball that broke to the inside and down. You know a spit ball was heavy and traveled fast. Lajoie hit the pitch hard down the third base line and it traveled so fast that it curved 20 feet, I'd guess, over the foul line and into the bleachers. There was strike one.

My next pitch was a spitter on the outside and Larry swung and tipped it foul back to the stands. Sully signed for another spitter but I just stared at him; I never shook him off with a nod or anything like that. He signed for the spitter twice more but still I just looked at him. Then Billy walked out to the box. "What's the matter?" Bill asked me. "I'll give him a fast one," I said, but Billy was dubious. Finally, he agreed. I threw Larry an overhand fast ball that raised and he watched it come over without ever an offer. "Strike three!" roared Silk O'Loughlin. Lajoie sort of grinned at me and tossed his bat toward the bench without ever a word. That was the high spot of my baseball days, fanning Larry in the clutch and without him swinging.

Well, we came home to finish out the season with three games against the Tigers. We still were in the race but we needed three straight for the flag. We got the first two. In the opener, Doc White beat the Tigers 3–1 and held Cobb and Claude Rossman hitless. I pitched the second and beat 'em 6–1 and allowed only four hits and that was my 65th game and 40th win of the season. And that left us a half game out of first and Cleveland was out of the race when it dropped the first game of a double-header to the Browns.

That brought it down to the final day of the season. We heard that Hughie Jennings and Harry Tuthill (Detroit trainer) had sat up to 4 o'clock in the morning putting hot towels on Bill Donovan's arm, trying to get it in shape to pitch. At game time we weren't sure Bill would pitch for he was visiting under the stands with Joe Farrell when Jennings came by and told him to warm up.

Most of us thought Jones would start Smith against the Tigers for he really had them handcuffed and always could be expected to pitch his best against them. We were startled rather than surprised when Jones said "Doc" White would pitch.

When Jones came in, I asked: "Are you going to pitch Doc?" He said "yes." Then I said, "That's a great injustice to a fine young man. You know White needs his full rest to be effective. I'll pitch if you want me to (I'd pitched in 65 games, my arm felt great and another game wouldn't hurt me). The man you should pitch is Smith . . . but you're mad at him."

I couldn't argue Jones out of starting White and "Doc" didn't last long. I'll never forget that first inning. Matty McIntyre singled. Donie Bush was hit by a pitched ball but the umpires wouldn't let him take first because he hadn't tried to duck the pitch. Then Donie fanned. There was a crowd around in the outfield and Sam Crawford hit a terrific drive into the fans for two bases. And then Cobb—Cobb the man who never could hit White—tripled, cleaning the bases.

I got down to the bull pen in time to get warmed up a bit and after Cobb's hit, Jones sent me to the box. The Tigers scored two more before I could stop them and then I pitched through the fifth. Then when I came to the bench, I threw my glove in the corner. "What's the matter with you?" Jones asked. "I'm through," I said. "Now you'll have to pitch Smith, the man who should have started." Smith finished but

THE BOX SCORE
(October 8, 1908)

CHICAGO	R.	H.	P.	A.	CLEVELAND	R.	H.	P.	A.
Hahn, rf.	0	1	0	0	J. Clarke, rf.	0	0	1	0
Jones, cf.	0	0	1	0	Bradley, 3b.	0	0	1	0
Isbell, 1b.	1	2	11	1	Hinchman, lf.	0	1	2	0
Dougherty, lf.	0	0	0	0	Lajoie, 2b.	1	2	1	0
Davis, 2b.	1	1	3	2	Stovall, 1b.	1	2	8	1
Parent, ss.	0	1	4	4	Bemis, c.	0	1	8	1
Sullivan, c.	1	2	8	4	Birmingham, cf.	0	1	2	0
Tannehill, 3b.	0	1	0	4	Perring, ss.	0	1	3	5
Smith, p.	0	0	0	1	Liebhardt, p.	0	0	1	2
Walsh, p.	0	0	0	0	Rhoades, p.	0	0	0	2
					N. Clarke	0	0	0	0
Totals	3	8	27	16	Totals	2	8	27	11

N. Clarke batted for Liebhardt in 7th.

```
CHICAGO      0 2 0 0 0 1 0 0 0—3
CLEVELAND    0 1 0 0 0 0 0 1 0—2
```

Errors—Dougherty, Tannehill (2), Bemis. Stolen bases—Davis, Sullivan (2), Perring, Bemis, J. Clarke. Two-base hits—Lajoie (2), Parent, Stovall. Sacrifice hits—Stovall, Liebhardt. Double play—Perring to Stovall. Hits—Off Liebhardt, 6 in 5 innings; off Rhoades, 2 in 2 innings; off Smith, 6 in 6 1-3 innings; off Walsh, 2 in 2 2-3 innings. Struck out—By Smith 4 (Bradley, Hinchman, Stovall, N. Clarke); Walsh 4 (Lajoie, Perring, Rhoades, J. Clarke); Liebhardt 6 (C. Hahn, Davis 2, Parent 2, Smith); Rhoades 2 (Jones, Tannehill). Bases on balls —Off Smith 3, Liebhardt 3. Wild pitch—Liebhardt.

the Tigers beat us 7–0 and there went the pennant. Donovan allowed only two hits and fanned nine and we dropped to third place when the Naps won from St. Louis.

I like to think back to the White Sox of those days. In 1906, we won the pennant and beat the Cubs in the World Series. Next season we were in the pennant race until the last days of September and in 1908 we fought them down to the final day of the season. There never was a fielding first base- man like Jiggs Donahue in 1908 when he set a record for assists. Sullivan was a great catcher, one of the greatest. It was a great team, a smart team. But the tops of all days was when I fanned Lajoie with the bases filled. Not many pitchers ever did that.

TED WILLIAMS

as told to Gerry Moore

Third among the all-time homer stars with a mark of 521, Ted Williams brought his distinguished career to an end after the 1960 campaign. He hung up a lifetime mark of .344, batting in a park which scarcely favored his left-handed stance. He was the last major leaguer to bat .400 (.406 in 1941).

Williams served with distinction in both World War II and the Korean War as a Marine flier. He was a controversial figure on and off the field and was always a dynamic lure at the box office.

He still retains his connection with the game as a talent

scout for the Boston Red Sox, the only team he played for during his career.

I GUESS I've had more than my share of thrills from baseball, but the greatest game in my own book still stands as the one played on Friday the 13th of September in 1946 at League Park in Cleveland.

That was the day I hit my first inside-the-park homer.

That unusual sock for the circuit in the very first inning provided the run that Tex Hughson preserved for a 1–0 victory and the first pennant in 28 years for our Red Sox.

It took some soul-searching on my part to place that incident above the many other great days I've enjoyed during my eight active years in the best game of them all.

Who could forget his first grand slammer? That happened to me on August 19, 1939 in Washington when I clipped Pete Appleton with the bases loaded. The best part of that was it helped us win an 8–6 decision from the Nats.

Then there was the All-Star Game in Detroit in 1941 when I bashed a homer against the top deck in Briggs Stadium with two out and two aboard in the ninth inning off Claude Passeau to give our American Leaguers a 7–5 win for the annual inter-league classic.

For a kid of twenty-two in those days, it was like a dream to be carried off the field on the shoulders of Joe DiMaggio, who had just crossed the plate ahead of me, and Bobby Feller, who was already in civilians after having finished his early three-inning pitching stint. My boyhood idols like Jimmy Foxx and Joe Cronin were mussing up my hair and tearing off my cap all during my free ride to the clubhouse that day.

All those things almost made me forget the record homer I had hit over the whole right field stands in the same Briggs Stadium two years earlier.

Along came the final day of that same 1941 season and we were playing in Philadelphia. After batting above .400 for most of the campaign, I had been whiffed three times on Saturday at Shibe Park by that old knuckle-baller, Roger Wolff, and had fallen just below the .400 mark.

I needed plenty of hits during Sunday's double-header to be sure to finish above that magic figure. I want to take the opportunity right now to thank Mr. Mack for instructing his pitchers on that occasion to pitch to me unless baseball strategy demanded otherwise.

I wound up with "six for eight" during that big twin bill

and a .406 figure for the season to become the first major leaguer to join the Four Hundred Club since Bill Terry belted .401 for the Giants back in 1930.

Next, my mind flashed back to the All-Star Game in 1946 at our own Fenway Park when we American Leaguers mauled our old rivals by a 12–0 count. Nobody could ask for a better day than I experienced before most of my home folks when I singled first time up, homered into the center field seats off Kirby Higbe next, lined a single into right, then another off Phil Cavarretta's shins and wound up the day by smacking Rip Sewell's famous "blooper ball" into the right field seats for another fourmaster.

Four hits, including two homers, in four official times at bat, four runs and five RBI's certainly represented a full afternoon.

However, only five days later was started the chain of circumstances that finally led me to choose Friday the 13th of September later the same big year as the red letter date on my personal baseball calendar.

In the first game of a double-header on Sunday, July 14th, at the same Fenway Park against the Indians, I connected for three homers in a single game for the first time in my career and batted across eight runs, which still stands as a RBI record for myself.

The third of my homers, which were my 24th, 25th and 26th of that season, provided the winning run for us of an 11–10 slugfest that was otherwise memorable because Lou Boudreau belted four doubles as well as a homer himself.

When I came up for the second time in the second game, which we also won, 6 to 4, Lou introduced the famous shift with which other teams have been trying to plague me ever since.

I managed to get a two-bagger in two official trips while facing the Boudreau shift for the first time, but I really caught up with it on that sweetest of Friday the 13ths in September.

Red Embree was the pitcher that famous day in League Park and I'll have to let eye-witnesses tell you how the Indians were placed the first time I came to bat. Three infielders were to the right of second base. Third Baseman Don Ross was almost on top of the middle bag. Center Fielder Felix Mackiewicz was on the right field side of center. Left Fielder Pat Seerey was almost behind third base, about 20 feet back on the grass and some 15 feet from the foul line.

I lost no time exploring the yawning left-center pasture. I lined Embree's first fat one in that direction and took off around the bases. People later told me that I was almost to third when Mackiewicz retrieved the ball from a gutter in front of the center field bleachers, more than 400 feet from the plate.

I wasn't looking because my heart was in my legs that day. I was thinking about all the years that Tom Yawkey and Joe Cronin had been trying to give Boston a pennant. There were plenty of us players who were getting tired of finishing second, too.

THE BOX SCORE

BOSTON (A)   CLEVELAND

(September 13, 1946)

	A.B.	R.	H.	P.O.	A.		A.B.	R.	H.	P.O.	A.
DiMaggio, cf.	3	0	0	1	0	Mackiewicz, cf.	3	0	0	4	0
Pesky, ss.	3	0	1	2	5	Ross, 3b.	4	0	0	1	2
Williams, lf.	3	1	1	1	0	Seerey, lf.	3	0	1	1	0
Doerr, 2b.	4	0	0	2	4	Edwards, rf.	4	0	0	3	0
York, 1b.	3	0	0	11	1	Fleming, 1b.	4	0	0	8	3
McBride, rf.	4	0	0	6	0	Boudreau, ss.	3	0	0	0	2
H. Wagner, c.	4	0	0	4	0	Mack, 2b.	3	0	1	3	1
Gutteridge, 3b.	2	0	0	0	0	Hegan, c.	3	0	0	6	0
Hughson, p.	3	0	0	0	3	Embree, p.	2	0	1	1	3
Totals	29	1	2	27	13	Totals	29	0	3	27	11

BOSTON (A)   1 0 0 0 0 0 0 0 0—1
CLEVELAND   0 0 0 0 0 0 0 0 0—0

Error—Embree. Run batted in—Williams. Two base hit—Mack. Home run —Williams. Sacrifices—Gutteridge, Mackiewicz. Left on base—Boston 6, Cleveland 5. Bases on balls—Embree 4, Hughson 2. Strikeouts—Hughson 4, Embree 3. Umpires—Grieve, Paparella and Hubbard. Time—1:28. Attendance—3,295.

I finally slid across the plate even though I guess I really didn't need to. I also later learned that Lou Boudreau's relay bounced away from the dish down the third base line and Catcher Jim Hegan had to step down and reach for the ball as I slid across.

After that big game when everybody was celebrating, a writer walked up to me and said: "I guess that's the easiest home run you ever hit, Ted."

Like fun, I said, it was the hardest.

My friend asked me why.

"Because I had to run for it," was my answer.

Run or not, it still stands as the greatest game I ever played in my own mind and probably will remain that way until maybe I can do something big to help the Red Sox win a World Series.

CY YOUNG

as told to Francis J. Powers

There's just no competition, Denton True "Cy" Young is too far ahead! Born March 29, 1867, in Gilmore, Ohio, Cy pitched 22 years for five clubs in both majors and hung up more victories, 511, and pitched more games, 906, than any pitcher in history. He tossed three no-hitters, just about par for the course. Young died in 1955.

A PITCHER's got to be good and he's got to be lucky to get a no-hit game. But to get a perfect game, no run, no hit, no man reach first base, he's got to have everything his way. There have been only seven perfect games pitched in the big leagues since 1880.

I certainly had my share of luck in the 23 years I pitched in the two big leagues because I threw three no-hitters and one of them was perfect. You look at the records and you'll find that Larry Corcoran, who pitched for the Chicago Nationals "away back when," was the only other big leaguer ever to get three no-hitters and none of them was perfect.

So it's no job for me to pick out my greatest day in baseball. It was May 5, 1904, when I was pitching for the Boston Red Sox and beat the Philadelphia Athletics without a run, hit or man reaching first. I'll be 78 next month, but of all the 879 games I pitched in the big leagues that one stands clearest in my mind.

The American League was pretty young then, just four seasons old, but it had a lot of good players and good teams. I was with St. Louis in the National when Ban Johnson organized the American League and I was one of the many players who jumped to the new circuit.

Jimmy Collins, whom I regard as the greatest of all third basemen, was the first manager of the Boston team and in 1903 we won the pennant and beat Pittsburgh in the first modern world's series.

Before I get into the details of my greatest day, I'd like to tell something about our Red Sox of those days. We had a great team. Besides Collins at third we had Freddie Parent at short, Hobe Ferris at second and Candy La Chance on first. You find some real old-timer and he'll tell you how great those fellows were.

In the outfield were Buck Freeman, who was the Babe Ruth of that time, Patsy Dougherty, who later played with the White Sox and Chick Stahl. Bill Dineen was one of our other pitchers and he'd licked the Pirates three games in the world's series the fall before.

Every great pitcher usually has a great catcher, like Mathewson had Roger Bresnahan and Miner Brown had Johnny Kling. Well, in my time I had two. First, "Chief" Zimmer, when I was with Cleveland in the National League, and then Lou Criger, who caught me at Boston and handled my perfect game.

As I said, my greatest game was against the Athletics, who were building up to win the 1905 pennant, and Rube Waddell was their pitcher. And I'd like to say that beating Rube anytime was a big job. I never saw many who were better pitchers.

I was real fast in those days but what very few batters knew was that I had two curves. One of them sailed in there as hard as my fast ball and broke in reverse. It was a narrow curve that broke away from the batter and went in just like a fast ball. And the other was a wide break. I never said much about them until after I was through with the game.

There was a big crowd for those times out that day. Maybe 10,000, I guess, for Waddell always was a big attraction.

I don't think I ever had more stuff and I fanned eight, getting Davis and Monte Cross, Philly shortstop, twice. But the boys gave me some great support and when I tell you about it, you'll understand why I say a pitcher's got to be awfully lucky to get a perfect game.

The closest the Athletics came to a hit was in the third when Monte Cross hit a pop fly that was dropping just back of the infield between first and second. Freeman came tearing in from right like a deer and barely caught the ball.

But Ollie Pickering, who played center field for Mr. Mack, gave me two bad scares. Once he hit a fly back of second that Chick Stahl caught around his knees after a long run from center. The other time Ollie hit a slow roller to short and Parent just got him by a step.

Patsy Dougherty helped me out in the seventh when he crashed into the left field fence to get Danny Hoffman's long foul; and I recall that Criger almost went into the Boston bench to get a foul by Davis.

Most of the other batters were pretty easy but all told there were 10 flies hit, six to the outfield. The infielders had seven assists and I had two and 18 of the putouts were divided evenly between Criger and La Chance.

Well, sir, when I had two out in the ninth, and it was Waddell's time to bat, some of the fans began to yell for Connie Mack to send up a pinch hitter. They wanted me to finish what looked like a perfect game against a stronger batter.

But Mr. Mack let Rube take his turn. Rube took a couple of strikes and then hit a fly that Stahl caught going away from the infield.

You can realize how perfect we all were that day when I tell you the game only took one hour and 23 minutes.

We got three runs off Waddell and when the game was finished it looked like all the fans came down on the field and tried to shake my hand. One gray-haired fellow jumped the fence back of third and shoved a bill into my hand. It was $5.

The game was a sensation at the time. It was the first perfect game in 24 years, or since 1880, when both John M. Ward and Lee Richmond did the trick. It also was the second no-hitter ever pitched in the American League. Jimmy Callahan of the White Sox pitched the first against Detroit in 1902 but somehow a batter got to first base.

During my 23 years in the big leagues I pitched 472 games

THE BOX SCORE
(*May 5, 1904*)

BOSTON	A.B.	R.	H.	P.	A.	ATHLETICS	A.B.	R.	H.	P.	A.
Dougherty, lf.	4	0	1	1	0	Hartsel	1	0	0	0	0
Collins, 3b.	4	0	2	2	0	Hoffman, lf.	2	0	0	2	1
Stahl, cf.	4	1	1	3	0	Pickering, cf.	3	0	0	1	0
Freeman, rf.	4	0	1	2	0	Davis, 1b.	3	0	0	5	0
Parent, ss.	4	0	2	1	4	L. Cross, 3b.	3	0	0	4	1
La Chance, 1b.	3	0	1	9	0	Seybold, rf.	3	0	0	2	0
Ferris, 2b.	3	1	1	0	3	Murphy, 2b.	3	0	0	1	2
Criger, c.	3	1	1	9	0	M. Cross, ss.	3	0	0	2	3
Young, p.	3	0	0	0	2	Schreck, c.	3	0	0	7	0
						Waddell, p.	3	0	0	0	1
Totals	32	3	10	27	9	Totals	27	0	0	24	8

```
ATHLETICS    0 0 0  0 0 0  0 0 0—0
BOSTON       0 0 0  0 0 1  2 0 *—3
```

Error—Davis. Two-base hits—Collins, Criger. Three-base hits—Stahl, Freeman, Ferris. Sacrifice hit—La Chance. Left on bases—Boston 5. Double plays—Hoffman to Schreck, L. Cross to Davis. Struck out—By Young 8, Waddell 6. Time—1:23. Umpire—Dwyer. Attendance—10,267.

in the National League and won 291, and then I went into the American League and won 220 there. So all told I worked 879 games and won 511 and far as I can see these modern pitchers aren't gonna catch me.

By the way, you might be interested to know that in my last big-league game I was beaten 1–0 by a kid named Grover Cleveland Alexander.